£2.50

Battleground Europe
YPRES 1914
LANGEMARCK

Battleground series:

Stamford Bridge & Hastings by Peter Marren
Wars of the Roses - Wakefield/ Towton by Philip A. Haigh
Wars of the Roses - Barnet by David Clark
Wars of the Roses - Tewkesbury by Steven Goodchild
Wars of the Roses - The Battles of St Albans by
Peter Burley, Michael Elliott & Harvey Wilson
English Civil War - Naseby by Martin Marix Evans, Peter Burton and Michael Westaway
English Civil War - Marston Moor by David Clark
War of the Spanish Succession - Blenheim 1704 by David Clark
War of the Spanish Succession - Ramillies 1706 by James Falkner
Napoleonic - Hougoumont by Julian Paget and Derek Saunders
Napoleonic - Waterloo by Andrew Uffindell and Michael Corum
Zulu War - Isandlwana by Ian Knight and Ian Castle
Zulu War - Rorkes Drift by Ian Knight and Ian Castle
Boer War - The Relief of Ladysmith by Lewis Childs
Boer War - The Siege of Ladysmith by Lewis Childs
Boer War - Kimberley by Lewis Childs

Mons by Jack Horsfall and Nigel Cave
Néry by Patrick Tackle
Retreat of I Corps 1914 by Jerry Murland
Aisne 1914 by Jerry Murland
Aisne 1918 by David Blanchard
Le Cateau by Nigel Cave and Jack Shelden
Walking the Salient by Paul Reed
Ypres - 1914 Messines by Nigel Cave and Jack Sheldon
Ypres - 1914 Menin Road by Nigel Cave and Jack Sheldon
Ypres - 1914 Langemarck by Jack Sheldonand Nigel Cave
Ypres - Sanctuary Wood and Hooge by Nigel Cave
Ypres - Hill 60 by Nigel Cave
Ypres - Messines Ridge by Peter Oldham
Ypres - Polygon Wood by Nigel Cave
Ypres - Passchendaele by Nigel Cave
Ypres - Airfields and Airmen by Mike O'Connor
Ypres - St Julien by Graham Keech
Ypres - Boesinghe by Stephen McGreal
Walking the Somme by Paul Reed
Somme - Gommecourt by Nigel Cave
Somme - Serre by Jack Horsfall & Nigel Cave
Somme - Beaumont Hamel by Nigel Cave
Somme - Thiepval by Michael Stedman
Somme - La Boisselle by Michael Stedman
Somme - Fricourt by Michael Stedman
Somme - Carnoy-Montauban by Graham Maddocks
Somme - Pozières by Graham Keech
Somme - Courcelette by Paul Reed
Somme - Boom Ravine by Trevor Pidgeon
Somme - Mametz Wood by Michael Renshaw
Somme - Delville Wood by Nigel Cave
Somme - Advance to Victory (North) 1918 by Michael Stedman
Somme - Flers by Trevor Pidgeon
Somme - Bazentin Ridge by Edward Hancock
Somme - Combles by Paul Reed
Somme - Beaucourt by Michael Renshaw
Somme - Redan Ridge by Michael Renshaw
Somme - Hamel by Peter Pedersen
Somme - Villers-Bretonneux by Peter Pedersen
Somme - Airfields and Airmen by Mike O'Connor
Airfields and Airmen of the Channel Coast by Mike O'Connor
In the Footsteps of the Red Baron by Mike O'Connor
Arras - Airfields and Airmen by Mike O'Connor
Arras - The Battle for Vimy Ridge by Jack Sheldon & Nigel Cave
Arras - Vimy Ridge by Nigel Cave
Arras - Gavrelle by Trevor Tasker and Kyle Tallett
Arras - Oppy Wood by David Bilton
Arras - Bullecourt by Graham Keech
Arras - Monchy le Preux by Colin Fox
Walking Arras by Paul Reed
Hindenburg Line by Peter Oldham
Hindenburg Line - Epehy by Bill Mitchinson
Hindenburg Line - Riqueval by Bill Mitchinson
Hindenburg Line - Villers-Plouich by Bill Mitchinson
Hindenburg Line - Cambrai Right Hook by Jack Horsfall & Nigel Cave
Hindenburg Line - Cambrai Flesquières by Jack Horsfall & Nigel Cave
Hindenburg Line - Saint Quentin by Helen McPhail and Philip Guest
Hindenburg Line - Bourlon Wood by Jack Horsfall & Nigel Cave

Cambrai - Airfields and Airmen by Mike O'Connor
Aubers Ridge by Edward Hancock
La Bassée - Neuve Chapelle by Geoffrey Bridger
Loos - Hohenzollern Redoubt by Andrew Rawson
Loos - Hill 70 by Andrew Rawson
Fromelles by Peter Pedersen
The Battle of the Lys 1918 by Phil Tomaselli
Accrington Pals Trail by William Turner
Poets at War: Wilfred Owen by Helen McPhail and Philip Guest
Poets at War: Edmund Blunden by Helen McPhail and Philip Guest
Poets at War: Graves & Sassoon by Helen McPhail and Philip Guest
Gallipoli by Nigel Steel
Gallipoli - Gully Ravine by Stephen Chambers
Gallipoli - Anzac Landing by Stephen Chambers
Gallipoli - Suvla August Offensive by Stephen Chambers
Gallipoli - Landings at Helles by Huw & Jill Rodge
Walking the Gallipoli by Stephen Chambers
Walking the Italian Front by Francis Mackay
Italy - Asiago by Francis Mackay
Verdun: Fort Douaumont by Christina Holstein
Verdun: Fort Vaux by Christina Holstein
Walking Verdun by Christina Holstein
Verdun: The Left Bank by Christina Holstein
Zeebrugge & Ostend Raids 1918 by Stephen McGreal

Germans at Beaumont Hamel by Jack Sheldon
Germans at Thiepval by Jack Sheldon

SECOND WORLD WAR

Dunkirk by Patrick Wilson
Calais by Jon Cooksey
Boulogne by Jon Cooksey
Saint-Nazaire by James Dorrian
Walking D-Day by Paul Reed
Atlantic Wall - Pas de Calais by Paul Williams
Atlantic Wall - Normandy by Paul Williams
Normandy - Pegasus Bridge by Carl Shilleto
Normandy - Merville Battery by Carl Shilleto
Normandy - Utah Beach by Carl Shilleto
Normandy - Omaha Beach by Tim Kilvert-Jones
Normandy - Gold Beach by Christopher Dunphie & Garry Johnson
Normandy - Gold Beach Jig by Tim Saunders
Normandy - Juno Beach by Tim Saunders
Normandy - Sword Beach by Tim Kilvert-Jones
Normandy - Operation Bluecoat by Ian Daglish
Normandy - Operation Goodwood by Ian Daglish
Normandy - Epsom by Tim Saunders
Normandy - Hill 112 by Tim Saunders
Normandy - Mont Pinçon by Eric Hunt
Normandy - Cherbourg by Andrew Rawson
Normandy - Commandos & Rangers on D-Day by Tim Saunders
Das Reich – Drive to Normandy by Philip Vickers
Oradour by Philip Beck
Market Garden - Nijmegen by Tim Saunders
Market Garden - Hell's Highway by Tim Saunders
Market Garden - Arnhem, Oosterbeek by Frank Steer
Market Garden - Arnhem, The Bridge by Frank Steer
Market Garden - The Island by Tim Saunders
Rhine Crossing – US 9th Army & 17th US Airborne by Andrew Rawson
British Rhine Crossing – Operation Varsity by Tim Saunders
British Rhine Crossing – Operation Plunder by Tim Saunders
Battle of the Bulge – St Vith by Michael Tolhurst
Battle of the Bulge – Bastogne by Michael Tolhurst
Channel Islands by George Forty
Walcheren by Andrew Rawson
Remagen Bridge by Andrew Rawson
Cassino by Ian Blackwell
Anzio by Ian Blackwell
Dieppe by Tim Saunders
Fort Eben Emael by Tim Saunders
Crete – The Airborne Invasion by Tim Saunders
Malta by Paul Williams
Bruneval Raid by Paul Oldfield
Cockleshell Raid by Paul Oldfield

Battleground Europe

YPRES 1914
LANGEMARCK

Jack Sheldon
and Nigel Cave

Series Editor
Nigel Cave

Pen & Sword
MILITARY

First published in Great Britain in 2014 by
Pen & Sword Military
An imprint of
Pen & Sword Books Ltd
47 Church Street
Barnsley
South Yorkshire
S70 2AS

Copyright © Jack Sheldon and Nigel Cave

ISBN 978 178159 199 4

The right of Jack Sheldon and Nigel Cave to be identified as Authors of this work has been asserted by them in accordance with the Copyright, Designs and Patents Act 1988.

A CIP catalogue record for this book is
available from the British Library.

All rights reserved. No part of this book may be reproduced or transmitted in any form or by any means, electronic or mechanical including photocopying, recording or by any information storage and retrieval system, without permission from the Publisher in writing.

Typeset in Times New Roman by Chic Graphics

Printed and bound in England by
CPI Group (UK) Ltd., Croydon, CR0 4YY

Pen & Sword Books Ltd incorporates the imprints of
Pen & Sword Archaeology, Atlas, Aviation, Battleground, Discovery, Family History, History, Maritime, Military, Naval, Politics, Railways, Select, Social History, Transport, True Crime, and Claymore Press, Frontline Books, Leo Cooper, Praetorian Press, Remember When, Seaforth Publishing and Wharncliffe.

For a complete list of Pen & Sword titles please contact
PEN & SWORD BOOKS LIMITED
47 Church Street, Barnsley, South Yorkshire, S70 2AS, England
E-mail: enquiries@pen-and-sword.co.uk
Website: www.pen-and-sword.co.uk

CONTENTS

Introduction 6

Chapter One **Preliminary Manoeuvres** 8
Chapter Two **20 October 1914** 21
Chapter Three **21 October 1914** 30
Chapter Four **22 October 1914** 73
Chapter Five **23 October 1914** 94
Chapter Six **24–31 October 1914** 121
Chapter Seven **1–9 November 1914** 132
Chapter Eight **The End of Battle** 136

Tours Introduction 153
Tour One: 157
Tour Two: 171
Tour Three: 178
Tour Four: 184
Cemeteries 191

A selective German Order of Battle 202
Bibliography 204
Acknowledgements 205
Selective Index 206

Introduction

Prior to 20 October 1914, the name of the village of Langemarck in West Flanders was not even obscure; it was totally unknown to the outside world. This agricultural community, surrounded by meadows, crisscrossed with broad and deep drainage ditches and sandwiched between the Steenbeek and the Broenbeek, was about to become notorious for the intensity of the battles which erupted around it and to gain undying heroic status as a bastion of the allied defence which prevented the German assault troops from bearing down from the north on the mediaeval town of Ypres. The British Official History defines the Battle of Langemarck as lasting from 21 - 24 October, but that is to take a narrowly Anglocentric view of events. Before the fighting died away in this sector on 11 November, the defensive battle for the village, conducted by the French army, which had gradually assumed responsibility for an ever-increasing length of frontage around Ypres, had drawn in formations of the German III Reserve Corps (which had recently captured Antwerp and had been involved in operations west of the Yser until the area was inundated) and also 9th Reserve Division, rushed north from the Verdun area. Due to problems with reorganisation and new formations brought up for the attack east and south of Ypres, the attack on that part of the front was delayed until 11th November, with perhaps fatal consequences for any hope of success there might have been. Instead of a powerful assault all around the Salient, it was split over two days and ended in minimal gains and certainly a far cry from what had been hoped.

The British involvement in this area was for a very limited period – after 24 October it would be several months before the BEF were seen again in any sort of numbers in the small villages and fields around Langemarck. Its involvement here began on the premise of an advance against a German open flank, one which was soon abandoned or at least limited when the strength of German opposition and, indeed, of the German's own offensive plans became apparent from the start of operations by I Corps. Still, there is a good story to tell and this book should also underline the considerable – the very considerable – part played by the French army in the defence of what soon became recognisable as the Ypres Salient.

To help readers follow experiences from the British and German point of view, as appropriate and practicable, we have indicated the two

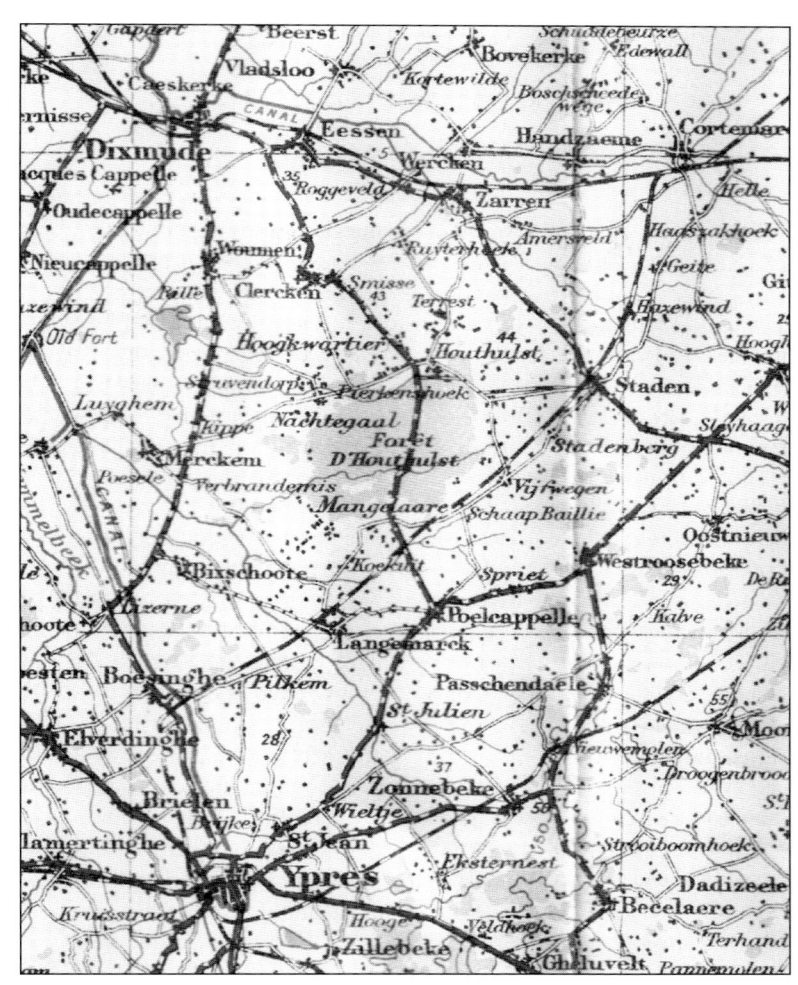

Contemporary map showing principal places covered in this volume.

sides by use of symbols, a British flat cap and the German *pickelhaube*; the French narrative is intermingled with the two; though, again, it should be emphasised that the allied involvement in chapters 6, 7 and 8 involved, almost exclusively, French troops on the allied side.

Spelling of place names was something of a challenge for both sides in 1914; in general we have left them as we have found them from the various sources; in the tours section the modern version is (we hope!) used, except for Ypres, which name has such a resonance amongst the British and Dominion troops. All times have been adjusted to that in use by the British.

Chapter One

Preliminary Manoeuvres

The battles which unfolded from Ploegsteert north to the sea at Nieuport in October and November 1914 represented the final, desperate, attempt by the German army to outflank, roll up and trap the allied armies on the Western Front before the war of manoeuvre became completely positional. The process began with the end of the Battle of the Marne and manifested itself from the German perspective as a series of right hooks, beginning in the southern sector of the Somme region during the last week in September and spreading rapidly north to Arras by 5 October and on into French Flanders. Much of the responsibility for these attacks was carried by the Sixth Army, commanded by Crown Prince Rupprecht of Bavaria and transferred north from Lorraine. However, once the Arras attacks began to bog down on 6 October, it was clear that additional forces would be required if the effort was to be sustained.

As an interim measure, Falkenhayn then massed all his available cavalry from the corps of Higher Cavalry Commanders 1, 2 and 4 and launched them into the area west of Lille and north to Ypres where days of inconclusive operations ensued, lasting in one form or another until nearly the end of the month. Despite the best efforts of the cavalry, it very soon became obvious that a major injection of manpower, no less than an entire army, would have to be deployed if the initiative was to be regained. The dilemma was where to find a pool of manpower that large at such short notice. The chosen solution was a gamble of breathtaking proportions. Six third rate reserve corps had been forming up in Germany since August. Composed for the most part of older reservists and men of the Landwehr and boosted by a large number of war time volunteers, they were poorly led, grossly ill equipped and had received only the sketchiest of training. Nevertheless, Falkenhayn decided to despatch four of these corps to join up with III Reserve Corps once the latter had completed the capture of Antwerp on 10 October and, beginning on 19 October, to launch them in a sweep parallel to the coast, designed to force the line of the Yser and then to swing south towards St Omer, with the aim of outflanking the Allied armies and encircling large numbers of troops.

To command this offensive, the original Fourth Army under Duke Albrecht of Württemberg was dissolved, then, on 9 October, a new one with the same number was created and established its headquarters at Ghent, where it attempted to give substance to Falkenhayn's grand design. Although even Falkenhayn himself described his plan as a 'gamble', his was not a 'winner takes all' decision; in fact he placed an each way bet, which suggests that his confidence that Fourth Army would be able to carry out this mission was less than complete. There were others, Crown Prince Rupprecht amongst them, who felt that the new manpower should have been used to bring depleted, but experienced, formations up to strength and that Falkenhayn should have waited until the Allies had advanced towards Ostend before smashing into their right flank and thrusting north to the channel coast. This would have been the riskier option and Falkenhayn was determined to ensure that, should his outflanking offensive fail, he would at least be in possession of a defensible line at the end of it.

Generaloberst Duke Albrecht of Württemberg, Commander Fourth Army.

The battle for Langemarck should be viewed against this

Advance of Fourth Army, October 1914.

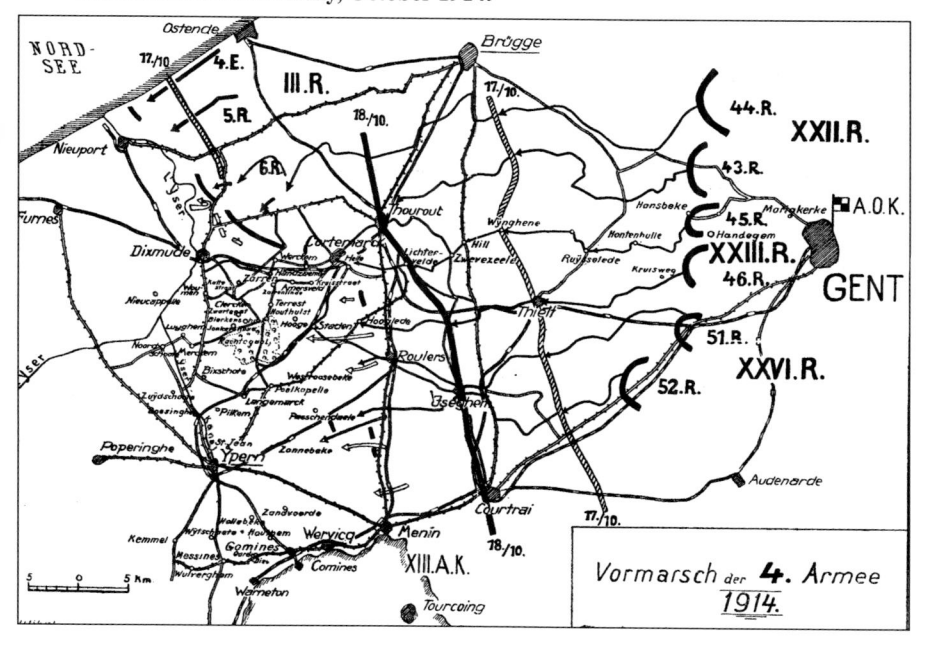

background. In the event, heroics by the Belgian army, which managed to evacuate 80,000 troops from beleaguered Antwerp and, boosted by French forces, to defend the line of the Yser for several days, throwing German timings badly out and ultimately, following the flooding of the polders, to bring operations in the north of the region to a complete halt. By that time Langemarck, defended briefly by the British army, had assumed great importance as the bulwark of the defence protecting the approaches to Ypres from the north. Possession of this vital ground was disputed intensely from 21 October to mid November, as the German XXVI Reserve Corps threw in attack after attack in an attempt to capture it. Its early naive attempts were utterly smashed with huge losses by the British defenders and then, once the British army was withdrawn on 24/25 October to concentrate its efforts astride the Menin Road, the French army furiously fought off all subsequent assaults by reinforcements from III Reserve Corps and 9th Reserve Division rushed north from Verdun, until the battle ended with both sides temporarily exhausted. The wrecked village was to remain in French hands throughout the whole of the following winter. The sacrificial gallantry of the raw troops of XXVI Reserve Corps, like that of the other German forces committed in Flanders, had all been in vain.

The bulk of the BEF, starting at the beginning of October, was moved north from the Aisne, which had already become a deadlocked section of what was rapidly developing into a line from the Swiss frontier to the sea. This move had not been without controversy; the Germans had the advantage of a single national command whilst the allies – French, British or Belgian – all had to consider their own national interests. From the viewpoint of the British C-in-C, Field Marshal Sir John French, the situation by the end of September was fairly simple. The bulk of the British Expeditionary Force was situated to the east of Paris. His three

Field Marshal Sir John French, Commander of the BEF.

corps were spread out along the line of the River Aisne, sandwiched between two French armies and at the end of a long logistical tail. To the north, a new British division (the 7th), formed mainly from troops that had been garrisoning various parts of the Empire and made up from the remaining regular troops in the UK, and a weak cavalry division (the 3rd) were preparing to engage in operations (they landed at Zeebrugge on 7 October) around Antwerp, which still held out against the Germans and containing within its fortified zone the bulk of the Belgian field army.

The situation around the Aisne stabilised by the end of the month, if still far from quiet, and no progress against the Germans was likely there.

As a consequence French urged Joffre, the French C-in-C, that the BEF should be sent to the northern flank, which would enable him to bring all the British formations back under his control, bring it closer to its supply bases and enable it to operate against the relatively open flank of the German army. The Indian Corps was en route and should shortly arrive at Marseilles; and the 8th Division was gradually being brought together in England, thereby substantially enhancing the BEF's fighting capability. With such a substantial force, it should be able to operate more effectively and even be a significant part of any enveloping movement against the German armies.

Marshal Joseph Joffre, Commander in Chief, French Army.

Joffre was not so enthused by the BEF's move: it would provide problems for the French armies operating on the Aisne, in an area that he considered to be still fragile. He did not want to tie up French rail transport with shifting the BEF (at least partial blame for the fall of Lille, a major railway junction, on 12 October was put down to the fact that no rail transport was available to move French troops north to aid its defence). Finally he had his own plans for an enveloping movement against the Germans and this did not necessarily involve a major role for the BEF, or at least the bulk of it – and certainly he envisioned a subsidiary part, under French direction. He almost certainly had worries about Sir John French's reliability, concerned that he might want to pull the BEF out of the line to refit and reorganise given any significant reverses, as he had threatened earlier on in the campaign. On the other hand he appreciated the political realities and agreed to the move.

So the BEF moved north; on 3 October the two divisions of Allenby's Cavalry Corps started on the long approach march to the Franco-Belgian border; by 10 October II Corps (Smith Dorrien) was situated west of Béthune and III Corps (Pulteney) was moving to concentration areas around St Omer and Hazebrouck, the final elements of the latter arriving on 11 October. However, also on 10 October, Antwerp formally surrendered. Belgian troops withdrew, with some difficulty, heading

Lieutenant General Edmund Allenby, commander of the newly created (9 October) Cavalry Corps.

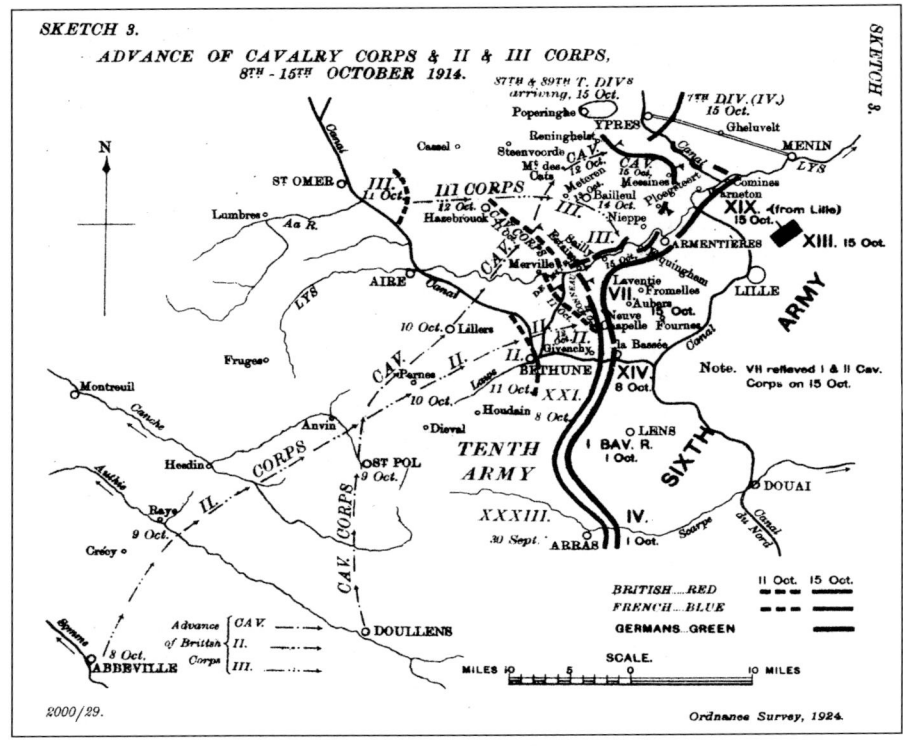

The move of the BEF to the north from the Aisne.

Situation map, evening of 18 October.

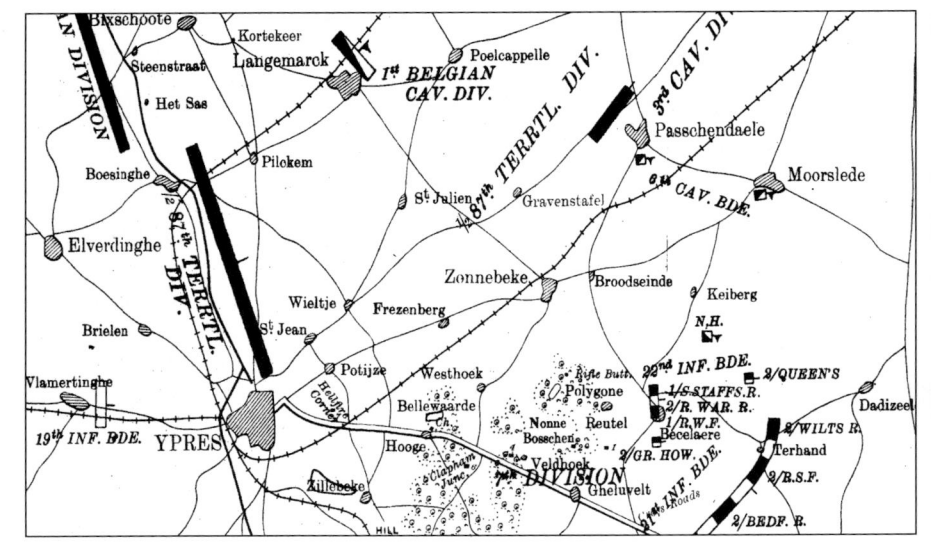

back to a defensive line based on the Yser. A day earlier IV Corps (7th and 3rd (Cavalry) Divisions), on the 10th split between Bruges and Ghent, was formed under the command of Rawlinson. It was making its way west towards Ypres, where it arrived about 15 October. The day afterwards, I Corps (Haig) began its move to the north, gathering around Hazebrouck on 17 and 18 October. With the Germans also moving very significant forces to the north, the final part of the war of manoeuvre was ready to begin.

I Corps.
This, the principal major British formation covered in this book, had taken considerable casualties during the Aisne fighting. It is instructive to look at what a fairly typical battalion which formed part of it, 1/South Wales Borderers, 3 Brigade, 1st Division, had endured since it left the UK on 12 August.

When the battalion went overseas it had 977 men, including twenty six officers, a warrant officer, forty nine sergeants and 911 men. It also had a '10%' reserve to act as first reinforcements, which came out to France a week later. Of this total, 631 were reservists. In the retreat from Mons the battalion suffered no casualties from enemy action, but it had marched at least 250 miles in just over a fortnight, with only two days of 'rest' (one of which included 23 August, during the Battle of Mons) and in close proximity to the enemy, with all that that entails. The average loss per battalion in 3 Brigade from sickness and missing, between disembarkation at Le Havre on 13 August and 10 September, was between seventy and eighty men. In the actions up to the end of the Battle of the Aisne the battalion had suffered about two hundred battle casualties – on 21 September these were thirty five killed, 131 wounded and some missing; it received a draft of reinforcements of 190 men, mainly special reservists, and a couple of officers, on 20 September. On 6 October the strength was 781 all ranks, with only ten officers doing duty with companies – battle casualties thus far had climbed to about 430: six officers and 110 men killed, five officers and 267 men wounded and thirty five missing; and this does not take account of the sick. A draft, its second, on 10 October brought the battalion over the 950 men mark and added another six officers: one regular, three special reservists and two who had been gazetted to the regiment after the outbreak of war. Nearly all the men of the draft were special reservists or re-enlisted old soldiers. By the time the battalion was preparing for the advance in Flanders, sickness continued to take an increasing toll, as the conditions of the last month took effect – for example two officers had to be evacuated sick on 20 October.

3 Brigade left the line on the Aisne during the night 15/16 October, a relief that was completed before dawn.

> The SWB's destination was Limé, in which village Battalion Headquarters were established in a most palatial chateau. But these comforts were not to be enjoyed long. That evening came orders to be at Fère en Tardenois by 5 am on the 17th ready to entrain and, thanks to Captain Paterson's skilful piloting of it in pitch darkness over an intricate and difficult road, the battalion arrived there to time, though after the long period in trenches the men found the unaccustomed marching very trying, and many had much difficulty in completing the march. By 8 am the battalion was steaming out of the station for a destination only revealed to the Adjutant at the moment of departure as being Étaples.

Thus the battalion, forming part of 1st Division's rearguard for its relief by the French, was in the line until the morning of the 16th, had completed a laborious march to the station (the distance today is ten miles on good roads), heading for an unknown destination, endured a rail journey of some twenty four hours before disembarking at Cassel and having another march (this time of five miles) to their new billets.

Almost immediately on arrival in the Flanders theatre (all but I Corps arriving by 11 October), the various elements of the BEF that had been on the Aisne became involved in fighting to the west of Lille and up to the Belgian border, with the Cavalry Corps operating on the left, extending into Belgium; British troops at one time or the other in the following days occupied positions in Fromelles and on Aubers Ridge that they were not to see again until 1918. By the time that Haig's I Corps arrived on the scene, Rawlinson's IV Corps, formed on 10 October and consisting of Capper's 7th Division and Byng's 3rd (Cavalry) Division, had moved to cover the eastern approaches to Ypres. Also about this time, on 11 October, General Foch was formally appointed commander of the French troops in the north – *Groupe des Armées du Nord* [*GAN*], with headquarters at that time at Doullens. His plan more or less fitted in with French's thinking – the Belgian and allied troops to the north of the British would head eastwards and for the coast; and the British I Corps and IV Corps and the French immediately to their north would launch an attack towards Ghent, with the aim of wheeling into the German right flank. Further to the south the rest of the BEF would continue to assist the major French effort before Lille; whilst the British Cavalry Corps would act as the connection between IV Corps and the Franco-British forces operating along the Yser.

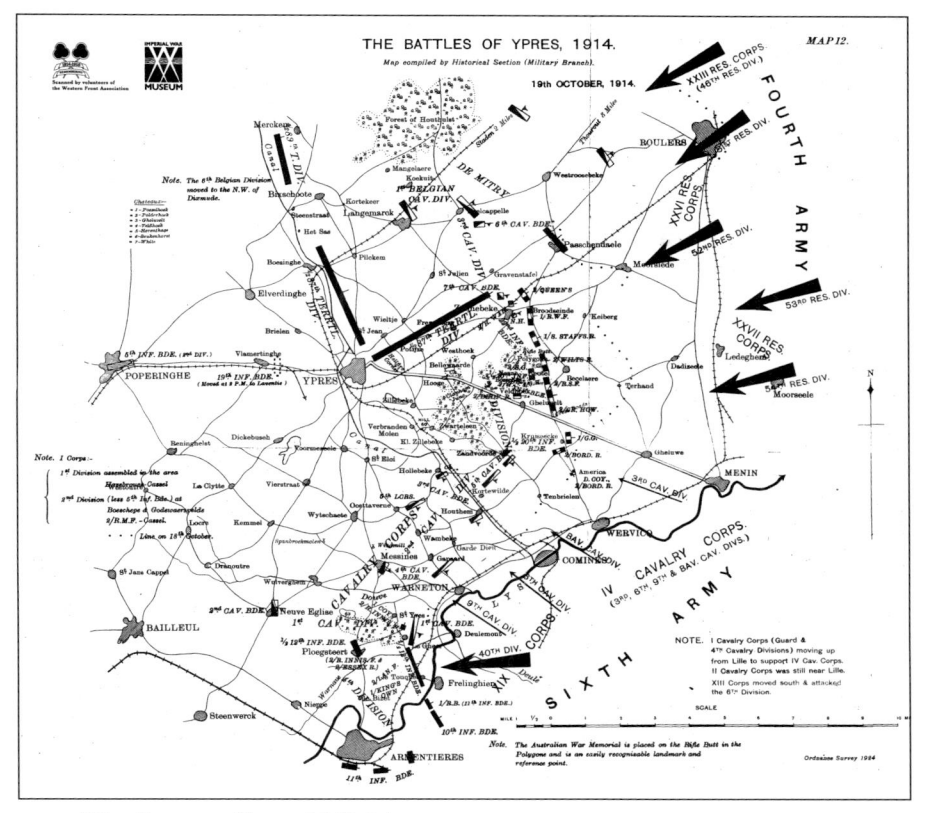

Situation map, Ypres, 19 October.

By the morning of 19 October I Corps had assembled around Hazebrouck and to its east (and 19 Brigade at Vlamertinghe); the BEF at this stage was holding a front of some twenty five miles. French made the decision not to reinforce his troops further south, by then already under considerable pressure, with I Corps (though 19 Brigade, in GHQ reserve, was sent and went on to occupy positions in Fromelles, behind French cavalry). He considered that there were only weak German forces (intelligence suggested that there was only a corps) to the east of I Corps.

IV Corps is also considered in this book, particularly those parts of it operating on I Corps' right flank, that is part of 22 Brigade (7th Division) and some of its screening cavalry from 3rd (Cavalry) Division.

22 Brigade of 7th Division had had a very difficult day; though it had started promisingly enough. An advance was made southwards, to within a couple of miles of Menin, brushing aside relatively easily the German opposition. However, there were problems developing on the

7th Division, 15 – 18 October.

right, as the screening cavalry of 3rd (Cavalry) Division came upon significant German forces. 7 (Cavalry) Brigade, on the extreme right of IV Corps failed to make the Roulers – Menin road and in the face of a developing German attack was ordered back to positions north of Moorslede. This impacted on 6 (Cavalry) Brigade, to the south, which withdrew south east of Moorslede and made contact with both French cavalry and French territorial troops, who were digging in on the Passchendaele ridge; from there 6 Brigade billeted for the night at Poelcappelle and the 7th to Zonnebeke, where it was able to provide a reserve for the left of 7th Division.

Given the loss of the screening cavalry, the threat from significant numbers of Germans and the possibility of a German thrust pushing through westwards and separating the bulk of the BEF from a meagre cavalry force, 22 Brigade received orders at about 1 pm to switch direction; instead of facing south towards Menin it was to swing left and hold a line from Terhand in the east (connecting with 21 Brigade) to

Moorslede. This was not easily done when in contact with the enemy, but it was achieved – helped by the largely ineffectual fire from the German artillery. As 3rd (Cavalry) Division continued its withdrawal, the whole of 7th Division moved back until it occupied positions from which they had, more or less, started that morning. 22 Brigade held the line north of Becelaere to the Broodseinde crossroads. It suffered by far the most of the Division's casualties on the day; for example just over half of the Division's 300 losses came from 1/Royal Welch Fusiliers alone, including eight officers, of whom two were killed. 2/Warwicks had sixty casualties and 2/Queen's twenty.

Meanwhile, on the British left, 19 October had seen considerable action along the Yser line, from Nieuport (artillery fire) and with

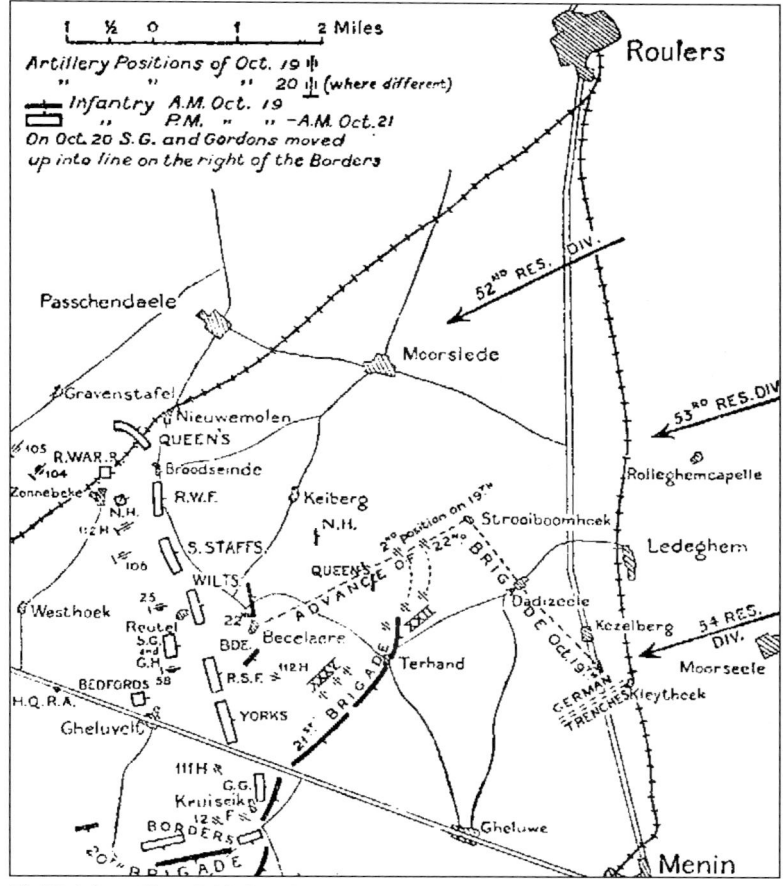

7th Division, 19 and 20 October.

Passchendaele and the surrounding country in 1916; notice the closer nature of the ground compared with today.

Brigadier General E Makins, GOC 6 (Cavalry) Brigade.

Major General Hon J Byng, GOC 3rd (Cavalry) Division.

Zonnebeke Chateau from the south.

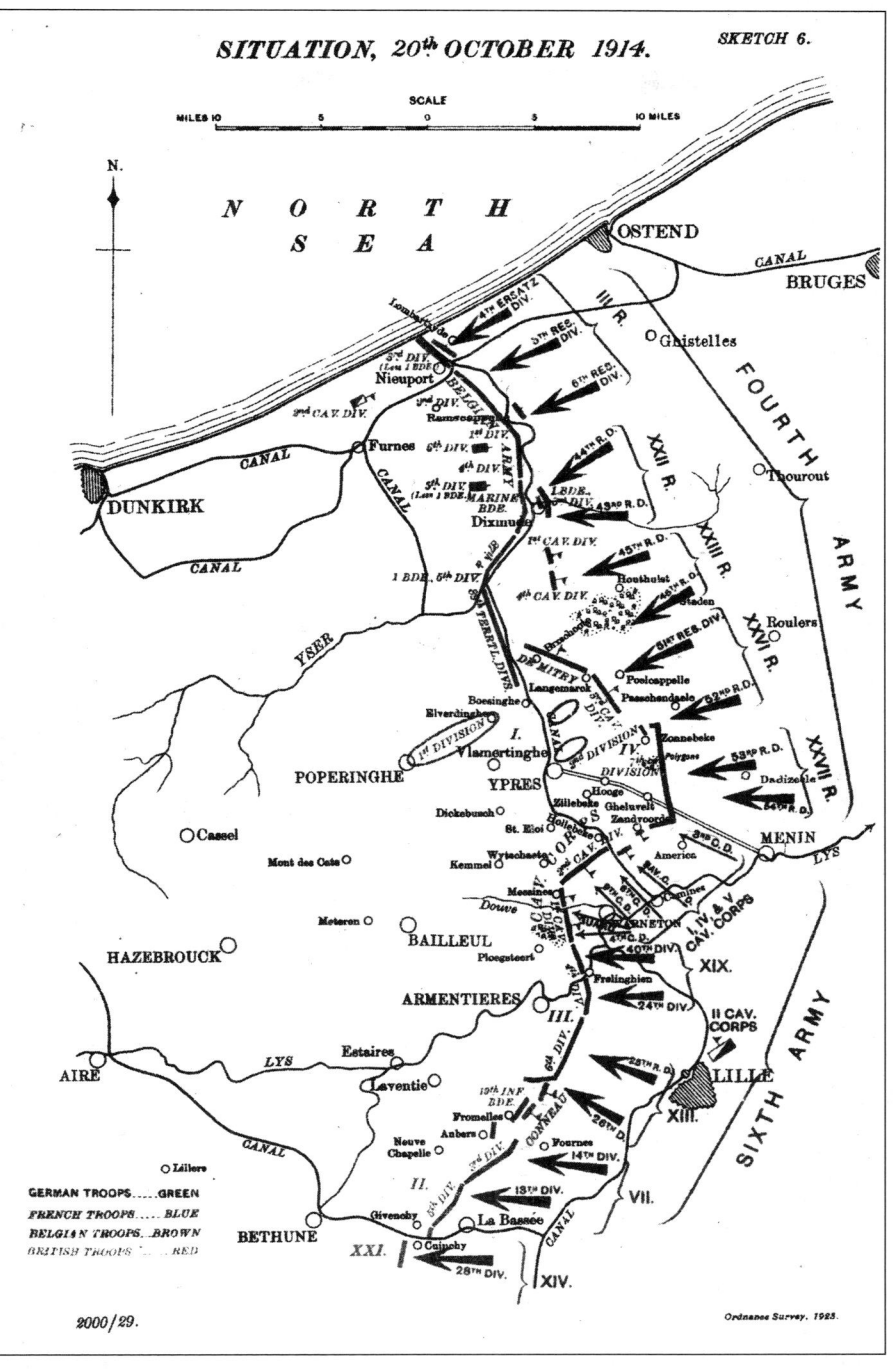

Situation map from La Bassée to the sea, 20 October.

infantry assaults (which had begun on the 18th) against Belgian outposts between Lombartzyde and Beerst, to the north of Dixmude. Joffre had concentrated much of his cavalry, four divisions worth, under the command of de Mitry, between the British and the Belgians, with a naval brigade on the Belgian's immediate right and two territorial divisions to help hold the line, one of these, the 87th, being located to the north of Boesinge and therefore forming the link with I Corps.

Persisting in the belief that the German forces in front of the proposed advance of I Corps were only light or ineffectual – or even both - that evening Haig was instructed by GHQ to advance on the 20th towards Bruges via Thourout, with his right passing through Ypres; and to attack German forces either north or north east out of Ypres (towards Courtrai), according to the situation. The 3rd Cavalry Division would screen the advance; however, the latter was given the option of capturing Menin if it did not compromise the covering of I Corps. 7th Division was to entrench along a line roughly Zandvoorde to Zonnebeke, some eight miles of front; whilst the remainder of the BEF was to continue operations to the south.

General Antoine de Mitry, GOC of the French II (Cavalry) Corps and cavalry along the Yser.

At 6 am on 20 October, I Corps began its advance eastwards, led by the 2nd Division from its billets in and to the west of Poperinghe, with 4 Brigade moving through Ypres itself. The town had been briefly occupied by German cavalry on 7 October (and the town paid a substantial indemnity to them for the pleasure), and 7th Division had also passed through on its way east; I Corps' arrival, at the time considered temporary, might be considered an early and significant event in the four years of Ypres' intimate association with the BEF and the beginning of its iconic status in British military history. Except for several months, from the tail end of November 1914 and the beginning of February 1915, when all or a significant portion of it was held by the French, the BEF held the great bulk of the Ypres Salient until September and October 1918, when the allies finally burst out of its confines.

Chapter Two

20 October 1914

Whilst the British deployments had been taking place, the newly raised reserve corps of the German Fourth Army had been manoeuvring into position and were ready by dawn on 20 October to go over to the offensive. On 20 October the divisions of XXVI Reserve Corps, under the overall command of General der Infanterie Freiherr von Hügel, were in position along the line Moorslede - Staden at 8.00 am and were about to attack the sector bounded by Zonnebeke in the south and Bixschoote in the north, which also forms the area covered by this guide. To the south XXVII Reserve Corps attacked towards Becelaere whilst, off to the north, XXIII Reserve Corps was operating. Here the inter corps boundary ran along the southern edge of Houthulst Wood. Langemarck itself, located roughly in the centre of the XXVI Reserve Corps' frontage, was thus far untouched by war as the men of 51st and 52nd Reserve Divisions prepared to advance.

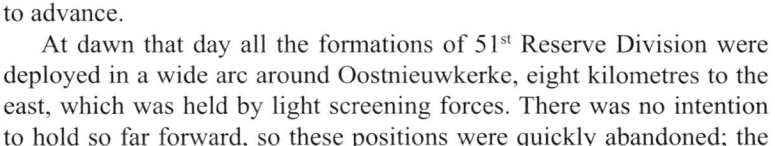

At dawn that day all the formations of 51st Reserve Division were deployed in a wide arc around Oostnieuwkerke, eight kilometres to the east, which was held by light screening forces. There was no intention to hold so far forward, so these positions were quickly abandoned; the

French prisoners of war being escorted to the rear by German cavalry.

troops involved withdrawing to advanced positions north and south of Westroosebeke. At that the attackers once more formed into two huge columns and continued to move west. Within an hour, however, they were brought under accurate artillery fire, so the infantry was forced to deploy into skirmishing lines and to take cover while the German batteries deployed to gun lines west of Oostnieuwkerke and began to engage the enemy batteries. After a two hour exchange of artillery fire, which underlined the deficiencies of the German gunnery training, the infantry regiments advanced shortly after midday but, unsurprisingly, the assault quickly bogged down, particularly on the right. XXIII Reserve Corps had encountered difficulties getting forward and unpleasantly accurate fire from French troops off to a flank began to cause casualties. The attack, having faltered on this exposed flank, was soon in trouble in the centre and on the left. In response, some German batteries were galloped forward to positions from which they could bring down direct observed fire.

Eventually the German gunfire enabled the infantry to advance once more and, by 3.00 pm, Westroosebeke was about to be outflanked. As soon as this became clear the defenders pulled out rapidly, pursued vigorously in the direction of Poelcappelle by elements of Reserve Infantry Regiment 235, which had been raised in Koblenz a few weeks earlier. In the process, no fewer than three officers and 103 men of the French Infantry Regiment 41 were captured. By nightfall Reserve Jäger Battalion 23 had advanced to Poelcappelle railway station, located some two kilometres northwest of the village itself. The Jägers then placed picquets several hundred metres to the front, taking care to establish a line of them along the southern edge of Houthulst Wood. (It is worth pointing out that Houthulst Forest was considerably larger in 1914, though less dense, than it is today; for example, to the west, it reached almost as far as Mangelaare.) This was known to hold enemy units which could threaten the Corps' right flank. By roughly the same time, leading units of XXIII Reserve Corps had also pushed up to the eastern edge of Houthulst Wood, where they halted; it being quite impractical to attempt to press on into the wood at night. Meanwhile the men of 51st Reserve Division bivouacked or found shelter in Poelcappelle, where orders were issued for a renewal of the advance towards Langemarck the following morning. With only three thousand metres to cover, confidence was general and morale high in the German ranks that night.

IV Corps, 7th Division, 22 Brigade
On the allied side, 7th Division had been ordered to carry out a reconnaissance in strength; for 21 Brigade this meant 2/Royal Scots

Fusiliers and 2/Wiltshires, with accompanying artillery, moving along the Terhand spur. Such a move would give flank protection to 3rd (Cavalry) Division, thinly holding a line from Nieuwemolen towards Westroosebeke. They cleared Becelaere of enemy troops. However, the pressure on 22 Brigade and the cavalry increased considerably and this probing advance was halted and, under fire, the British returned to their original line.

This pressure was such that, by midday on the 20th, Byng's cavalry had to withdraw as a result of the French cavalry having to fall back themselves as a result of German pressure. De Mitry's Cavalry Corps had been driven back from its positions north and east of Houthulst Forest so that it now lay west of it. This had a knock on effect on 3rd (Cavalry) Division, which had to bring its left flank back to a position

The right of 7th Division, 20 October.

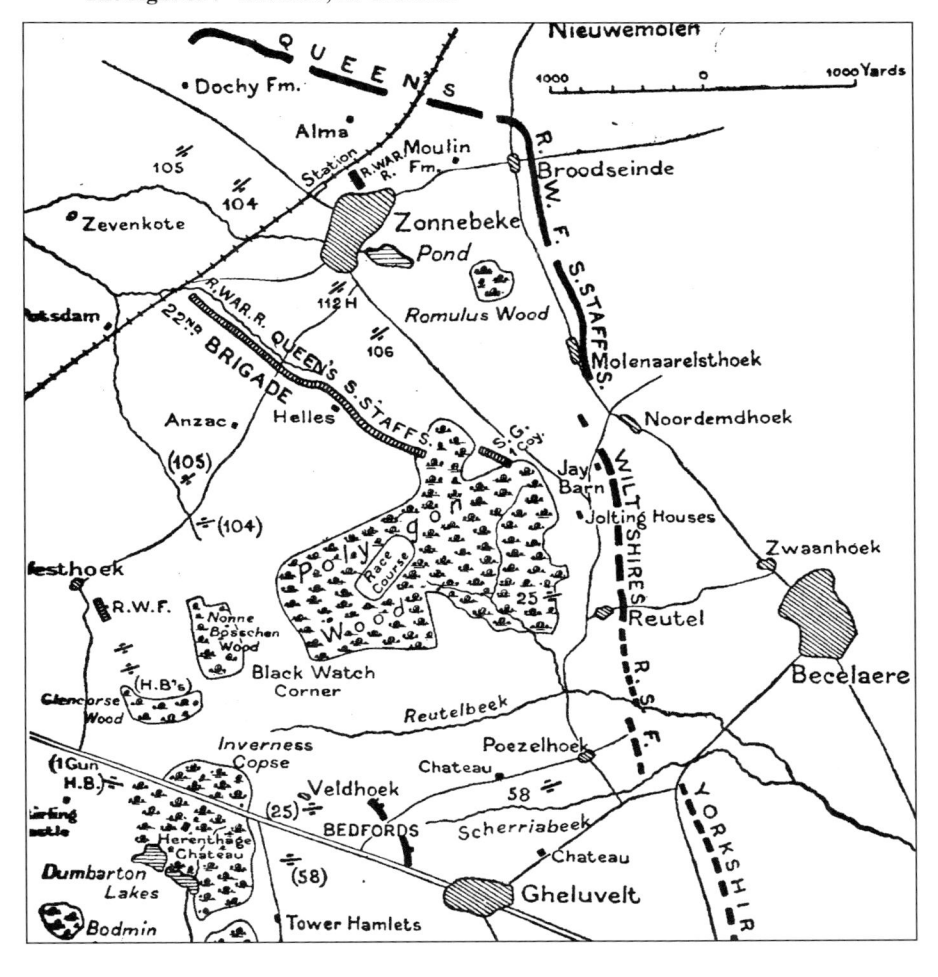

south of Poelcappelle from north of Passchendaele. Early on that morning 6 (Cavalry) Brigade had dug trenches with commandeered tools – a consistent and loud complaint from both sides in these early stages of the war was a lack of decent entrenching tools – to the west of the Westroosebeke – Passchendaele road. By 8 am these positions were under attack but were held relatively comfortably, supported by effective artillery fire; but as the French cavalry pulled back from Westroosebeke at about 11.30 am, so the Brigade fell back towards Poelcappelle. Coming under sustained shell fire in the afternoon, accompanied by infantry attacks and exposed by French withdrawals on the left, the Division drew back its left flank in line with French infantry units holding Langemarck.

This made 22 Brigade particularly vulnerable on its left flank. Major Ralph Hamilton, The Master of Belhaven, at the time watching the advancing Germans from an observation post behind 1/South Staffs' position, took some satisfaction in being able to take some action:

I shall never forget seeing some twenty or thirty Germans running across a green field which was divided in two by a fence, probably barbed, as I noticed that on reaching the wire fence they all concentrated and ran through a gate in it. Our lines of fire were already laid out, and from the map we were able to get the range to a yard. The next time we saw a party crossing the field and making for the gate, Bolster [Major George Bolster, CO of 106 Battery RFA, died of wounds on 23 October and buried in Ypres Town Cemetery] *ordered a round of gun fire. At this short range (2,800 yards) with my Zeiss glasses I could almost see the faces of the Germans, it being a gloriously fine, sunny day.*

Just before they reached the gate, he gave the order to fire. The guns, which were hidden behind us, loosed off and we heard the shells whining away. As the Germans clustered in the gate, a shell from No 1 gun burst immediately in front of them. The whole lot at once lay down, and at first I thought that they were taking cover until our fire stopped. However, I watched them for some hours, and not one of them moved again. I counted fifteen in a circle of some twenty yards' diameter.

Already under fairly heavy shellfire, from about 2 pm the Brigade came under infantry attack as well. 2/Queen's was moved up to occupy a covering position on the left, from an area north west of the Broodseinde crossroads to the railway crossing not far east from today's Tyne Cot cemetery. The main problem for them was artillery fire; as evening fell the battalion withdrew to its old positions to the west of and parallel to the Zonnebeke-Langemarck road; though a company occupied the space between the railway line west of Zonnebeke and the Passchendaele road. The main pressure on the Brigade was felt most strongly by 1/RWF, holding the line around Broodseinde. However it was able to withstand the attack of the German infantry. In these early days of the war the artillery was not yet sophisticated enough to be able to cover advancing infantry with a barrage; rather it attempted to plaster an area, cease firing and then the infantry would launch an assault. As most of the attack was coming from the left and as 1/RWF's right flank was covered by 1/S Staffs, it was possible to place the battalion's two machine guns on the left flank. Between them and rifle fire from the various rifle-slits (in no way was there a trench line as understood later in the war; nor was the position wired), the advancing Germans were beaten off relatively easily. Even before night fell, the German artillery had become both heavier and more effective, as Hamilton found out when asked to take a message by Brigadier General Lawford to the CO of the South Staffs.

> *With some difficulty I got there, crawling the last twenty yards, perfectly flat. I found that the Staffordshire Headquarters had made themselves extremely comfortable in a very big bomb-proof, which one approached by going down several steps. The colonel told me that his pioneer sergeant was a coal miner and I at once recognise the pitman's work by the way in which the roof of the bomb proof had been propped.*

After tea and a cigarette, he set off to return to his horse, back at the gun lines a half mile away.

> *I had scarcely left the Staffordshires' bomb-proof when a shrapnel burst just behind me and on my right, the bullets striking some ten yards to my right. Ten seconds later the second shell of the pair arrived, and burst ten or twenty yards to my left. Had I been ten yards to the right or to the left, one or other would have got me.*

Lieutenant Hindson, of the Royal Welsh Fusiliers, noted:

> *During the night there were several violent outbursts of fire, lasting some time, but nothing followed. The enemy were blowing bugles and whistles most of the night, but with what object I am unable to say.*

Be this as it may, it was quite clear by the evening of 20 October that the situation on the left of the BEF line was precarious. Thus, what had been planned as an advance was soon to be transformed into what became an encounter battle.

Much of the action on this sector of the front took place in what was the southern half of the XXVI Reserve Corps sector, where 52nd Reserve Division had gone into action. Its objective was the area bounded by Passchendaele, Keiberg, Broodseinde and Zonnebeke. Formed up into two huge bodies of troops, with Reserve Infantry Regiments 238 and 240 in the south and Reserve Infantry Regiments 237 and 239 advancing to their right, it made for the high ground. Unfortunately, the moment the advance guard of the northern group emerged from Moorslede shortly after dawn, they were forced into cover by accurate rifle and machine gun fire. They took up fire positions, attempted to locate the enemy and, as the units moving in rear of them made their way forward to reinforce, became involved in an intense fire fight and so made only limited progress. Reserve Infantry Regiments 238 and 240 had a similar experience astride the Moorslede – Zonnebeke road.

Oberst z.D. Freiherr (Baron) von Beaulieu-Marconnay, Commander Reserve Infantry Regiment 239

Eventually a slackening of the defensive fire permitted Reserve Infantry Regiments 239 and 237 to mount an attack on Passchendaele at 1.00 pm. Following bitter hand to hand fighting the village was secured then, profiting from this success, regiments to the south resumed their advance. By the time night fell Reserve Infantry Regiment 238 was occupying farm buildings on the eastern edge of Broodseinde and Reserve Infantry Regiment 240 had pushed on through a wooded area just to the southeast. Casualties, though not negligible, were not high considering the intensity of the battle earlier in the day; and the distant prospect of the towers and spires of Ypres was good for overall morale. Outposts were established and all those not on sentry or other duty attempted to get as much rest as possible prior to the resumption of the advance the following morning.

I Corps

Meanwhile, back in the allied rear area, Haig's I Corps (1st and 2nd

Divisions) set off eastwards early on 20 October: 2nd Division heading east from Poperinghe, with its left boundary on Elverdinghe; whilst 1st Division moved from its concentration area around Hazebrouck, through Poperinghe and towards Elverdinghe, with the aim of covering the Corps' left flank.

3/Coldstream of 4 (Guards) Brigade moved from its billets at Boeschepe at 6 am and took up its positions at St Jean before being ordered forward to St Julien. Its progress had not been easy, as the regimental history notes:

> The whole place seems to have been full of French troops, large numbers of whom were passing back through our lines. But besides this the march of our troops had been obstructed by thousands of unfortunate refugees who had been burnt out of their homes, and were hurrying along the roads; persons huddled together in farm carts, wagons, and even perambulators, with little money and little food – all were fleeing from the destructive invaders, they knew not whither. The scene is described [in 3rd Battalion's War Diary] as one of the most terrible ever witnessed.

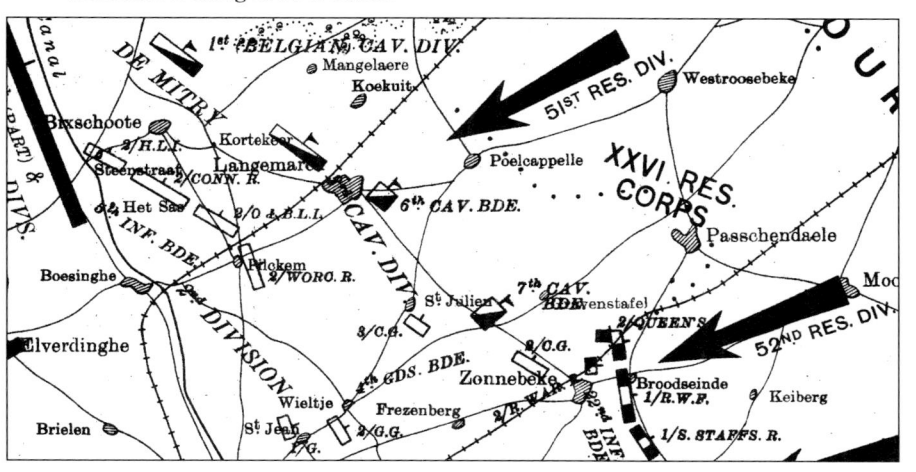

Lieutenant General Sir Douglas Haig, GOC I Corps.

It soon became clear that there would be problems; 7th Division needed support on its left wing and Haig, in the afternoon, sent two battalions from 4 (Guards) Brigade to assist it – 3/Coldstream to St Julien and 2/Coldstream to Zonnebeke.

Situation evening of 20 October.

Belgian refugees

5 Brigade had arrived in the Poperinghe area about midnight on the 19th and were billeted there; their rest was but a short one and it was on the move again early the next morning, acting as flank guard for the division, moving up to the front via Boesinge and then, after a halt there, moved on to Pilckem Ridge, which at the time was occupied by French territorials. The brigade then set about entrenching a line on the crest of the ridge, holding a position from Pilckem to Steenstraat. The Worcesters' history notes:

> *All that day a distant thunder of gunfire had been heard to the southward. As evening came on, the French territorials withdrew behind the line of the British brigades and an ever-increasing swarm of refugees came thronging westward through the entrenched position. A chilling drizzle ushered in a dark, wet*

night, which passed without incident save for the intermittent flash and rumble of gunfire on the Menin Road.

By the end of the day, 2nd Division occupied a line from Wieltje to Steenstraat, screened forward by 3rd (Cavalry) Division and to the left by French territorials, with 1st Division behind, billeted in the Poperinghe – Elverdinghe area.

On the positive side the build up of allied forces continued on 20 October; the increasing commitment of the French army to the northern flank was signalled by the creation of *Le Détachement d'Armée de Belgique* [*DAB*] under General d'Urbal and the arrival near Nieuport of General Grossetti's 42nd Division. Also becoming clearer was the extent of the German forces; although there was intelligence about the presence in front of IV Corps of *XXVI Reserve* and *XXVII Reserve Corps*, both the British and French higher commands either doubted what they were told or considered that they were, as the British Official History puts it, 'improvised and hastily trained formations of limited value'.

General Victor d'Urbal, commander of Le Détachement d'Armée de Belgique (DAB).

Chapter Three

21 October 1914

The whole of 7th Division's front came under heavy attack on 21 October. This account of British operations confines itself to the left of 22 Brigade's front, where the German 52nd Reserve Division had the task of outflanking Broodseinde and occupying the high ground to the west, from which positions it would be able to bring fire to bear on the right flank of the defenders opposite 51st Reserve Division; and so provide flank protection for entire Fourth Army operation, which had crossings of the Yser as its objective.

The German artillery opened up early and with greater accuracy than hitherto; particularly trying was fire coming from the newly won ground around Passchendaele, which enabled the Germans to fire in enfilade on 22 Brigade's left flank. Early on 21 October, all the regiments of 52nd Reserve Division, arranged in two large groups (brigades had not at that point been established) advanced west. The northern group, Reserve Infantry Regiments 237 and 239, moved parallel to the Roulers – Ypres

The church in Passchendaele in about 1900; newly constructed then, after the war and its total destruction, the rebuilt church appears to be identical to its predecessor.

railway, deeply echeloned to the right and maintaining contact with 51st Reserve Division. Off to the south, Reserve Infantry Regiments 238 and 240, together with Reserve Jäger Battalion 24, advanced either side of Broodseinde. The intention was that once that village had been captured they were to fight through the woods south of Zonnebeke (ie Polygon, Reutel and Nonne Bosschen woods), whilst also maintaining contact with XXVII Reserve Corps, which was fighting hard to the west of Becelaere. 'The enemy is to be attacked energetically', stated the divisional operation order for that day. Setting off at 5.30am, and with its 1st Battalion pushed forward as an advance guard, 2nd and 3rd Battalions Reserve Infantry Regiment 237, which were following up at about 750 metres distance, made to outflank Broodseinde to the north; but in less than half an hour the 1st Battalion was heavily engaged and suffering a significant number of casualties. The regimental commander reacted by deploying 3rd Battalion in extension of the 1st Battalion line to the north, and 2nd Battalion moved forward to buttress the centre of the 1st Battalion line.

To counter this, 2/Queen's had come up on 1/RWF's left flank and to its rear, to hold a refused line north west of Zonnebeke; but there was confusion in communications and the Queen's centre company withdrew to a line further back, leaving the left flank company to face heavy enfilade fire almost unsupported and having to withdraw in the early afternoon under its weight; however, C Company, in trenches west of the Broodseinde road, between the railway and the Passchendaele road, held on grimly all day and in the late afternoon it was joined by the rest of the battalion, previously holding the ground between (and in rear of) 1/RWF and 1/S Staffs.

Major Hamilton, in an instructive passage on the use and effectiveness of shrapnel, commented on the increasing volume of the German shelling:

> *About midday, the enemy began to bombard the town itself for some hours, but only with shrapnel. This did not do very much damage, but was very alarming, as the bullets from the shrapnel and the pieces of the shells flew about the streets like hail. They were firing in bursts – that is to say six shells arriving at a time. The air was thick with the flying lead, fragments of steel, slates from the roofs, glass and bricks. The noise was appalling; one could hardly hear oneself speak. One really wondered how anything could live in such an inferno, the more so as the main street of Zonnebeke was a prolongation of the German line of fire, and rifle bullets were continuously whining down the street.*

A pre war view looking east down Yperschesteenweg (modern Ieperstraat) in Zonnebeke before the war.

> In the open, when a shrapnel bursts there is the sudden and violent tearing noise peculiar to these shells, a puff of white smoke and nothing else. But in a town or on a road, in addition to the foregoing, there is also the violent patter of the bullets striking the ground. As a shrapnel, to be effective, must burst fairly close to the ground, shells which explode a hundred feet or so in the air are comparatively harmless. Fortunately for us, a very large proportion of the German shrapnel burst too high; in fact I hardly saw any burst on percussion, except in the cases where they struck the roofs of houses.

Off to the north, Reserve Infantry Regiment 239 was advancing, but with great difficulty. The entire area was under heavy fire, making progress slow. A quick reconnaissance showed that the British were occupying the Langemarck – Zonnebeke road and the farm buildings in front of it. Unfortunately the terrain very much favoured the defence but, despite all the problems and now with some awareness of the locations, 3rd Company Reserve Infantry Regiment 239 was sent to manoeuvre forward until it was in a position to attack Zonnebeke. Unfortunately, despite exploitation of the available cover, the movement was detected. Enfilade fire was brought down and enemy artillery fire, shrapnel in particular, caused great difficulties. Commander 2nd Company was wounded in the chest by a rifle bullet and many other men had to be evacuated with wounds from shrapnel balls.

The situation was similar throughout the divisional area and forward movement was restricted to small bodies gradually working their way forward using fire and manoeuvre, whilst the reserves closed up. By the early afternoon, these tactics were beginning to be effective and some troops could be observed pulling back towards St Julien. Making the most of this apparent wavering, Reserve Infantry Regiment 237 pushed ahead. Unfortunately, the other regiments were in no position to conform. The right hand battalion of Reserve Infantry Regiment 239, for example, was caught up in the panicky move to the rear of Reserve Infantry Regiment 235. Despite the efforts of Oberstleutnant Bronisch, commanding officer 1st Battalion Reserve Infantry Regiment 239, who did his best to provide an example of calmness under fire, by the time all his men were under control again some sub units were well on the way back to Poelcappelle and under unpleasantly accurate shrapnel fire. The right flank of Reserve Infantry Regiment 237 was in the air and the men tried to dig in quickly to escape the fire. Their efforts were in vain; within less than two hours the entire regiment was forced to withdraw a further 800 metres and to dig in once more there.

From a start line on the Gravenstafel Ridge, there was an attempt to renew the attack at about 3.00 pm but it achieved very little. Simultaneously, heavy fighting involving Reserve Infantry Regiments 238 and 240 of 52nd Reserve Division was still taking place around Broodseinde. Reserve Infantry Regiment 238 had advanced to the eastern edge of the village, where it waited for the Reserve Infantry Regiment 240 attack to begin. Its commander, Oberst von Wartenberg, gave the order at 10.00 am then, with 1st Battalion Reserve Infantry Regiment 240 left, 2nd Battalion right and the battalions of Reserve Infantry Regiment 238 deeply echeloned on the left flank, quite rapid progress was made. It seemed as though the defenders had been expecting the main effort to come directly against the village and so they concentrated their fire against Reserve Infantry Regiment 238, which had adopted hasty defence position and which held on until at about 2.30pm. 1st Battalion Reserve Infantry Regiment 240 was then ordered to launch a frontal attack on the village. Despite the obvious danger, the order came almost as a relief to the hard pressed men. Within minutes the leading sections were clashing with troops who were holding out in the first of the buildings.

The German artillery did not perform well during this battle, enabling the British troops to resist Reserve Infantry Regiment 240 north of the village, but pressure from Reserve Infantry Regiment 238 was followed by the waving of white flags and there were numerous surrenders. Some of the less experienced German troops had wanted to race forwards at the sight of the white flags; more cautious counsel prevailed. There was in fact no abuse of the white flags and eventually entire infantry sections surrendered until more than one hundred prisoners were being directed to the rear. Reserve Infantry Regiment 240 lost heavily that day. Major von Blücher, commanding 1st Battalion, was killed, Hauptmann Waldschmidt, commanding 1st Company, was wounded and Oberleutnant Hieronimus of 4th Company was also killed. So, in only forty eight hours of battle, the commanding officer and all four company commanders had become casualties and the adjutant, Leutnant Reunert, assumed command. To the south of the village, where British troops appeared to have established themselves along the line of the road from Broodseinde to Keiberg, there were also continuing problems in the face of obstinate defence.

At about 3 pm the town of Zonnebeke came under high explosive fire (what Hamilton calls 'Black Marias'):

> *Zonnebeke has a church, standing in a small 'place', with a very high steeple, and evidently the Germans, knowing our [Brigade] headquarters were in the centre of the town, were using the church steeple as a target. This bombardment in the streets of a town by high explosive shells was, I think, the most alarming part of the whole experience. Everything in the town shook when one of these shells burst. The whole ground appeared to tremble, as in an earthquake, even when the explosion was a hundred yards away.*

Zonnebeke has a church, standing in a small 'place', with a very high steeple … A photograph from about 1890.

1/South Staffs came under heavy attack all day. The 7th Division's history notes:

> ... *they held on, and thanks to the good cover offered by their narrow and deep trenches – the battalion contained many miners and prided itself on its digging – their casualties were low, while they had the satisfaction of inflicting heavy losses on their opponents, especially with the machine guns... Luckily the German artillery fire, though very heavy, mostly just went over the trenches; indeed more trouble was caused by a farm house on the right and by unlocated machine guns. On the left the Germans got within about three hundred yards, but found it impossible to advance further in face of the battalion's musketry, and a field battery which came forward boldly into the open to shell the Welsh Fusiliers* [on the left] *at short range gave the Staffords' left company a target of which it promptly availed itself.*

The 7th Division's history continues:

> *The Welch Fusiliers were soon in sore straits; their position was enfiladed from the left, the sandy soil made good trenches hard to construct, while about the worst result of the bombardment was that the sand tended to get into rifles and machine guns and put them out of action. By 9 am both the battalion's machine guns had been disabled and the heavy shelling made it extremely difficult to keep the firing line supplied with ammunition.*

The Regimental history, quoting Lieutenant Hindson – who was to languish in a German PoW camp until sent to internment in Holland in February 1918, describes the action:

> *At about 10 am the enemy began to bombard us with 'coal-boxes', having previously sent an aeroplane over. They soon began to find the exact range and began to flatten our trench very systematically. The brunt of the fire fell on the trenches either side of the Broodseinde-Moorslede road held by A Company, who lost heavily, the occupants being killed or buried in the trench.*

Reinforcements, in the shape of several platoons and the battalion's machine guns, came up at midday from the reserve battalion, 2/Warwicks; but the position was becoming hopeless. The Germans were working

Station Road, Zonnebeke, with the church in the distance; in the opposite direction the road led to Langemark.

A mill in Zonnebeke pre 1914, which was on Kleine Molenstraat (the street name lives on, if not the mill), west of the town.

their way around the battalion's left flank; a counter attack on a wood to the front of the position, from which the Germans appeared to be gathering before assaulting, came to grief, with only a few of the large assaulting party, of whom sixty or so reached its edge, managed to make their way back. Hindson continues:

> *As the day wore on, it became more and more difficult to get messages to and from Battalion Headquarters, and for two hours before we were taken we had lost touch; our only means of communication was by runner... After the bombardment* [of mid morning] *we found it impossible to use many of the rifles and we had to hammer our bolts open with entrenching tools; our maximum rate of fire was about three rounds per minute. In the afternoon we were being shelled from our left rear with shrapnel – at the time we thought our own guns were bursting short, but apparently they were German guns... About 4.30 pm I was captured with two other officers and forty two men; we had been holding about a hundred yards of trench.*

At about 5 pm, Hamilton got news that Major Malony, CO of 104 Battery, had been hit through his director whilst observing from the trenches north west of Zonnebeke, at the foot of the mill.

> *The medical officer at once went off to try and find a motor ambulance, and I rode up to the* [railway] *station. The fire was so hot in the street that I decided to leave Bucephalus under a large porch and I continued my way to the windmill on foot, keeping close in to the walls of the houses on the side from which the shells were coming. So long as the houses in the street were continuous, they afforded me complete protection from shrapnel or rifle bullets, and I was only hit by bricks and mortar from the walls of the houses; but, as I neared the outskirts of the town, the houses became detached one from another, and then it was very unpleasant having to cross the spaces between them. The shrapnel was bursting at intervals of ten or fifteen seconds, and it was impossible to judge when they would come. However, I found that by waiting until a shell had just burst, I usually had time to run like a hare to the next house. The rifle bullets, of course, could not be legislated for at all.*
>
> *I eventually reached the windmill close to Malony's observation post. Here I found a young officer of, I think, the Queen's, who was sheltering under the mound of the windmill with*

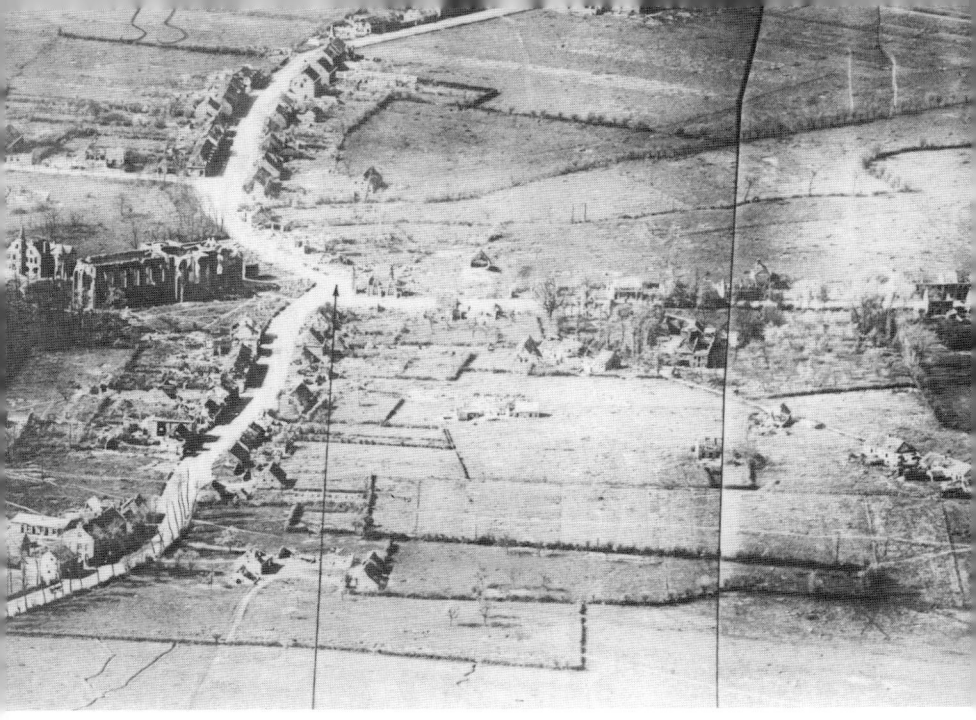

An aerial view of Zonnebeke taken in April 1916.

> some twenty men. He told me that he and his men were all that were left of a company of 250. He also told me that Malony had been dragged out of his trench and was lying behind a cottage on the other side of the road. On reaching this, I found that he had already been moved back towards his battery [positioned near the level crossing to the west].

Hamilton decided to return to get his horse and ride up to the Dressing Station, an ambulance having collected Malony:

> By this time the Germans had got the range of the church very accurately, and the open 'place' which I had to cross was thick with white smoke from bursting shrapnel. I never expected to cross it alive. The street was paved with round cobbles and covered with slimy mud – a place, under ordinary circumstances, I should have hesitated to ride along at a walk. However, on this occasion we negotiated it, including a right-angle corner, at as fast a gallop as poor old Bucephalus was capable of, and regained the cover of the narrow streets untouched.

By the time he got back, the perils of the situation were plain and the consequences inevitable:

> Our infantry were all this time being subjected to appalling fire both by shrapnel and 'Black Marias', the trenches in many parts being completely blown in, and the men in them buried alive. They dug out as many as they could, but when the cover was gone the survivors were exposed to view, and as nothing can live under fire unless entrenched, I fear that many of the men were buried alive. [...]
>
> By nightfall it was obvious to General Lawford that our position was becoming untenable, and it was decided to withdraw as soon as it was dark. By this time we had no supports, the supports and reserves having long ago been sent up into the trenches. Even the General's own headquarters guard had gone up too. The only men available were some belonging to a company of the RE. These hastily threw up a little shelter trench at the level crossing [west of the village], and if the worst came to the worst we hoped to be able to hold the crossing until the remains of the infantry got through.

Brigadier General Lawford obtained permission from Rawlinson to bring back his line, to a position from the railway crossing west of Zonnebeke, there connecting with 1/Irish Guards (itself withdrawn west of the Langemarck road) on I Corps' right and then continuing its front beyond a farm, Helles. A tributary of the Hannebeke (later known as Brands Gully) was used to provide cover against artillery, which however only gave a limited field of fire for the defending infantrymen. The brigade managed to carry out this move in relatively good order from about midnight; 2/Warwicks were on the left near the level crossing to the west of Zonnebeke, then 2/Queen's and 1/South Staffs. In the process of the retirement, however, the South Staffs (amongst others) managed to lose their transport – blissfully unaware of the situation, it was decided to get to the new positions via the Broodseinde crossroads, only to be welcomed and captured by the

Royal Welsh Fusiliers' officer casualties of the defence of Zonnebeke: Lieutenant Edwin Hoskyns, killed 20 October; he has no known grave.

Captain William Vyvyan RWF, wounded on 21 October and died as a prisoner on the 24th. He is buried at Bedford House.

Lieutenant Hugh Ackland-Allen RWF, kia on 23 October; he has no known grave.

German occupants. Although this loss might sound trivial, 1/South Staffs had literally lost everything except what they stood up in – the Germans captured their cookers, water carts, mess cart and GS wagons.

1/RWF suffered heavy casualties on this day; five officers were killed, three were wounded, six were missing – all taken prisoner; whilst there were over 300 casualties amongst the men – though only thirty seven of these were killed. Only two of these men have a known grave – the rest are commemorated on the Menin Gate. During the night 21/22 October it pulled back into Brigade reserve, in positions west of Nonne Bosschen Wood; there 1/RWF could muster only six officers (including the CO, adjutant and quartermaster) and 206 other ranks.

Night fell on the battlefield but Reserve Infantry Regiment 238 continued on south in the darkness to try to reach Zonnebeke though, for some time, it was virtually impossible to make meaningful progress. Fire was going in all directions, but German attackers kept up the pressure and eventually forced the defenders out of their positions; most of them escaping into the night. At that and despite the fact that it had already been in action for twelve hours, 1st Battalion Reserve Infantry Regiment 238 pushed on, reached the Moorslede – Zonnebeke road and then advanced towards Zonnebeke itself, capturing several farms on the way. During the course of the follow up, 1st Company, commanded by Leutnant Mattenklott, took three officers and 115 other ranks prisoner; whilst Offizerstellvertreter Riedmüller's 10th Company Reserve Infantry Regiment 240 also took prisoners: three British officers and forty eight other ranks. A little while later, with the men tired out, a halt was called for what was left of the night. Pickets and listening posts were sent out. This not only ensured against surprise. Such was the confusion that night, that the heavily laden British supply train mentioned above, which found itself in amongst German troops, was captured shortly before dawn. Random firing went on all night, but this caused very casualties, because the troops had all found some form of shelter or natural cover.

The 2nd Division

The Division advanced that day with 4 (Guards) Brigade on the right (more or less astride the Zonnebeke to Langemarck road, up to the area of what was to become Kansas Cross) and 5 Brigade on the left (to the future Vancouver Corner and about a kilometre towards Langemarck), with 6 Brigade held in reserve astride the road at Wieltje.

4 (Guards) Brigade's two forward battalions came from the Coldstream Guards. 2/Coldsteam on the right advanced to make contact with 7th Division, 22 Brigade, whose left flank ended near Zonnebeke

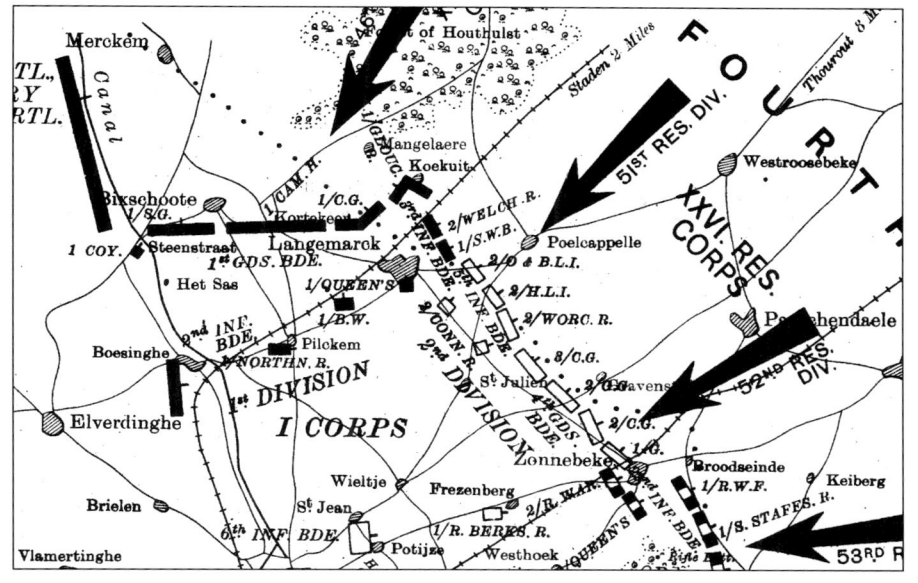

Situation evening of 21 October.

station; whilst 3/Coldstream advanced from its start area south of St Julien on the left; the divisional cavalry (15/Hussars) acted as a linking force between the two divisions. 2/Coldstream came under heavy enough fire to have to deploy as it crested the small rise near Zonnebeke, but by 11.30 am it had crossed the Zonnebeke-Langemarck road; it then halted in the face of stiff opposition. 3/Coldstream faced problems on its right but successfully managed to fight its way up to the ridge on which sits Gravenstafel; however, as troops to its flank could not come up to them, the two forward companies were withdrawn to a line forward of the Zonnebeke-Langemarck road. 3/Coldstream suffered quite heavy casualties, losing about a hundred men (sixteen killed), including the CO, Lieutenant Colonel G Feilding, who was wounded in the early afternoon.

7th Division, under increasing pressure during the afternoon all along its extensive front, was having difficulty holding its left flank; cavalry had already been used to reinforce it without decisive effect and so in the afternoon it was replaced by 1/Irish Guards; whilst 2/Grenadiers were also moved up in the afternoon, slotting in between 2 and 3/Coldstream and thus thickening up the whole line of 4 (Guards) Brigade. The final dispositions, by 2 pm, were two companies 3/Coldstream on the left, one company 2/Grenadiers in the centre and one company of 2/Coldstream on the right, all east of the Hanebeek; and one company 2/Coldstream thrown back to try and keep contact with 7th Division. A company of Irish Guards was sent to fill the gap to 7th Division and restored a line in Zonnebeke itself, cleared away a number of German snipers, taking shelter behind the seemingly ubiquitous hay stacks that feature so prominently in memoirs and regimental histories of this period, burying some of the dead of 22 Brigade and engaging, 'by order', in 'a lot of futile digging'.

Finally, shortly after midnight, 22 Brigade warned that it was pulling clear of Zonnebeke, taking up positions from the railway crossing west of Zonnebeke to the northern edge of Polygon Wood; this meant that 1/Irish Guards and 2/Coldstream had to fall back somewhat, back to Point 37 (to the west of today's Dochy Farm cemetery), to ensure that the divisional line was secure; a move they executed at about 1 am on the 22nd.

A participant in these proceedings was Major GD 'Ma' Jeffreys, second in command of 2/Grenadiers; his interesting diaries of the early months of the war form the basis of JM Craster's *Fifteen Rounds a Minute*.

'Ma' Jeffreys, after the war, as a major general.

> *After dark the whole sky to the east was lit up by the glare of fires, presumably lit by the Germans, who made a counter attack on our positions about 10 pm. As they approached, someone called out, 'Don't fire, we are Coldstream', but as their spiked helmets could be clearly seen against the light of the fire, our men were not taken in, and they were repulsed with heavy loss.*

Langemarck

In order fully to appreciate the way the events of the day unrolled near Langemarck, it is instructive to note what the Germans were trying to achieve in this area. Orders for 21 October were issued during the previous night. The Fourth Army's aim was to seize bridgeheads across the Yser, north of Ypres, so the orders to the three reserve corps were to clear up to the river. This was easier said than done. Intense fighting was going on for Becelaere and XXIII Corps was stalled east of Houthulst Wood. In an attempt to unlock the impasse, its 46th Reserve Division was directed to advance west, north of the wood, then to swing south until it met up with 51st Division; whilst the latter was ordered to drive hard to the west, ignoring the situation on its flanks and securing the approaches to the Yser. The Germans were aware that they would have to fight hard for Langemarck, which was in a state of defence.

It was not just the defences and garrison of the village that were a cause for concern. The terrain on all the approaches to Langemarck, with its wide drainage ditches, embankments and numerous buildings located on slightly higher ground, offered numerous defensive advantages in terms of covered fire positions and long fields of fire. It was quite obvious that all the approaches to Langemarck were potential death traps. The sole method of counteracting these difficulties, it was felt, was to rush the defences with massed forces and hope that the aggressive momentum so generated would be sufficient to overcome the problems. Given the state of training of the formations involved, this was highly optimistic.

Notwithstanding any reservations, 51st Reserve Division was ordered to launch forward from its positions around Poelcappelle at 8.00 am on 21 October. For speed and cohesion, it was to advance in four regimental columns towards Het Sas and Pilckem, and seize the entire length of the Yser from Bixschoote south. So as to provide maximum fire support, every gun was moved forward during the night into gun lines between Westroosebeke and Poelcappelle and, once in position, was to bring the heaviest possible weight of fire down on Langemarck from dawn until the attack closed up on the village.

As part of the preparations, Commander 51st Infantry Division issued the following order:

> *1. The enemy opposing the Corps is located at Langemarck and Broodseinde.*
>
> *2. The offensive will be continued tomorrow. The neighbouring corps to the right will advance completely to the north of Houthulst Wood. 52nd Reserve Division will attack the enemy to the south and, in so doing, will protect the flank of 51st Reserve Division.*
>
> *3. 51st Reserve Division will attack in four columns as follows:*
>
>> *- <u>Northern Column</u> (Reserve Infantry Regiment 234, Reserve Jäger Battalion 23, half of Cycle Company, 1st and 2nd Batteries Reserve Field Artillery Regiment 51 with a light ammunition column) is to advance from Poelcappelle Station via Koekuit, Bixschoote to Steenstraat.*
>>
>> *- <u>Second Column</u> (One battalion from Reserve Infantry Regiment 236, Reserve Jäger Battalion 24, 3rd Battery Reserve Field Artillery Regiment 51) from Poelcappelle Station via Goed ter Veste, Weidendrest and Kortekeer to Steenstraat.*

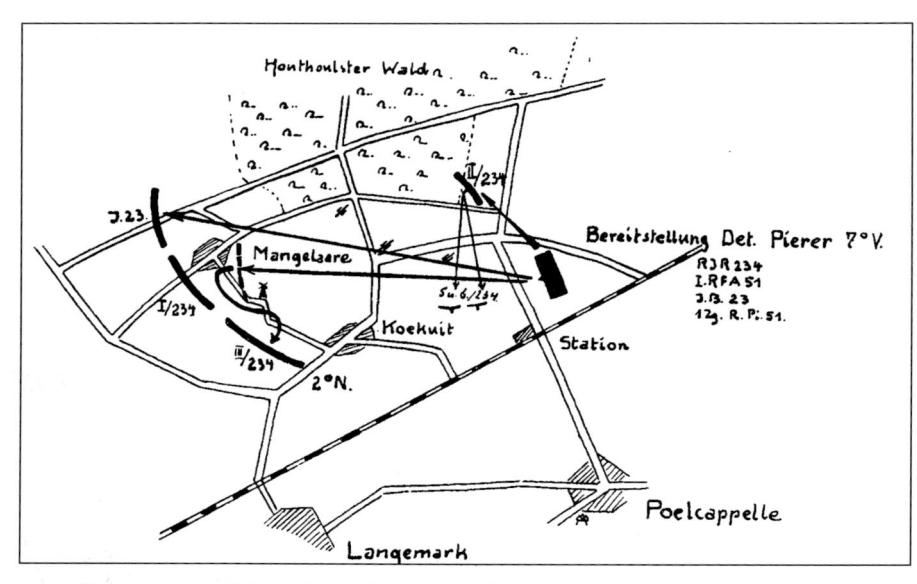

Situation near Mangelaare, 2.00 pm 21 October.

- *Third Column* (Two battalions Reserve Infantry Regiment 236, 4th Battery Reserve Field Artillery Regiment 51) from the northern edge of Poelcappelle village, north of Langemarck to Het Sas.

- *Southern Column* (Reserve Infantry Regiment 235, 3rd Battalion Reserve Field Artillery Regiment 51, Reserve Engineer Company 51 with 51st Reserve Division Bridging detachment on call) from Poelcappelle, south of Langemarck to Pilckem then Boesinghe.

The columns are to be at their start points, unobserved as far as possible, by 6.00 am. The advance is to begin at 6.00 am.

4. 4th Company Reserve Infantry Regiment 235 is to remain at the disposal of the Corps Commander, together with two field gun batteries (5th and 6th Batteries Reserve Field Artillery Regiment 51) and two thirds of the second light ammunition column.

5. Light ammunition columns are to be deployed as follows:

   - 1st Light Ammunition Column, reinforced by the remainder of the 2nd Column, with the Northern Column

   - A third of the 2nd Light Ammunition Column with the Third Column

   - 3rd Light Ammunition Column with the Southern Column

6. *The heavy artillery (100mm guns and Field Howitzers) is to reconnoitre positions between Poelcappelle and Westroosebeke, so as to be able to bring fire down on Langemarck and are to occupy these positions by 8.00 am.*

7. *I shall be located to the east of Poelcappelle by the main road. A telephone link is to be established to that point as soon as possible.*

I Corps:

As we have seen, to the south of I Corps the BEF was now very much on the defensive, fending off as best it could increasing German pressure; the limit of any eastwards advance had been reached on 19 October, although orders to advance continued for some days.

Haig had been instructed to advance eastwards, protected by 3rd (Cavalry) Division on his right and French cavalry on his left. In fact he was not to enjoy the benefit of Byng's cavalry division for any length of time, as it was withdrawn to assist Major General Capper's beleaguered right flank (and on the 25th became a part of Allenby's Cavalry Corps). He was told that there was still only one German corps within striking distance, though both I and IV Corps HQs felt that they would meet a larger enemy, even if they were newly raised. Haig's orders were for his two divisions to advance to Passchendaele – Poelcappelle and thence on to Westroosebeke. 2nd Division was already in place, but the 1st had to move up from its rear positions to get to the start line, a move delayed by fleeing refugees and the movement of French territorials. The result was that it did not get to the Langemarck line until 8.30 am and so, instead of I Corps moving forward at the planned 7 am, the advance began at 9.20 am.

Major General Thompson Capper, GOC 7th Division; he died of wounds received during the Battle of Loos and is buried in Lillers Communal Cemetery.

The Official History comments that the Germans were assisted by the 'country':

> ... though nearly flat – such low ridges as there were did not show up – was enclosed and intersected by streams, and high thick hedges, very difficult to get through; whilst views were further obstructed by labourers' cottages, trees in the hedgerows and small copses.

The Langemarck battlefield. Note the small enclosed fields and drainage ditches.

This is a salutary point to bear in mind when viewing the battlefield today; apart from the expansion of villages in this prosperous part of Belgium, changes in farming techniques have resulted in the ripping out of hedgerows and copses, making it more challenging to visualise the problems faced by the soldiers on the battlefield. As commented elsewhere, the Germans considered that the ground aided the defence!

There were also problems of manoeuvre for the troops of 51st Reserve Division as they attempted to get forward for the assault towards Langemarck. In fact there was a mad scramble throughout the night as troops deployed forward into their assembly areas. Such was the overcrowding of the few routes and so chaotic the movement that there was some doubt if it would be possible for everyone to be in position on the start lines in time. It took Reserve Infantry Regiment 235 no less than five hours to cover the four kilometres from Westroosebeke to Poelcappelle. At every halt exhausted infantrymen sagged to the ground and it was only with great difficulty that they could be got back on their feet. Then, when they finally arrived at Poelcappelle, the place was so crammed with troops that the regiment had to press on into open country and it was already nearly 3.00 am before there was any chance of a snatched doze before the attack was due to begin.

As a demonstration of the strain on the infantrymen before the assault even got underway, a member of Reserve Infantry Regiment 234 summarised the situation in his forward assembly area thus:

> *Stand by to assault Langemarck!... By about 5.00 am we were occupying a field to the right of the railway line leading to Langemarck. Still enfolded by the night, we sat on our knapsacks and propped our heads in our hands. Our whole beings were consumed by utter weariness. Klaus lay stretched out on the grass snoring. Nobody gave a thought to the day ahead... What lay ahead was as dark as the night itself. But there were odd feelings inside... what was it? Hunger? Thirst? Neither of those. Desire for sleep? Possibly! No, there was a feeling of anxiety – really sharp anxiety that bit and gnawed away at us ...*

Vizefeldwebel Frischauf Reserve Infantry Regiment 236, who was an early casualty, later recorded his impressions as the attack began,

> *Despite the fog, the enemy found out what was happening, some shrapnel shells began to explode over the houses and roads and a few men were wounded. Commands could be heard everywhere, but nobody really knew what was happening ... Doubling forward through gardens with some difficulty, the platoons and companies left the built up area and began to deploy into skirmishing lines. There was an immediate increase in the rifle and machine gun fire of an invisible enemy, who could not be engaged effectively by us. The firing of our batteries, which had closed up at high speed and had gone into position behind our lines, added to the noise of battle. Soon wounded, with pale faces and shiny dressings were returning in ever-increasing numbers. Some of them were being carried on rifles or slung in groundsheets, whilst other propped themselves against houses as their wounds were dressed. At long last my outpost, reinforced by the platoon which had been held back in the trenches they had manned the previous night as regimental reserve, was sent into battle."*

As the leading elements prepared to set off in the direction of Langemarck, the men of Reserve Infantry Regiment 233 which, together with two batteries of Reserve Field Artillery Regiment 51, was held back in Corps reserve and which had been on full alert and ready to move from 2.00 am, advanced their positions slightly. How much of an impact they

German infantry in hasty defence north of Langemarck in October 1914.

would be able to make remained to be seen. They began the day already feeling extremely tired and hungry. Their regimental historian later noted that they had not had a hot meal for three days, that they still lacked field kitchens and that had had to subsist on odd rations abandoned by the Belgians during their withdrawal. They could be no clearer proof of the totally inadequate preparation of the new reserve regiments.

Initially the ground mist and drizzling rain with attendant poor visibility facilitated the occupation of the divisional forming up places just in rear of the start lines. However, when at about 9.00 am the lines of infantry stood up ready to move off towards their objectives, the sun was beginning to burn off the mist. Langemarck by this time had disappeared behind clouds of dust and smoke thrown up by the continuing bombardment and shells continued to pour down to cover the move of the mass of infantry, as the regiments closed in as rapidly as possible on it but if the attackers expected to arrive swiftly on their objective they were rapidly disabused. Within a few minutes of crossing the start line they came under a torrent of accurate rifle and machine gun fire from various defended localities, including buildings on the edge of the village.

In the face of this fire German casualties began to mount rapidly and the advance quickly stalled. Maintaining direction proved to be very hard. As has been emphasised, there was almost no relief, whilst copses, hedges, fences and walls interfered with the fields of view. In addition to the boggy terrain there were numerous broad drainage ditches which blocked free movement. An almost total lack of topographical maps was an additional problem for the company officers, who were attempting to keep control and press on with the attack. Despite these difficulties, continuous attempts were made by individual sections and platoons to get forward, but the element of surprise had been lost. Fire support was scanty or non-existent and the defence took an enormous toll on the attackers. Eventually, hugging the ground, the survivors began to dig shell scrapes and to wait for darkness to fall. It is not difficult to see in retrospect how British plans for the day had served to frustrate the German advance.

5 Brigade's (2nd Division) advance began when 1st Division's 3 Brigade came up at 9.20 am, the South Wales Borderers being on the latter's right flank. At first things went smoothly enough, but once the Langemarck road had been crossed three battalions of the Brigade (from south to north, 2/Worcesters (sixty casualties, as recorded by the regimental history; another source suggests seventy five), 2/Highland Light Infantry [HLI], who came up as the fighting intensified (113 casualties) and 2/Ox & Bucks (220 casualties) were hit in enfilade by sustained enemy fire.

The day had started early in the morning, as the two leading battalions of 5 Brigade set off, **2/Worcesters** on the right and 2/Ox & Bucks on the left, followed by 2/Connaught Rangers and 2/HLI. The Worcesters' history notes:

> *2/Worcesters moved forward from the Pilkem Ridge to the crossroads north of St Julien* [Vancouver Corner]*, which they reached shortly after 6 am. There a long halt was made while the 1st Division came up into line on the left. British cavalry reported that the enemy were close in front and intermittent firing could be heard, but trees and hedgerows obscured the view.*
>
> *By 9.30 am* (sic) *all were ready to resume the advance; but the long delay had enabled the enemy's advanced troops to push forward almost up to the position of the halted brigade. The leading platoons of the Worcesters had advanced only a few hundred yards when their movement was checked by sharp bursts of fire from the hedges in front. A confused fight followed, with much rushing of small bodies of troops from hedge to hedge. Reinforcements were hurried up by both sides, and rapid firing became general all along the line. Many men were hit, advance*

became more and more difficult, and the platoons were forced to dig cover with their entrenching tools.

By nightfall all four companies of the battalion had been drawn into the firing line, which was extended among the hedgerows about a mile north east of St Julien. Picks and shovels were brought up after dark, and the troops set to work to make their position more secure. Throughout the night they laboured. Firing continued at intervals, and the work of entrenchment was interrupted by several minor attacks, all of which were beaten off.

The Worcesters' line was stiffened on the right by the deployment of two companies of 2/Connaughts, with the two others in reserve. The Connaughts suffered four killed and thirty wounded; they were fortunate not to have lost more:

> At about 6 pm the area was heavily shelled by the Germans. One of the enemy HE shells hit a small estaminet about a thousand yards behind where C and D Companies were stationed, in which Battalion Headquarters had been established. The Commanding Officer, Adjutant, and some four other officers were in the house at the time. The shell landed in an adjoining room and wrecked

The line of 2/Worcesters on 21 October.

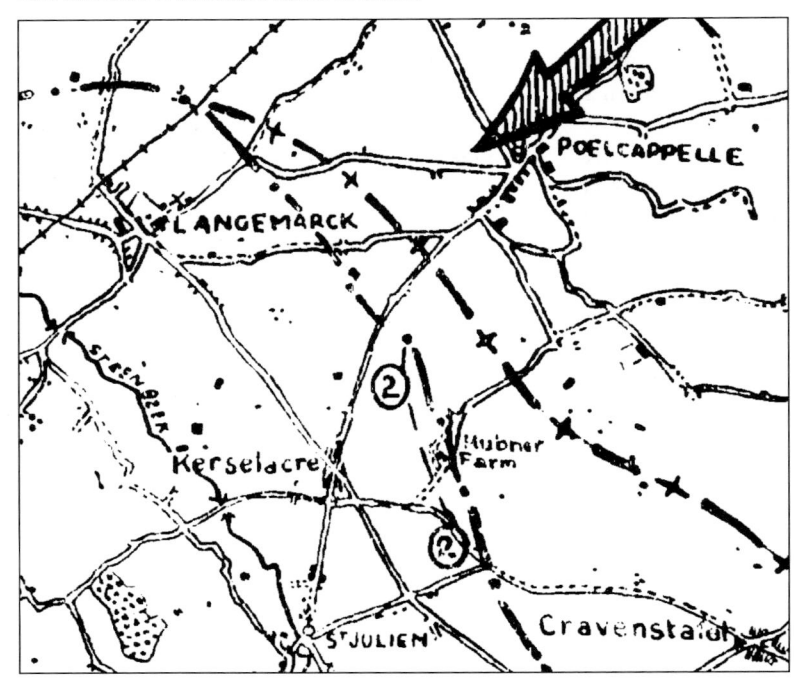

half the building and blew down the roof. All in the house were blown down by the explosion, but, fortunately, none were seriously hurt. During the bombardment all the rations and other stores, which had been laid out in a barn ready to be taken up to the companies in the trenches, were blown up.

2/Ox & Bucks, the left hand battalion, suffered considerably during the day's fighting: sixty one men and five officers were killed (one of whom died of wounds) – to which should be added three men missing, presumed killed.

The battalion was on the left of the division's line and attempted to keep contact with the South Wales Borderers on its left, which latter, it will be recalled, formed the right of 1st Division. Lieutenant Colonel HR Davies, the CO, wrote of the opening stages of the advance towards Passchendaele:

By this time [ie 9.20 am] *shrapnel had begun to fall, but it did not do a great deal of harm. The advance began, the men going forward under fire excellently. Bullets came almost at once, and it soon became evident that most of our losses were from fire from the left front, from ground which the 1st Division were to attack. A good many men were hit, but in spite of losses we advanced quickly and steadily, delay being caused chiefly by the difficulty of getting through thick fences.*

Indeed it was in getting through one of these fence-cum-hedge obstacles that the battalion suffered many of its casualties. D Company was held up short of a small stream, the Hanebeek (which has a bewildering number of different spellings in the various sources). Lord Ernest Hamilton, in his popular history of the early days of the war, published in 1916 – it went through twenty one 'editions' by early 1918 – notes that the battalion was checked:

... by a long hedge, interwoven with barbed wire. In the middle of the hedge was an open gateway, apparently offering the only opportunity for advance. Every officer and man, however, who attempted the passage of the gate was mown down by machine gun fire. ... Eventually Captain Tolson and Lieutenant Spencer succeeded in running the gauntlet of the gateway and got through. At the same time the hedge was broken down in more than one place...

Hamilton appears to have exaggerated as, according to the regimental account, 'only' about thirty men became casualties in this particular location and quite possibly none of these were an officer. But he does illustrate graphically some of the issues in advancing in this type of country – country for which at least some of the battalion commanders seem to have had available only a 1:100,000 map.

Captain HM Dillon of A Company, the follow up company on the right of the battalion's advance, wrote of his experiences to his sister; the letter was subsequently published in the Oxford Mail and in the regimental chronicle.

> *As soon as we got into line ready to advance they turned their guns on to us like a hose. We had to wait a bit to let the first line get on, and a good many people got hit. When the first line got on, I went forward at once and ran until I got to a ditch and put fifty men into it. All the officers of the front line company in front of me, bar one, were down by now, so the only thing was to get on at all costs and get our rifles into the devils. Went on again, but the men fell fast as we advanced. Collected some hundred men at some haystacks, but the wounded were rushing in from all sides for cover. Got to farm buildings with twelve men and had a few minutes rest. Went on again into lane, where I found four officers, and it seemed impossible to get on, and I found that only three of my men had got on. I had to go back to the farm to try to collect some men but when I got there I could find nobody, and I don't know now* [this part of the letter was written during the afternoon of the 22nd] *where they got to. Started coming back, when I saw a there was a deep furrow in a field on my right with some men in it, which I thought must be them, so went through. There was no shell fire now, but we were fairly snowed on by rifles and machine guns from God knows where, and had to crawl on elbows. When I got on about sixty yards I found they were not my men, but some of another regiment* [almost certainly from 2/Worcs]. *While I was debating what to do, a man ran to me; he had six holes in him and asked me to bandage him. He had no dressing, but I covered all the wounds bar one, for which I had no dressing – not a very good start for a battle, as I got covered in blood and shall not have a chance to wash for perhaps a week. Got on to hedge and at last discovered German position. Opened fire at, I suppose, 10 am...*
>
> *One could not move hand or foot all day, but in the evening went down and got some men of a Scotch* [sic] *regiment* [from 2/HLI]. *This made three different lots in my command. If we could*

have got another hundred men we could have rushed the Germans, but they did not want us to, as the next troops on our left [3 Brigade] *were left behind. A great pity, as the Germans evidently had had enough, and we could have got through. Dug deep trenches all night.*

The fire this first day was beyond belief. High explosives, shrapnel, machine guns and rifles blended into one unending roar. I was completely deaf through the first part of the night...

At about 8 pm the firing died down and he sought orders from Colonel Davies:

He told me to take command of all the troops I had with me, get the wounded away if possible and dig. We did dig, and got the wounded away before morning. The dead we pulled out into a field and covered them up; also got some rations and water. There was nothing to be done but await events.

With the advance held up, the battalion had begun to entrench at dusk. The CO and his adjutant, Captain RB Crosse, went to investigate the hedge line in front of the farm that was being used as Battalion HQ and to make contact with D Company, which straddled the Poelcappelle road:

Captain Harden [OC D Company] *saw us and ran across the road to us, although the Colonel called out to him not to come. He came, however, and was explaining where his Company was, when a bullet went straight through his head and killed him at once. On our way back we saw a man who told us that Lieutenant Murphy* [C Company] *had just died of his wounds and that his body was about fifty yards away under a haystack.*

Captain Allan Harden, 2/Ox & Bucks, killed 21 October; he has no known grave.

Colonel Davies continues his account:

During the night we were able to get up rations and ammunition, also the big entrenching tools from the tool wagons; and water bottles were filled at the farm [which later became known as New Houses] *where I had my headquarters. A great many wounded were brought into our farm, but there was some delay in getting up the ambulances, owing, I believe, to a mistaken order having been given to them by someone to turn back when on their way up.* [This perhaps not too surprising, given that the farm was practically a part of the new British front line.] *Having some fifty wounded in the farm, with the probability of its being shelled, was a great anxiety; but to my intense relief some motor-ambulances arrived just in time, and we were able to get all the wounded away before daylight.*

In addition, at 8.30 pm, thirty six of the men were marched down to St Julien, by that stage a mile and a half away, to the advanced dressing station by the wounded Major Eden, the Battalion's senior major. 2/HLI had moved a company forward on the left of the Ox & Bucks as the fighting developed; for the night they had two companies on the left, forming a contact with 1st Division, the other two forming a close reserve. 6 Brigade remained throughout the day at Wieltje although, because of the difficult situation developing around Zonnebeke, 1/Berks was moved up to Frezenberg so that it could be in a better position to intervene should this become necessary.

The 2nd Division had had a rather indifferent day; it had certainly failed in its aim of taking Passchendaele; this was mainly a consequence of the difficult situation into which 1st Division had become embroiled soon after it began its advance from Langemarck towards Poelcappelle. In fact it had had its heaviest fighting of the Battle of Langemarck on

The ruins of St Julien church and village, taken later in the war, from near the Hanebeek.

A British ammunition waggon blown off a bridge at St Julien.

this day (suffering a total of 578 casualties); the subsequent hard fighting was to take place for the most part on its flanks, on the fronts of 7th and 1st Divisions.

The 1st Division

1st Division moved very early in the morning from its billeting area around Elverdinghe, and the forward brigades crossed the canal at Boesinghe. The advance guard comprised three battalions (from 3 Brigade, Brigadier General Landon), a couple of batteries of artillery, some cavalry and cyclists, as well as medical and engineer units; in support was 1 (Guards) Brigade, with 2 Brigade held back as a Corps reserve in the Boesinghe area. Lieutenant J Hyndson, who was in B Company of 1/Loyal North Lancs, describes the initial moves:

> *21* [he seems to have put 20 and 21 October together] *October: We begin our march towards Ypres, passing through the village of Steenevoorde and Poperinghe, and in this latter*

Brigadier General HJS Landon, GOC 3 Brigade; on 26 October, with a number of others, he was promoted to major general and took temporary command of 1st Division after Lieutenant General Lomax was wounded (he died after some months) at Hooge Chateau on 31 October.

55

village our troops, having surrounded some 200 Germans inside the church, are patiently waiting for them to surrender. […] *On we go again, and finally, after having covered some eighteen miles in all, we billet in houses by the roadside* [a few kilometres short of the Boesinghe area]. *Room is somewhat cramped, and the whole company, two hundred and fifty strong, sleep the night in one small house built to accommodate a family of five!*

The start line for the advance proper was Langemarck; delays were caused by the great congestion on the roads, especially at the choke points of the bridges on the Yser. 2nd Division had at least the advantage of being much closer to their start line, whilst the whole of 1st Division had a tiring march – there is nothing much worse than the 'stop start' that characterised the move of about nine miles or so. 1/Queen's (Royal West Surrey) led the column, followed by 1/SWB and 1/Glosters; they had to pass the brigade start point at 3.40 am, clear Elverdinghe by 5 am and be through Langemarck by 7 am. In fact it was 6.30 am before it got to Boesinghe and 8 am by the time it got to Langemarck. French territorials were still present in the village; but what was to be of great practical assistance in the event were a couple of French batteries armed with the very effective 75s.

The delayed move on Poelcappelle began at about 9.20 am: 1/Queen's (left), headed towards Poelcappelle station, about a mile or so north of the village itself; and 1/SWB (right), headed on the eastern road out of Langemarck, aiming to make contact with 2/Ox & Bucks on its right.

A French 75mm field gun battery in action near Ypres

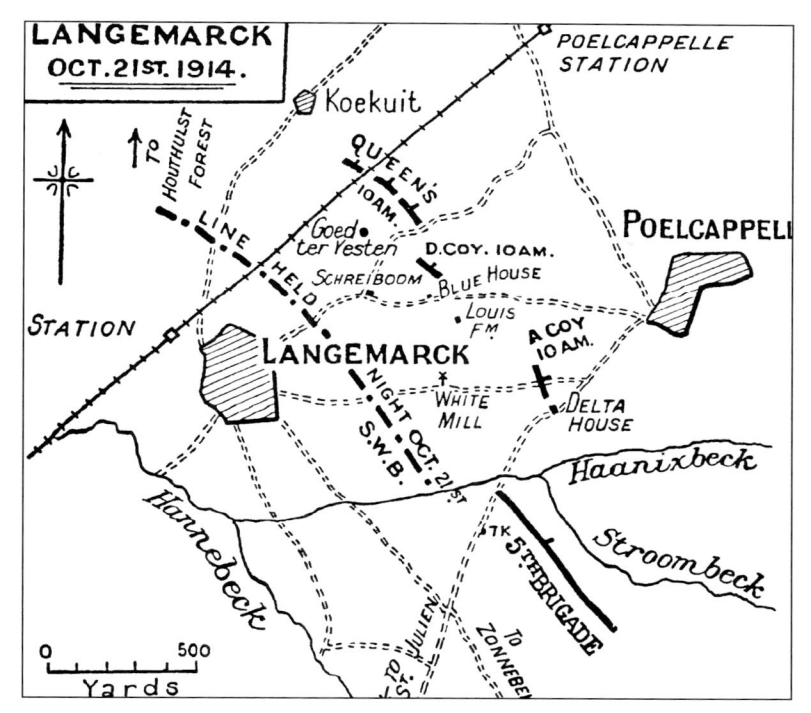

The right of 1st Division, 21 October.

1/SWB began its advance under heavy German shell fire, which was, however, neither very accurate or effective; progress was made easier by the closed nature of the country and effective British and French artillery support, but the ground soon became much more open, at which time rifle fire became a problem, particularly for the second line. By 10 am the Queen's had got about half way to their objective, with the SWB keeping up; the Germans, indeed, seemed to be pulling back to the north. In the midst of this progress, German units from *46th Reserve Division* launched their attack from Houthulst Forest and were clearing the French (mainly cavalry) before them. 1/Queen's had to switch resources to the left flank, which under the original scheme would have been covered by the French. This meant that 1/SWB, whilst continuing to move forward, eventually lost contact with 1/Queen's, about an hour after the advance had begun. The Glosters were put on the left flank of the division's advance and occupied Koekuit; 1 (Guards) Brigade, instead of pushing on the attack towards Westroosebeke, as originally planned, was now becoming enveloped into the developing battle north and east of Langemarck.

French hussars passing French infantry near Ypres.

By early afternoon, 1/SWB was under increasing pressure from German attacks, especially on the left and by mid afternoon – at about 2.15 pm – the forward companies were forced back towards Langemark. Reinforcements from 2/Welch helped to stabilize the situation on the left and two companies managed to occupy a line about 500 yards north east of Langemark; the gap between these and A Company, which was well ahead on the right, was effectively covered by a machine gun. One advantage of the forward nature of A Company's position, along with the fact that it had a good field of fire and at least some cover, meant that it was able to keep German advances out of Poelcappelle westwards under control. However, its isolated position and the fact that it had suffered significant casualties – twenty five killed and missing, fifty or so wounded – meant that at about 5 pm it was ordered back (which it accomplished a few hours later), to bring it into alignment with 2/Ox & Bucks on the right and the new configuration of 3 Brigade. For by this stage all pretence at advancing had been abandoned and 1 (Guards) Brigade was now fully occupied in holding the division's left flank. By the end of the day the battalion had lost nineteen men killed, sixty five missing – though, as it turned out, slightly over forty of these had been killed, with over sixty wounded. Of the dead, all but ten or so have no known grave. Captain Barry had a narrow escape:

> [He] *was at first reported missing* [and] *owed his life to the devotion of some of his men who refused to give up searching for him, and eventually found him seventy two hours after he had been wounded, disabled by a badly damaged knee.*

1/Queen's had as its objective the road running from the railway station at Poelcappelle, extending towards the village. Its progress was halted at about 10.30 am by flanking and frontal fire and they dug in at that point. In the early afternoon, at about 2.30 pm, there was confusion in the right forward company (B), when the line had to be inclined back to conform with that of 1/SWB, which led, for whatever reason, to a withdrawal being made by the whole company; the company on the left, being notified of the move, in turn withdrew, along with its support company – and in the process suffered considerable casualties. The new line was established where the support company (2/Welch) had their positions; and at 7.30 pm the battalion was removed to reserve positions, west of Langemarck and south of the railway. The day's action had cost it two killed and one wounded officer; thirteen other ranks killed, sixty eight wounded and six missing.

Soon after the advance began, fighting developed further to the north of Langemarck; a threat was perceived to be coming from the area of Koekuit, a tiny hamlet on the left flank of the division. **1/Glosters**, at about 10 am, sent half a company to occupy it and the rest of the battalion entrenched behind it and also attempted to make contact with the Queen's on the right. Now the whole of 3 Brigade had been committed. It was also becoming clear that considerable bodies of French troops were withdrawing from the division's left. The Glosters were warned by French cyclists of 7th *Cavalry Division* of the major German advance coming from the north east. A number of German thrusts were made against Koekuit and the left flank; one, a major effort at 11.45 am, came from the direction of Mangalaere, but the position was held, the Germans getting no closer than about 600 yards. Having failed, they fell back to Mangalaere. More men from the Glosters moved up, shortening the gap between them and 1/Queen's; from these position the Glosters were able to give support fire to the Queen's, who were suffering, in particular, from German artillery fire from Poelcappelle. A second, bigger attack was made on the hamlet at about 2 pm, this time from the direction of Staden, the number of defenders was fast dwindling and then the movement backwards of 1/Queen's in mid afternoon led to Koekuit being abandoned.

Perceiving the threat to the left flank of the division, 1/Coldstream was sent up to prolong the line along the Kortebeek, a small stream north of Langemarck, here running more or less east to west and several hundred metres behind Koekuit. With the help of the Coldstream (and some men from 1/Scots Guards), the Glosters recaptured the hamlet an hour or so after its abandonment. By 4 pm Koekuit was reoccupied and the Glosters' line was extended three hundred yards to the south west, to

Grutesaele Farm; the battalion's position now resembled a 'U' bend with the apex at Koekuit, vulnerable to attack from flanks and front. The final major German attack came soon after 4 pm, when German columns were seen advancing from the area of Poelcappelle Station; rapid bursts of fire broke these up, but the accompanying artillery barrage accounted for a number of defenders, including several wounded, who had been put in a ditch until they could be evacuated.

The Glosters held on to Koekuit until dark, when it was again given up as it was too far in advance of the rest of the line and the position vulnerable in the extreme. By midnight, after delays in getting the wounded evacuated, the battalion withdrew to Varna Farm, south west of Langemarck, in reserve. Given the intensity of the fighting, they had extraordinarily few casualties, losing three officers and forty eight other ranks.

Major General (soon to be Lieutenant General) Samuel Lomax, GOC 1st Division.

Because of the increasing threat from German troops coming out of Houthulst Forest and from Mangalaere, Major General Lomax (GOC 1st Division) about noon ordered Brigadier General FitzClarence VC (GOC 1 Brigade) to send a company of 1/Cameron Highlanders (the brigade reserve), with supporting artillery and a small group of cavalry, to take up defensive positions around Kortekeer Cabaret, which sat on the crossroads on the Langemarck-Bixschoote road, and in particular the crossings of the St Jansbeek – sometimes written as St Jans Beek – and Kortebeek (now the Broenbeek). Hardly had A Company got itself in position than it was joined by the rest of the battalion. This was moved up from their reserve position to the north of what became known as Iron Cross, where the men had been dispersed to rest in scattered platoon groups 'as a precaution against 'aimed' (ie observed) artillery fire from aircraft'. Soon afterwards 1/Scots Guards was sent to cover the left flank of the Camerons and 1/Black Watch was brought up to cover any gaps between the Coldstream and the Camerons as necessary and to act as a reserve.

Brigadier General C FitzClarence VC, in his younger days, GOC 1 (Guards) Brigade.

This situation had come about because of developments on the French front, to the left of I Corps. Its advance had been based on the premise of its flanks being secured – by IV Corps on the right and by the French Cavalry Corps on the left. Even before the advance began on 20

A German post action photograph of Kortekeer Cabaret and the crossroads.

October it was clear that 7th Division was rapidly becoming over extended; now the protection of the French cavalry was withdrawn by an order issued at about 2 pm. The reason for the latter decision was because of the weight of the German attack on the Yser to the north of Steenstraat and because of the German forces coming through Houthulst Forest, notably its northern edge. Fortunately for I Corps, the GOC (General Hely d'Oissel) of the French *7th Cavalry Division* refused to carry out this order until he received a formal order so to do, as he realised the potentially fatal consequences to I Corps if its flank were to be uncovered suddenly; his division remained in the Bixschoote area until the British had taken suitable action. This involved the deployment of 1 (Guards) Brigade along the line from the rear of Bixschoote to close to Koekuit, with 1/Scots Guards on the left, the Camerons in the centre and 1/Coldstream on the right. Indeed groups of French troops, including some artillery, remained for some time after in I Corps' sector. Hely d'Oissel, is one of the unsung heroes of 1st Division on 21 October – his name is not noted in any British account that we have seen. He went on to command a corps, which he was still doing when the war ended.

A Company of **1/Camerons** was deployed forward and to the right of Kortekeer Cabaret; there was sporadic shooting, but casualties were chiefly caused by shellfire – either German or from French

General Hely d'Oissel, GOC of the French 7th (Cavalry) Division, a robust and dependable ally.

shrapnel shells bursting short – an uncomfortable situation shared by a company of French territorials, who also held part of the line of the streams. When the rest of the 1/Camerons came forward the companies were deployed in a half circle around the Cabaret – which itself became the Battalion's headquarters. To prevent these extended positions being overrun under the cover of darkness, the CO, Lieutenant Colonel MacEwen, drew the circle inwards, closer to its centre. D and B Companies covered the left of the circle, A and C the right.

So, by nightfall, 1st Division had been forced to deploy two of its brigades and held a refused and extended left flank that looked vulnerable.

By the end of the day, I Corps had suffered 932 casualties which, in the circumstances and given the scale of the German losses, were light. It held a front of between seven and eight miles from the western edge of Zonnebeke to south of Koekuit (five miles) and from there to just south of Bixschoote and the canal at Steenstraat. What is called a 'line' is not to be confused with the line after trench warfare set in by the end of 1914, even less so with the increasing sophistication of such lines as the war progressed. Essentially, those of I Corps at this stage consisted almost exclusively of independent rifle pits, fairly shallow – maybe three feet deep – often providing mutual fire support or covering gaps between units. These gaps could be quite wide, anything up to a couple of hundred yards. They were almost never protected by wire and, although they could cover any gaps during daylight hours, such gaps were vulnerable to infiltration at night or in heavy mist or fog conditions, not unusual at this time of the year. In addition, they provided minimal cover against adverse weather; there was plenty of drizzle and heavier rainfall during First Ypres and the temperatures could be low. So the men of all armies were weary – very weary – and, to make things worse, both sides had difficulty in maintaining adequate rations, the Germans probably more so than the British.

Not only did the German soldiers suffer from failure of their administrative tail to supply and feed them, the inexperienced soldiers of 51st Reserve Division had simply been out of their depth and outfought on the eastern approaches to Langemarck that day. One veteran of Reserve Infantry Regiment 235, referred to only as 'Unteroffizier B', later wrote in his diary:

Who today and during the days that followed had any idea about what was happening and what either we or the enemy intended? Our company commander was as much in the dark as I, or even the dumbest recruit. *In fact the last named would have been best placed by far. He knew absolutely nothing and, therefore, could not even get hold of the wrong end of the stick. Quite suddenly bursts of shrapnel spread death and destruction on our positions. There was no holding on any more. There was no order. I had no clue where our platoon commander was, nor did I know if those of us who could still move should launch ourselves further forward, or if it would be better to head to the right and cross the road to see if that offered protection. Men were falling all around me; we were in a witches' cauldron of artillery fire. There was nobody in charge, none who could have stated whether or not we were to hold on at all costs.*

My own thoughts were not to pull back but to go forward and to the right, so that we should leave the artillery fire behind. There were no formed sections or platoons any more, nor was there any sort of unified advance. What I saw and experienced that day and later was amongst the sort of image that the wildest imagination can dream up. What was left of our division, of the four regiments which we had deployed? One thing was sure. In every piece of meadow, behind every hedge, were bands of men, some large, some small; but what were they doing? What could they do? Visibility over the ground was strictly limited by all the hedges. Some claimed to be under fire from the right flank; others from the left. The battle situation was totally unclear. The only leaders left were unteroffiziers; and we knew little more than the men.

As the day wore on, deadly accurate shrapnel fire from the allied batteries burst above the German troops and entire groups of soldiers were seen to fall to this, the primary killer of 1914. The situation became ever more critical when NCOs and platoon officers were killed or wounded. There was insufficient expertise or experience amongst the soldiery, many of whom milled around aimlessly or sought cover in the numerous buildings dotted around the countryside. Reserves continued to be committed to the battle but they, like those who had gone before, could make no impression on a resolute defence. Despite the hornet's nest of fire, some German field artillery batteries were rushed forward to the front line, from where they brought down fire with varying amounts of success against point targets in or near Langemarck. At one time the blue uniforms of French territorial soldiers, who were deployed alongside the British, were seen to be pushed out of their outpost line, but there was no general withdrawal and the situation remained critical as the allied troops poured devastating rifle and machine gun fire on the attackers.

In response, fresh forces were sent forward from Poelcappelle, but this simply led to a hopeless intermingling of largely leaderless survivors from several different units and almost insurmountable problems of command and control. At about midday, the Corps Commander deployed his final reserve - Reserve Infantry Regiment 233 - but it achieved nothing at all. The experience of Kriegsfreiwilliger Kleysteuber of 9th Company was absolutely typical:

> *We advanced on the enemy at about midday. Together with Julius Schleiden from my home town, a few other comrades and Offizierstellvertreter Grothe, we moved as a covering party about fifty metres in front of the company. We made our way forward by pushing through gardens and hedges. It was flat countryside,* [comprising] *fields, meadows and numerous gardens, all surrounded by hedges and fences, which made it extremely difficult to advance. Suddenly, we came under fire and bullets whistled all around us. There was, however, absolutely no sign of the enemy. An enemy machine gun joined in and then the fun really began!*
>
> *We threw ourselves down and crawled into a ditch and stayed there for a full half hour, whilst the machine gun systematically raked the entire area. Exercising the greatest care, we managed to get to a farmstead, looked for cover behind a ditch and dug in to some extent. We then had a chance to look behind us at our own men and were able to see what havoc the machine gun had wrought. Our dead were lying there in rows and we were not in a secure position either! An aircraft flew over and betrayed our position. Artillery fire began to come down and shrapnel shell after shrapnel shell burst above us – a fuze landed a mere three metres to my left.*
>
> *Schleiden and I sought cover behind a willow tree, which was hit repeatedly and splinters of wood splashed into our faces. We felt ourselves all over, but it was nothing. There we stayed for some considerable time under a dense rain of shrapnel balls. In order to get clear of it we moved right, but only succeeded in moving out of the frying pan into the fire. It was even worse there. One man came up to me with a bleeding hand and another was lying behind me. Hit in the leg by a shrapnel ball, he was unable to walk and had to pull himself forward with his hands. Sauer arrived, hit in three places. We tried once more to launch an assault, but we were simply beaten back.*

The situation was the same all along the attack frontage, so it was hardly surprising that these disorganised, inexperienced troops began to pull back in increasing numbers. As always, the movement began with individuals and small groups, but there was soon the very real risk of panic and wholesale retreat. Only heroic efforts by the few surviving commanders prevented this from happening for the time being. Survivors amongst the German infantry were almost unanimous that they had never imagined that such a weight of fire could conceivably have been brought down from the buildings on the eastern edge of the village, whilst their gunners freely admitted that their attempts at counter-battery fire were almost impossible. They could not find places where they could observe allied gun lines beyond Langemarck directly and, at that time, there was no other means of bringing accurate fire to bear. The allied gunners, less concerned about the German artillery than the threat posed by their infantry, only had to fire shrapnel into the area forward of Langemarck to be able to cause death and destruction on a huge scale.

As the day wore on the commander of 51st Reserve Division struggled hard to maintain the momentum of his attack. It was largely in vain. Most orders never reached their intended recipients and, even where runners did get through, all attempts to give substance to them failed as the regiments withered away in the storm of fire on the approaches to Langemarck. By the early afternoon, having suffered appallingly and with all its officers killed, wounded or missing, Reserve Infantry Regiment 235 broke. Panic-stricken, the survivors ran to the rear, totally out of control and pursued by bursting shrapnel all the way to Poelcappelle. 'Unteroffizier B' of Reserve Infantry Regiment 235 later described the scene from his perspective.

Later it became – allegedly – impossible for us to hold on where we were and on the word of command, 'About turn!' an unstoppable move to the rear began. We moved back until, just before the village, [Poelcappelle] *we bumped into the Oberst of Regiment X* [Oberst Wilhelmi, Reserve Infantry Regiment 236]. *He stopped us in our tracks, turned us about and drove us forwards once more. Had we been gathered together, reorganised, given a clear mission and placed under suitable leadership, things would probably have turned out better. For hours I had not seen a single familiar soul. Soon we set off forwards, then deviated to the right and soon we turned back. There was no sign that men were willing to stand up like German soldiers on campaign, willing to defend what was right and to act as the terror of the enemy. Rather the feeling was that we had been senselessly sacrificed and were being treated like cannon fodder in the most contemptuous meaning of the word.*

Responding to urgent requests for support from 51st Reserve Division, XXVI Reserve Corps allocated it the last reserves, which only amounted to one infantry battalion and a single field artillery battery. In addition, members of the divisional staff went forward to try to hold and then rally the retreating troops. This was successful in places, but all the impetus had gone; there could be no question of even equalling the previous limit of the advance. The unfolding disaster was watched by the commander and staff of the neighbouring Reserve Infantry Regiment 236. Oberst Wilhelmi, the commander, went out into the open to rally the troops, but was himself wounded in the process. Poelcappelle became crammed with aimless stragglers and shirkers who were eventually gripped by a few officers and NCOs, who deployed them into the trenches to the west of the village and remained with them in order to ensure that they stood firm.

As the day wore on, 1st Battalion Reserve Infantry Regiment 236 was designated the divisional reserve and sent to a holding area near Westroosebeke, but it soon it had to redeploy forward once more to fill a gap between Reserve Infantry Regiments 235 and 236 just forward of Langemarck. Its commander, Hauptmann Schöler, was killed in the process and there were many other casualties. One man who did survive was Kriegsfreiwilliger Willi Kahl of 7th Company, who later wrote,

> We had imagined that our baptism of fire would be somewhat different. There can be nothing more depressing than the very

A German cemetery in Westroosebeke in the early days of the fighting.

Westroosebeke whilst under German occupation.

public failure of an attack launched as though on exercise against an invisible enemy. Unthinking, section after section ran into the well-directed fire of experienced troops. Every effort had been put into our training, but it was completely inadequate preparation for such a serious assault on battle-hardened, long service colonial solders. Only through consideration of the extraordinary moral tension of the morning of 21 October can there be comprehension of the moment during the afternoon when the enemy hove into view for the first time. Of necessity, due to the increasing loss of our commanders, the individual was thrown back ever more on his own resources and, to some extent, it was possible to proceed beyond the drills which had been learnt and so cope with the hidden terrain and the constant surprises the battle itself threw up.

After two rounds fired standing unsupported, as if on the range, the inevitable happened. Just as I was taking the first pressure on the trigger, I was hit in the left buttock and I immediately felt the effects of the last strenuous days of marching – days for which we had not in the slightest been prepared – and the loss of blood from the wound weakened me far more than should have been the case. Everywhere there was confusion. Men were flooding back from the front, it was impossible to miss what was happening. Was it withdrawal? Had there been an enemy counter-attack? Would we be able to advance once more; would we wounded not have to be cared for? Yet again we were back to the total hopelessness and paucity of thought which had marked our attacks from the very beginning.

The day ended with parties from Reserve Infantry Regiment 236 and a few sections of Reserve Infantry Regiment 235 clinging on in rough shell scrapes and trenches in amongst houses on the edge of Langemarck. They were completely isolated and in a critical position. There was no possibility of renewing the general attack, though there was a failed attempt to capture the gas works, during which a few British soldiers were taken prisoner. A discussion between the few surviving leaders after night fell led to the decision being taken to abandon the gains and to withdraw to Poelcappelle, taking all the wounded and prisoners with them. This was achieved relatively easily, but the day as a whole had been a bitter, bloody fiasco.

Leutnant Brendler of Reserve Infantry Regiment 233 subsequently recorded his impressions of the day.

Darkness fell! – the battle stalled! We could sense that the enemy had beaten off our powerful thrust. The enemy was still harassing the area with shrapnel and firing at the great straw stacks until they caught fire and lit up the battlefield. By the light of these fires we could make out a few figures as they moved around, whilst the enemy, doubtless sheltering in well concealed trenches, immediately brought down fire on them. The figures moved towards us; they were men of the 233rd. We went forward and linked up with a further twenty men. Far to our right and left there was no sign of any Germans. In the meantime the night had become inky black.

Young *Kriegsfreiwilligen* on the march in Flanders: *There had been no time to equip the troops with anything more than the rudiments of infantry soldiering ...*

> Seeking to make contact, we suddenly came under murderously heavy fire which cracked around our ears. There was no need for words of command. Everyone threw himself to the ground and tried to worm his way deep into it. Those who had no spades dug with their helmets or bayonets. None of us had any idea where we were; there were no maps and, even if we had had, we could not have read them in this darkness and the use of light would have been ill advised! ... Ever since we moved into the assault we had received orders from neither regiment nor battalion, so it was a matter of acting independently. I then led this detachment, about fifty to sixty men strong and composed of men from all the battalions, back to Poelcappelle.

Not all groups of survivors were fortunate enough to have an officer or NCO to provide leadership and guidance. The day had been an exhausting, emotionally draining and shattering experience for the majority of those engaged. The way the battle developed and total failure of the attack underlines brutally the deficiencies in the training and preparation of these new formations. There had been no time to equip the troops with anything more than the rudiments of infantry soldiering, so that as soon as commanders were killed or wounded minor tactics and battlefield discipline fell apart. The result was near, or actual, panic that day near Langemarck and there were also scenes of drunkenness and ill-discipline amongst the leaderless soldiery who had made their way back to the shelter of Poelcappelle.

Away from the fighting, in the relative calm of Ypres, meetings took place which involved, at one stage or the other, French, Haig, Rawlinson, de Mitry (French cavalry) and Bidon (French territorials). Rawlinson made clear the precarious nature of his position around Zonnebeke and the thrusts along the line of the Comines Canal on his southern flank. With the considerable enemy activity on I Corps' left flank, it was clear that the Germans were making a determined attack from the south east and north east on Ypres, not to mention a massive assault on the Belgian positions to the north, on the Yser. So, by mid afternoon, Haig realised that there was no question, at the moment, of continuing his attack much beyond the original preliminary objectives of Poelcappelle and Passchendaele, an assessment with which French agreed. French also revealed that Joffre intended to launch an offensive eastwards, in conjunction with Belgian troops, on I Corps' left, but would need time to locate and position the necessary troops: *IX Corps*, of two infantry divisions was being sent immediately to Ypres, more would follow later; however, such an attack could not commence before the 24th.

General Bidon, GOC the French 87th (Territorial) Division, part of de Mitry's II (Cavalry) Corps.

GHQ's orders to the various corps of the BEF went out at 8.30 pm, instructing that the general line was to be held, 'which will be strongly entrenched'. But, as the Official History points out, in its last comment on the day's actions, '... for such entrenchment, as we know, both material and man power were lacking'.

On the German side, later that evening Headquarters XXVI Reserve Corps, for its part, issued an order whose wording suggested either that the chain of command was totally out of touch with events on the battlefield or had taken an unrealistic view of the reports passed up the line.

Southern Exit, Westroosebeke, 21 October 1914

1. I am delighted that today the Corps, during its first serious battle, has beaten off and driven back the enemy all along the line.

2. Tonight the Corps is digging in in the captured positions, reorganising, and replenishing with food and ammunition. Strong forces, also dug in, are echeloned back on the flanks and are preparing to resume the offensive in the morning. Throughout the night there is to be constant patrolling against the enemy, timely reporting if they withdraw, including information concerning the direction in which they are pulling back. Should the enemy still be in position along the front in the morning, the attack is not to be launched until a special order has been issued. During the attack artillery reserves are to be held back until the decisive moment, but individual guns or sections can be used in enfilade against enemy lines of infantry.

3. 51st Reserve Division is to withdraw a large reserve during the night and is to decide when and where its deployment is likely to promise final success.

4. 52nd Reserve Division is largely deployed outside the boundaries of the Corps. The division is to leave only weak forces dug in against the enemy in the Broodseinde sector and the main force is to move in to the area bounded by Mosselmarkt – Kerselaar and Moorslede – Brielen.

5. From daybreak the heavy artillery is to be ready to fire in its current positions.

6. Headquarters will be located at the southern exit of Westroosebeke from 6.00 am tomorrow.

Always assuming that the substance of this order filtered down to the troops, which is most unlikely, they must surely have been puzzled how paragraphs 1 and 2 could have been written, bearing in mind that they were surrounded by all the confused and costly evidence of failure. At a higher level, the orders to move a large part of 52nd Reserve Division in the dark must have led to a collective shaking of heads. To have given substance to this in the circumstances would have been totally impossible and those drafting it should have known that. The fact that such an order was even issued just goes to show that from top to bottom the new formations were far from ready for operations at the time they were deployed. By the end of 21 October the entire German chain of command should have been aware that the results of this day of battle had been hugely disappointing. The standard of training of their troops, coupled with difficult terrain and obstinate fighting resistance by the allied defenders had seen optimism replaced by a severe blow to morale and ignominious panicky retreat in places. Operations in this sector were off to a most inauspicious start.

Chapter Four

22 October 1914

During the night 21/22 October, Headquarters XXVI Reserve Corps reviewed its earlier instructions for the following day. Once the extent of losses and the poor morale of the survivors became clearer, there was a realisation that it would be pointless to launch another frontal assault on Langemarck. Staff checks suggested, however, that there might be scope for the left hand formations of the Corps to press on towards St Julien and then to advance towards Langemarck from the southeast. This plan rather overlooked the fact that, although there had been some success near Broodseinde, the right flank of XXVII Reserve Corps was experiencing severe difficulties near Becelaere and Reutel. Furthermore, 52nd Reserve Division on the southern flank had been pulled so far to the south during the previous day that the linkage between 52nd and 51st Reserve Divisions was extremely vulnerable, should the British launch a counter-attack. As a result, the orders were that the various formations were to redeploy so that the left flank of the Corps was anchored on the northern edge of Broodseinde, with the right more or less along the southern edge of Poelcappelle.

Headquarters Fourth Army accepted the logic of this assessment, but directed that Langemarck was nevertheless to be attacked on 22 October, it being vital that the pressure on XXVII Reserve Corps be relieved. In addition, inaction was deemed inadmissible in case it put at risk the operations of XXIII Reserve Corps against Bixschoote and the Ypres Canal. However, it was accepted that the fighting strength of XXVI Reserve Corps was greatly reduced so, although there were risks, 46th Reserve Division of XXIII Reserve Corps was directed to drive in a southerly direction on 22 October and, having crossed the Broenbeek, to assault Langemarck from the rear.

So far as that part of the BEF was concerned in what might now be justifiably called the Ypres Salient, this day was dominated by threatened attacks against IV Corps on the right, an attack along the Comines Canal and against the junction of 21 and 22 Brigades; on 2nd Division, against its positions to the south east of Langemarck; and, most notably, against 1st Division, especially its left flank. The French launched an unsuccessful attack in the morning with a brigade (and supporting artillery) of *87th Division*; its aim was to attack in the flank any German troops attempting to cross the canal between Bixschoote and Dixmude. Apparently the British had no notice of this attack, which caused some confusion to the left of 1st Division, as first there were the French territorials coming through their positions in the morning; and then, when fought off by the Germans, again as they withdrew at 2 pm.

Because of the perceived threat against the southern flank of 7th Division, information obtained by cavalry and air reconnaissance. Haig ordered 2nd Division to be prepared to support 22 Brigade at Zonnebeke and sent his Corps troops to the south, near Hollebeke, in support of the cavalry holding the line there. When a wireless intercept was received, at about 2.30 pm, much of IV Corps' reserve was moved forward to anticipate a major attack and Haig, at 4 pm, sent two battalions from 6 Brigade, 2nd Division's reserve brigade, from St Jean south to Klein Zillebeke.

2nd Division

As things turned out, the Germans failed to take any advantage of the capture of Zonnebeke after it had been evacuated by the British in the early hours of the 22nd; the nearest significant action was against the junction of 22 and 21 Brigades and a battle for the control of Reutel, to the east of Polygon Wood. Thus **4 (Guards) Brigade** faced no infantry assaults but did come under persistent artillery fire.

In the early hours of the morning, around 1 am, the right of the brigade had to comply with the withdrawal of 22 Brigade through Zonnebeke to the west. This was not a completely straight forward operation; easier for 1/Irish Guards, closest to Zonnebeke, but rather more difficult for 2/Coldstream, the adjacent battalion. However, they managed the withdrawal, got themselves suitably dug in and also had a good field of fire.

> ... the enemy, contrary to expectations, did not show the same activity as on the previous day; his infantry made a few minor attacks which lacked weight and cohesion and were easily repulsed by our guns and rifle fire, though his artillery kept up a continual bombardment with both shrapnel and high explosive shells. The results were, however, insignificant, either because the fire was wild or because the men kept well under cover in their new trenches, and casualties only came to one man killed and one wounded.

The pulling back of the Irish Guards and 2/Coldstream meant that the Germans took control of the road out to Langemarck for a distance of about a mile. 2/Grenadiers and 3/Coldstream, on the other hand, were able to retain the positions they had consolidated the previous day and were able to venture out over some of the ground they had given up after their advance on to part of Gravenstafel Ridge.

> ... It was reported at dawn that some of our wounded in the advance of the day before were lying out near a German picket, and as soon as possible a party of stretcher bearers went out and successfully brought them in. In the afternoon, however, the Battalion underwent a severe shelling which killed two men and wounded eleven others.

The day before, 3/Coldstream had suffered most heavily amongst the battalions of 4 (Guards) Brigade; so it was intended that on the evening of 22 October to pull it out of the line and send it back to billets, with the bulk of their trenches being taken over by 2/Worcesters. However, an attack in force on 5 Brigade in the evening put paid to that move, and the battalion remained in the line.

By comparison, **5 Brigade** faced determined German infantry attacks. The two battalions on the right were least affected, but came under persistent, if intermittent, shell fire. The Connaughts remained with two companies up and two in reserve; their casualties of three killed and five wounded would have been almost entirely due to the shelling. On the left, though, the **Worcesters** had a more challenging time:

> At dawn on October 22nd the enemy opened a furious bombardment and the work of completing the trenches was continued under a rain of shells and bullets. The enemy's infantry had been reinforced and made several attempts to get forward, but each time they were beaten back by the musketry of the British battalions, who held their ground all day in spite of a heavy bombardment from the German howitzers. The trenches dug overnight provided adequate cover and the actual casualties were not heavy (two killed, four wounded and one missing), but the constant concussion of bursting shells in all directions made the defence of the position most trying. As darkness fell, the enemy's infantry [from 51st Reserve Division] swarmed from their trenches and charged. The main force of the attack struck against the left of the Brigade line. ... the Worcestershire had small difficulty in driving back by fire the enemy on their front. Night fell, but the bombardment and the attacks did not cease, and firing continued intermittently all through the hours of darkness.

We are fortunate that for **2/Ox & Bucks** there are individual accounts in its regimental chronicles. Most significant of these is that of Lieutenant Colonel Davies, the CO of the battalion (who went on to command 3 Brigade and then commanded 11th Division for the last eighteen months of the war).

During the day there was not much infantry fire, nor was there much artillery fire on our portion of the trenches. I was still able to live in the farm [later known as New Houses] *most of the day. The companies in our lines were much mixed up, and I did not try to sort them out. It was much better for the men to remain in the trenches which they themselves had dug, and watching ground which they knew. Officers were in charge of different parts of the line, usually with some men of their own company and men of other companies mixed up with them. On the right of the main road* [ie the St Julien-Poelcappelle road] *was Dillon; on the road, Tolson; on the immediate left of the road, Baines; further to the left, Kirkpatrick (who, in spite of wounds in the neck and shoulder, stuck to duty for 24 hours after being hit* [he was subsequently killed on 15 May 1915])*; and, on the extreme left, Ponsonby* [killed in September 1915]*.*

In the late afternoon the Germans began to shell us. They made rather a special mark of the farm, and soon succeeded in setting it on fire. However, I had a good trench already dug behind the farm, and into this the Regimental Headquarters moved, without having any casualties.

Soon afterwards (about 5.30 pm), just as it was getting dark, a fairly heavy attack was made, on the part of the trenches near the St Julien-Poelcappelle road, by about a battalion of Germans. The bulk of the attack was delivered a little to the right (east) of the road and was well enfiladed by some men under Tolson who lay along the road. Three men were actually lying in the culvert by which the Haanixbeek crosses the road, and did good execution. The leading Germans got within 25 yards of our trenches, but then could stand it no longer and ran back. [Captain Dillon noted, the following day, that there were four German wounded near the trenches and he brought them in; and the company were able to count seventy of them lying dead.] *In this attack the Germans came on in thick lines, but our men were very steady, and we lost only one killed and one wounded* [in the attack]*. Another six men were killed and eight wounded at other times in the day.*

During the day I had orders that the Worcestershire and ourselves were to retire after nightfall to a position about half a mile behind, so as to be in line with the 1st Division. I protested strongly against this as we were well able to hold our position and it did not appear difficult for the 1st Division until level with us. My protest was forwarded by Westmacott [temporarily commanding the Brigade] to General Monro ... who replied that although he appreciated our disinclination to give up the ground gained, it was necessary for us to retire, so as to conform to the general line of the army. To my great relief, however, the order to retire was cancelled at night – possibly because of the attack which the Germans had made. A considerable part of the night was spent in burying our dead of yesterday.

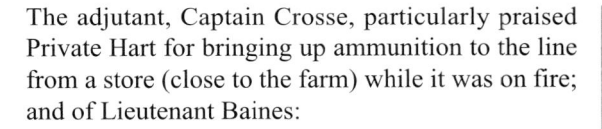

Lieutenant Colonel (soon to be promoted colonel) CB Westmacott was acting GOC 5 Brigade, replacing Brigadier General Haking, who had been wounded on the Aisne.

The adjutant, Captain Crosse, particularly praised Private Hart for bringing up ammunition to the line from a store (close to the farm) while it was on fire; and of Lieutenant Baines:

... in the late afternoon the enemy's infantry could be distinctly seen moving about in the root fields on our left front. Lieutenant Baines's part of the lines [just left of the road] was badly shelled, and he saved a great many casualties by very cleverly withdrawing his company to the steep bank of the stream in rear and occupying the shell holes, which he connected up and made into a trench as soon as the shelling ceased.

Major General Charles Monro, GOC 2nd Division.

The Fourth Army directive to XXVI Reserve Corps for 22 October was that it was to be prepared to move against Langemarck as soon as 46th Reserve Division had made recognisable progress. The need for speedy action was emphasised; 46th Reserve Division was to launch its attack at 6.00 am, so that Langemarck would be in German hands by midday. As a result XXVI Corps released a second operation order, the content of which was still a poor reflection of the current situation.

1. The enemy, which advanced against the Corps on 21st, has been outflanked by the corps to our left and right and, in places, has been forced back to the vicinity of the Yser. To our north, at 6.00 am, the neighbouring division (46th Reserve Division) will launch an attack on Langemarck, with its left flank anchored on Mangelaere.

2. The Corps is to join in with the general attack. 51st Reserve Division is to assemble to the west of the line Poelcappelle Station – Poelcappelle – Stroombeek ready to attack. The evacuation of Langemarck by the enemy is to be reported immediately.

3. 52nd Reserve Division is to link up with 51st Reserve Division and is to report direct to Corps Headquarters when the junction point with 51st Reserve Division is established.

4. Both divisions must be in contact with one another and be ready to advance westwards from 7.30 am.

5. The heavy artillery is to remain initially in its present locations and is to reconnoitre positions to the east of Langemarck as soon as that place is free [of enemy], *from where fire can be brought down by heavy field howitzers and 210mm howitzers against Steenstraat and Boesinghe (destruction of the bridges there). The*

The attack on Langemarck, 22 October.

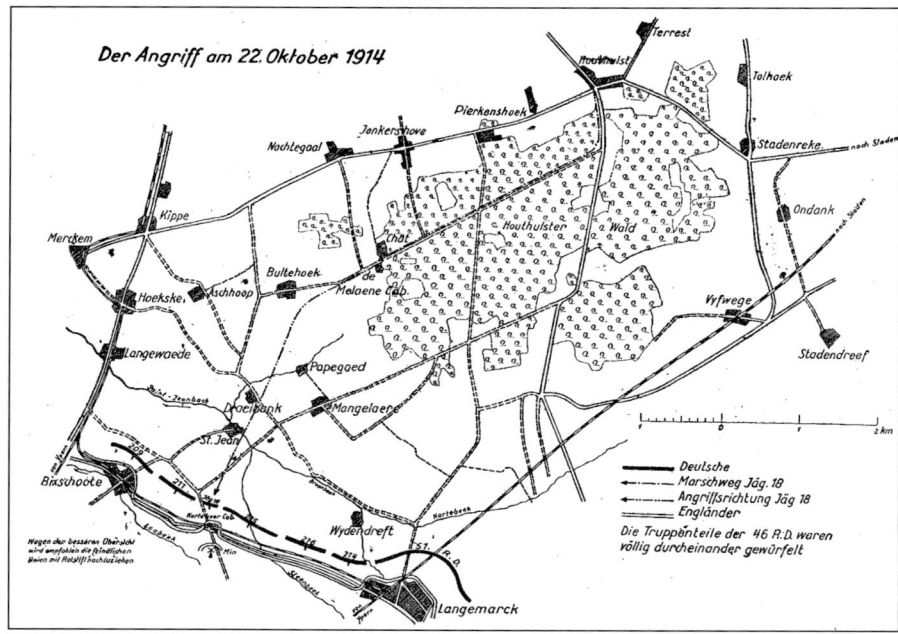

100mm battery will be given the task during the further advance of taking up a position from where it can bring the road Luzerne – Boesinghe under enfilade fire.

There was in fact too little time available to give substance to this plan, in particular because units and formations were already manoeuvring in accordance with previous instructions.

1st Division
The issues facing 1st Division on this day were considerable. It will be recalled that its advance on 20 October on the left flank was to be covered by the French; but they had been forced back, not only by the threat of German advances from Houthulst Forest but also because of the considerable pressure being faced by the Franco-Belgian forces along the canal line to Dixmude and beyond. Therefore, on 21 October, resources had to be devoted to this flank, though on 21 October these were relatively few.

It did mean that the division had to provide cover for a distance of some three to four miles, back to the canal line at Steenstraat. The morning of 22 October was relatively uneventful; Langemarck was heavily shelled, but the British positions were outside the village; in the area of Bixschoote, a German advance from the east was dealt with by French artillery. After the French thrust by part of *87th Division* in the morning had failed and they withdrew through the southern part of 1st Division's line, the Germans were then able to turn their full attention to the thinly held line of the division. The developing attack sucked in more and more troops from the divisional reserve; but, despite some very difficult moments, the line held except at Kortekeer Cabaret, where a withdrawal of about half a mile was made; it was only in this area that I Corps was forced to fall back on 22 October.

The right hand battalion of 3 Brigade, 1/SWB, found itself in the fortunate position of being in between the two major thrusts of the German attack; perhaps this was just as well, as the battalion's withdrawal on 21 October had left it in positions which did not offer a good field of fire.

The evening of the 21st had left **1/Coldstream** with two companies holding defences to the left of 3 Brigade, strung out along the Broenbeek (also known as the Kortebeek). The withdrawal, at about 6 pm, by the Camerons from Kortekeer Cabaret and its forward defence line, left the Coldstream left flank in the air and enfiladed, and No 4 Company was driven out of its trenches on that flank. No 1 Company was warned of what was happening and were able, in turn, to fire on the Germans from the flank as they surged forwards. Two companies of 1/Black Watch were rapidly despatched to assist, the German advance was halted and No 4 Company was able to reoccupy its positions, although on a smaller front. No 2 Company was brought forward to thicken up and extend the line to the right, in order to connect up with 3 Brigade, but it was too dark to be able to do this effectively. However, men of 26 Field Company RE (about which more below) worked hard through the night to dig a trench connecting 1 (Guards) and 3 Brigades.

Earlier German heavy artillery had opened fire on Langemarck and St Julien from 7.00 am. Reacting swiftly, the British brought fire down on Keiberg and around Poelcappelle all morning. As the exchanges of fire went on, 51st Reserve Division waited anxiously for the attack of 46th Reserve Division to make progress. Several contact patrols were sent to try to detect the sounds or actions of battle off to the northwest, but there was no sign at any point during the day of an attempt to cross the Kortebeek [Broenbeek on the modern map]. The units of 51st Reserve Division therefore kept in cover and tried to dig their positions deeper. There were some signs of movement in the British trenches that afternoon. Then, just after 52nd Reserve Division got into position, the British launched a limited counter-attack. It took an hour of close quarter battle before this attack was driven off with heavy casualties and the British remained active throughout the following night.

It was not until much later that the non-appearance of 46th Reserve Division was explained. For most of 21 October it had been tied up in minor actions north of Houthulst Wood. By nightfall the advance had arrived at Nachtegaal, to the northwest of the wood, and a halt was called for between that place and the hamlet of Ashoop to the southwest. Preparations then began for the advance towards Bixschoote the following morning, when orders arrived to swing the axis ninety degrees to the south, so as to come to the aid of 51st Reserve Division in its battle for Langemarck. Although the situation around Nachtegaal was relatively calm, the sound of battle coming from Langemarck and Broodseinde could be heard clearly. Speed was clearly of the essence and the commanders of Reserve Infantry Regiments 213, 214, 215 and 216 under the direction of the divisional staff quickly issued orders for the new situation.

It was no easy matter to organise so large a change in direction and, in addition, the terrain was not conducive to military movement. The various watercourses, flowing generally westwards, posed very real difficulties. Passing over the Kortebeek and the railway embankment northwest of Langemarck were obviously going to be very tricky moments. Nevertheless, the advance began early on 22 October, with Reserve Infantry Regiment 213 and Reserve Jäger Battalion 18 forming an advance guard. The intention was to reach the Kortebeek by 6.00 am, but this was not possible; although by that time leading elements were advancing south towards Mangelaere, southwest of Houthulst Wood, they came under effective enemy fire about 1,000 metres north of Mangelaere and were forced into cover as reinforcements moved up.

At roughly the same time Reserve Infantry Regiment 215 started to advance to the west of Reserve Infantry Regiment 213, but by now the defenders were thoroughly alerted. The 215th had no sooner left Nachtegaal that it came under heavy artillery fire from the direction of Bixschoote and were forced into cover. The fact that its companies were still formed up in close column when this happened meant that British

46th Reserve Division's attack towards Kortekeer Cabaret, 22 October.

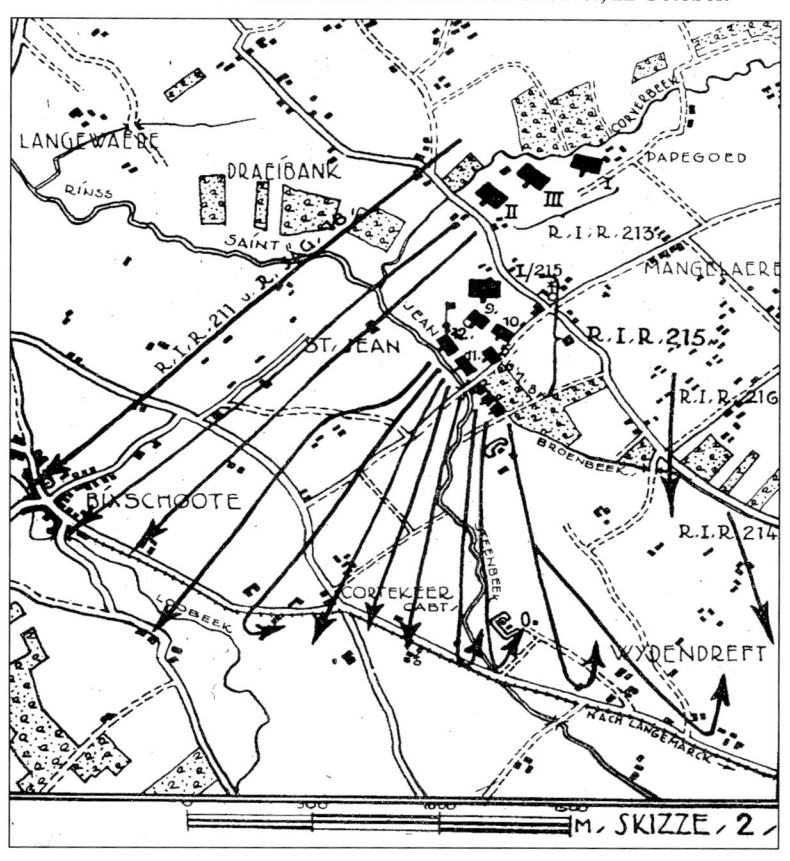

shrapnel was finding densely packed targets and there were numerous casualties. The companies were forced to race forward in a confused manner to take cover in a small wood to the south and it took until 1.00 pm to reorganise, shake out before leaving the cover of the wood and attempting to close up on Reserve Infantry Regiment 213 and Reserve Jäger Battalion 18. To add to the difficulties, the entire area was dotted with farm buildings, from which British troops brought down heavy fire.

There was a rumour that Belgian *franctireurs* were responsible and, although this was quite baseless, it provoked a furious reaction in the German ranks and they pushed on as far as the Draaibank area where British infantrymen, concealed behind hedgerows and in buildings, tore great gaps in the attackers from short range. Whilst the subsequent heavy fire fight continued, orders arrived at around 2.00 pm that the Kortebeek was to be crossed and an assault launched against Langemarck. Every effort was made to give substance to these orders, but it was all in vain. The rifle companies suffered huge casualties, and reinforcements were constantly moved up to maintain their strength so, although eventually some men did get across the Kortebeek, the scene on the opposite bank was one of total chaos. Command and control of this random assortment of men was nigh on impossible and the entire area was under constant shrapnel fire. However, those still on their feet pressed on in the face of the desperate defensive efforts of the British, who were resisting fiercely and, by 3.00 pm, with bullets cracking everywhere, the fighting was almost hand to hand. Oberst von Oertzen, commander Reserve Infantry Regiment 215, personally led a charge which gained a foothold in the forward British trenches near Bixschoote, but the battle soon degenerated into a slogging match for every metre of progress.

One kriegsfreiwilliger of 9th Company Reserve Infantry Regiment 215 later wrote home:

> *I felt a sense of utter fatigue and exhaustion. I was barely able to pull a few beets out of the ground. I bit into them and I can still remember their earthy taste. We crawled on, the hedges and houses looming up out of the dark background. We could see the flash of the rifles and the machine guns. 'On your feet! Double march!' We made some progress, but the majority were hit. To the rear were burning buildings. I looked around and saw two men still on their feet. We threw ourselves down and pressed our faces against the cold earth. There was an eerie rustling in our ears. It was the sound of bullets cutting through the leafy tops of the beets.*
>
> *I scraped a hole for my face with my bare hands then began to return fire. Beside me an old officer groaned and pressed his hand*

against his body, as though he could reduce the intense pain of a stomach wound by so doing. To my rear, a second assault wave was launched forward. It did not even get level with my position. All I could hear were screams and groans. A third wave threw themselves to the ground to my front. 'Achtung! – Go!'... Dear God, Thy will be done... 'On your feet! Go!' Ten metres further on, the entire wave was mown down, a mere fifty metres from the enemy. Close to me someone was screaming out loudly, but I was such a coward that I could not bring myself to go to his aid ...

The Cameron Highlanders are blessed with a superb regimental history – a detailed text, very good maps and a first class index. Volume 3 covers the activities of the 1st and 2nd Battalions in the Great War; and it gives a detailed account of the part of 1/Camerons in the fighting around Kortekeer Cabaret, on the left flank of I Corps.

The morning was fairly quiet; the Germans had come forward during the night and, shortly before midday, some of the more outlying positions to the east were withdrawn back towards the Langemarck-Bixschoote road.

The rifle fire had now become much heavier, and the British artillery was firing on the Germans who, where the country was open, could be seen at distances of 900 yards and over, advancing in extended order in successive lines. These glimpses of the enemy were taken full advantage of by A and C Companies, who used their rifles and rangefinders with marked effect. Two sections of C Company, which held the trench below the windmill on the Langemarck road [about five hundred yards to the right of the cabaret], *made excellent practice, their fire being directed by the observer from the top of the mill. The Camerons machine guns were also in action, their position north of the Inn* [ie the cabaret] *in a farm enclosure during the forenoon, beginning about 11.30. The Germans, however, established a firing line which ran roughly along the Hannebeek* [the south western extension of St Jansbeek] *in front of A Company.*

On the left of the battalion's line the Germans started appearing in considerable force; significant fighting started here at about 12.30 pm and occupied the attention of much of B Company. By 3 pm one platoon had run seriously short of ammunition and (the history states) 'about 12,000 rounds' were brought up to it, in the process of which two ammunition carriers were killed. An hour later, things became serious:

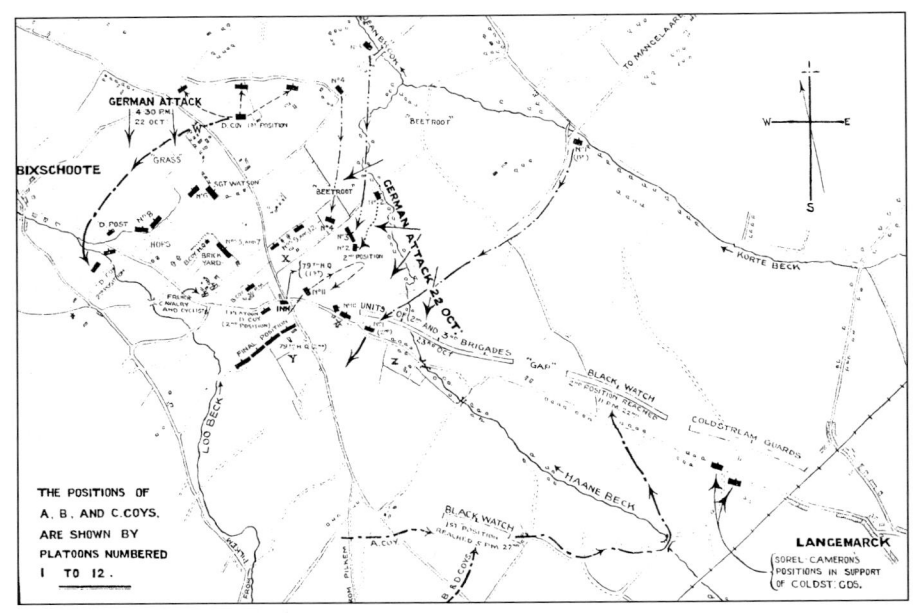

The defence of Kortekeer Cabaret (Inn), 22 October.

[The Germans] *reached a point about 200 yards from No 8 Platoon's trench. Here they lay down. The ground in front of the Camerons was open grass without obstacles, and it soon became clear to B Company that the Germans meant to come on, and that as no British reinforcements arrived they would have to face the coming assault without other help. The men behaved in a splendid manner, firing steadily all the time. Some bayonets were lost owing to the mud preventing them from fixing properly.*

At about 4.30 pm three battalions of Germans assaulted Second Lieutenant Leah's [No 8 Platoon] *trenches; they came on with two Colours flying and a band, and they were all singing. The Camerons emptied ten rounds a man into the approaching mass, which nevertheless completely overran the trenches. The first German column simply jumped over the trench and pressed on, and the remnants of Leah's command moved off left and joined the adjacent platoon of D Company under Lieutenant L Robertson, which had already been forced to retire.*

The hop field behind No 8 Platoon's trench delayed the German advance for a short time, and then they overran Lieutenant Stewart's platoon in a similar manner, not stopping to clear up the trench or to use their bayonets. This action on the part of the enemy enabled the remains of the platoon to get back to the brickyard where Captain Orr had his [B] *Company*

Headquarters. As the enemy came through a gap, Captain Orr and three men of his company, without hesitation, charged into them with cold steel... The heroic four were completely overwhelmed by the tide of Germans, and were never seen again by their comrades.

Captain Orr, aged 35, had fought in the South Africa War and at the war's outbreak was at Staff College. The loss of officers like him, staff trained and experienced, was to be one of the British army's greatest obstacles in producing a large scale, continental sized army. Probably the other highly significant loss in these first four or five months of warfare on the Western Front was the wealth of seasoned NCOs.

Captain J Orr, Cameron Highlanders, killed on 22 October; he has no known grave.

After this a few men who had collected at the back of the brickyard under Lieutenant Stewart and CSM Fleming found their attempt to retrieve the position frustrated by being taken in rear by some of the enemy who had swept past their flank, but at about 6.30 pm they managed to get back and to lie down twenty yards behind a barbed wire fence, which ran east and west about a hundred yards south of the brickyard. The Germans collected and charged this small party, but they were hindered by the fence and lost heavily in their attempt to cross it.

Stewart then attempted to make contact with some – any – part of the battalion, and came across the machine gun officer, Lieutenant Donald Cameron, with about a hundred men, holding the line on the road west of the cabaret. What remained of B Company joined up with them; several small scale German attacks on them failed.

On the eastern side of the road to Bixschoote and north of the cabaret, A Company, reasonably secure behind the parapets of the trenches that they had dug the previous night, came under regular fire from the Germans, who were massing on the other side of St Jansbeek. All these events, the attacks or threatened attacks, against D, B and A Companies, were observed,

...from the top of the windmill on the Langemarck road. Strangely enough, this rather obvious observation post did not attract much attention from the enemy until about 2 pm, when there was a

distinct movement from the Germans in that direction. This was a serious moment, for the gap between the Camerons' right and the 1/Coldstream left offered an easy opening to an assaulting enemy. At the right moment (about 2.30 pm) Lieutenant Chalmers of the Black Watch [the Brigade's reserve battalion] *arrived with a machine gun and this was installed in the second storey of the mill.*

The gun was fixed and steadied with bags of meal and the detachment got the range at once and made such excellent practice amongst the Germans that their advance was checked for a time, and they repeatedly put up white flags. [This might well have been a means of signalling to their artillery.] *The gun was moved from window to window to engage different targets. ... Up to about 3 pm the Black Watch machine gun had it, comparatively speaking, all its own way, as there seems to have been some obstacle to the Germans replying; but at about 3.15 pm they brought three or four machine guns to bear on the windmill and the detachment had great difficulty in getting their gun away, one man being wounded in doing so. The windows of the mill became quite untenable.*

The windmill area was reasonably strongly held – there were two sections of C Company, without an officer, in a trench in front of the mill, with another two sections in support in a house a short distance back from No 10 Platoon under Lieutenant Barber. About a quarter mile east was No 1 Platoon of A Company, positioned on the road. Strangely enough, the position had not been shelled by the Germans thus far. But things were to change.

About 3.45 pm No 1 Platoon retired from its place on the road and the Germans poured across it under cover of a very heavy rifle fire. They got through the gap on the left of the Coldstream Guards and the Cameron right was turned. The German advance was strongly supported, large numbers being seen coming on over the ridge beyond the Hannebeck [sic; or St Jansbeek]. *Lieutenant Barber's two sections* [from C Company] *were then sent forward to take up a fire position in front of some houses on the left front of the windmill.*

At this moment about fifty Germans who had got into the low ground suddenly sprang up and tried to rush one of the three platoons of A Company. They came on in the most intrepid and gallant manner, but all were shot down, the last man falling about fifty yards short of A Company's trench.

At 4.15 pm the remaining platoon of C Company [the Battalion's reserve] *was sent out to extend the line on A Company's right and to fill up part of the gap* [between them and the mill position]. *They went out a little to the right of the inn, but before they got any distance half were hit... The survivors took up a position about fifty yards in front of and to the right of the inn.*

The hostile fire at the windmill began to slacken as the afternoon got darker, and a farmhouse Z, about 450 yards east of the mill, was burning fiercely. ... The Black Watch, who had been in Brigade reserve, counter attacked the wedge that the Germans had driven in past the Coldstream left. After dark the result of this counter attack became visible in the light of the burning farm Z, the gratifying sight of Germans retiring across the road in spite of the efforts of their officers to urge them in the opposite direction. Heavy and continuous fire was going on near the inn. About 6.30 pm it died away, and the strains of the 'Wacht am Rhein' could be heard instead, an unwelcome sound which caused some anxiety about Battalion Headquarters.

As might be imagined, this fighting caused many casualties to the junior officers and NCOs of the German regiments involved and the overall objective had still not been captured. Oberst von Oertzen of Reserve Infantry Regiment 215 did what he could to improve the situation. Pressing on along the line of the Hanebeek as darkness fell, the advance finally crossed the line of the railway embankment. Listening posts were sent even further forward during the hours of darkness. Reorganisation was problematic. There was no food of any kind. The field kitchens could not get forward and the rations carried into action had already been eaten. Worse, the aid posts were overwhelmed by the casualties and hardly any of them could be evacuated. Musketier Scheidhauer of 8th Company Reserve Infantry Regiment 215 recalled,

Never again did I experience so tough an assault as this one. Whistles blew to signal the start. A warrant officer was lying to my front. 'Herr Feldwebel, we must get going!' I pulled at his foot, but he lay there stiffly. He was dead. At the end of the next bound an Unteroffizier was lying down on the ground. I pulled at his clay covered boot. Stiff – dead. I shuddered all over. I raced diagonally across the road into the ditch on the right hand side. It seemed to me as though a woodpecker was pecking at the telegraph pole next to me; fine chippings of wood were falling on me. I then realised that I was lying in the beaten zone of a machine gun and its bullets were gradually felling the pole. Further forward a voice bawled, 'On your feet! Double march!' It was hard to make the decision to move. My rucksack was digging into my neck. Apathetically, I jogged slowly forward. Shot cows were bellowing in the fields. I ran with death at my throat and tore myself free of a wire fence as bullets whistled around me. Beads of nervous sweat stood out on my brow. Near a farm building I met up with an Offizierstellvertreter and about thirty men. Mentally and spiritually we were totally spent ...

Generalleutnant Schoepflin, GOC 45th Reserve Division.

Oberst Riedel, the commander of Reserve Jäger Battalion 18, was involved in one of the later attempts to inject momentum into this operation and wrote about it subsequently.

About 4.00 pm we advanced together with Reserve Infantry Regiment 211 of 45th Reserve Division. [Our] orders were to attack the enemy dug in on the far bank of St Jans Beek. Reserve Infantry Regiment 211 forded the beek, with the Jägers, some of whom crossed by a bridge to their left. The battalion moved forward and then lay down on the ground. Behind a house stood General [major] Herhudt von Rohden. He advised against a further advance and suggested waiting for darkness to fall. However, once the signal, 'Fix bayonets!' was heard by means of a trumpet call from the right, there was no further delay. The battalion advanced, 1st and 3rd Companies shook out and led off, with battalion headquarters next, followed by 2nd and 3rd Companies in a second wave.

"With truly colossal daring, a way was forced through the murderous rate of fire, the front line was reached and a way was forced further forward. Several farmsteads, their buildings on fire, were stormed. After a short pause the battalion pushed on and, as darkness fell, together with men drawn from the entire division and despite heavy enemy fire, the houses of Kortekeer were stormed ...

Just over a kilometre northwest of this action, Reserve Infantry Regiment 211 was still trying to force its way into Bixschoote. Night had long since fallen and groups of soldiers were picking their way with difficulty through the darkened streets, where they risked exchanges of fire with their own side. In response they resorted to shouting loudly in German and sang patriotic songs. Its history claims that it was one of the first to sing *Deutschland über Alles!* for this purpose.

As the evening drew on some more British reinforcements came up to the mill position; besides welcome additions to the manpower, they also brought some very limited supplies of ammunition and also the news that the battalion had retired, position unknown; and that the inn was occupied by the Germans in force.

It was now pitch dark, and a patrol sent towards the inn from the windmill came back at once with the information that there was a large part of the enemy advancing down the road from that direction. Major Sorel-Cameron [2 i/c of the Battalion and in charge at the windmill position], being out of touch with Battalion Headquarters, decided to march towards Langemarck, and started with the German officer [captured earlier by a patrol] and the German soldiers under escort in the rear. The NCO of their escort, however, moved off the wrong way in the dark, and marched straight into the Germans advancing from the inn. The confusion and firing which resulted enabled the column to slip away eastwards without fighting, until between 7 and 8 pm they ran into a Coldstream Guards picquet on the Langemarck road, which was now held by that regiment, with the Black Watch on their left, the latter brought forward earlier in the afternoon – along with some French cyclists – to help to restore the situation.

A Company received orders to withdraw from its positions after dark, by-passing the cabaret by crossing the Langemarck road between it and the windmill. There they joined a new defensive line – now straight rather than a semi circle, which ran east west through Y Farm, south of the cabaret. Perhaps the word 'line' gives the wrong idea; in fact what was produced was mainly sufficient to cover soldiers lying down, scraping the surface with entrenching tools. This position had been heavily reinforced, and the line now included men from 1/Northamptons, a company of the Coldstream and the Camerons. The three platoons of D Company and Lieutenant Leah's group were also brought in at about this time and, finally, at about 8 pm, the remainder of B Company.

> *Everybody felt more secure in the new position, which was practically a straight trench. The position just left had been almost semi-circular, and there was always an uncomfortable feeling that if the enemy got through anywhere he would take the rest of the half circle in reverse. The anxiety caused by this feeling has to be experienced to be appreciated.*

An attack by 1/Northamptons, along with the Coldstream company, to recapture the cabaret that night was ordered; but it was too dark to be able to act effectively, though the line was advanced closer towards the Langemarck road. Apart from an attempt by some of the Camerons to cross an intervening beet field and reoccupy part of the south side of the Langemarck road (an attempt abandoned because of a complex ditch system, impossible to discern in the dark), this was how the position remained overnight. 22 October 1914 became a 'battalion anniversary' for 1/Camerons – and for good reason.

To 1/Camerons' left, at the beginning of 22 October, were 1/Scots Guards. The regimental history gives very little space to the events on the left flank of 1st Division near Bixschoote – noting the heavy fighting going on on its right flank, and the activity of the French in the earlier part of the day, but merely commenting on 'a miserable, sleepless night [that of 22/23 October], haunted by false accounts saying the rest of the Brigade had been separated from them, and that at any moment they might expect to be surrounded by the enemy'.

In fact there were severe concerns at higher command levels about the safety of the left flank of 1st Division, indeed the left flank of the BEF. Haig made decisive decisions about recovering the relatively small amount of territory that had been lost to the Germans. He pulled together the equivalent of an extra brigade – 2/KRRC from Corps reserve and 1/Queen's from 3 Brigade reserve, who were to support 1 Brigade; whilst 1/Loyals [Loyal North Lancs], 2 Brigade's reserve and 2/South Staffs from 2nd Division's reserve were to be at Pilckem by 2.45 am. The whole, with the addition of the Nothamptons, was put under the control of Brigadier General Bulfin of 2 Brigade, who was to launch a counter attack at dawn to retrieve the lost ground. Lieutenant Hyndson described the move of 1/Loyals:

At the time, Brigadier General Bulfin, GOC 2 Brigade; promoted to major general on 26 October.

> *22 October: As the night draws in the sky is lit up by a distant glare of burning houses, set on fire by the Hun artillery* [naturally, not by British or French artillery as well!]. *Before we are able to settle down, we are hurriedly called out, and march off without the slightest idea of where we are going. After trudging along a*

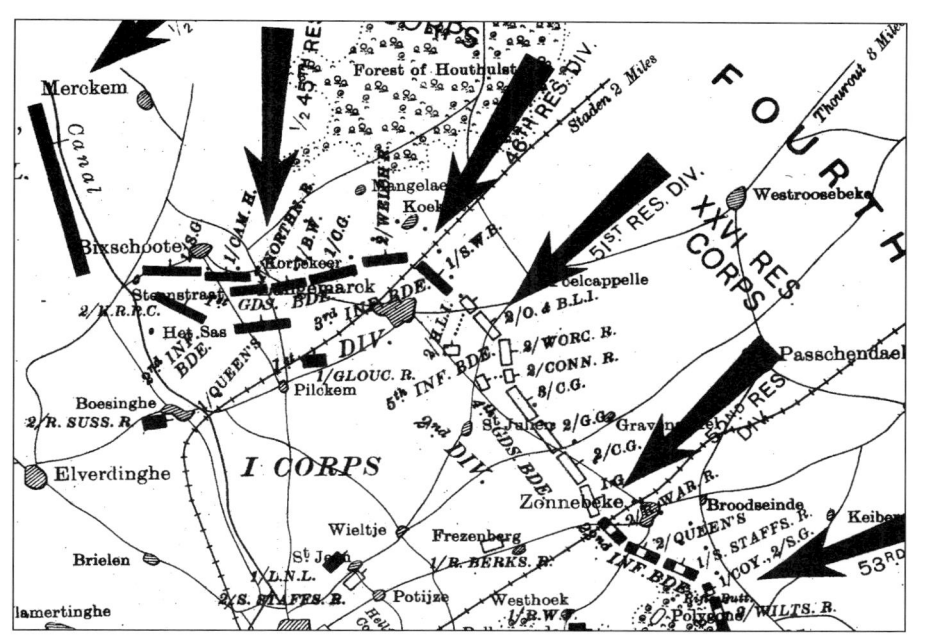

Situation map, evening 22 October.

twisting road for a few miles, we land up at St Jean [at 8 pm], where we pass a few hours in sleep. Called out again at ten o'clock, we march to Pilckem, where we halt again, and as soon as daylight appears we move into a turnip field and lie down in close column.

This gathering together of battalions and other units from a variety of brigades and even divisions, placed under a specifically appointed commander and usually for either only a limited time or for a specific purpose, was known as 'puttying up', even at the time. To work successfully it required high levels of training and competence at all levels of command and someone at the top with a firm grasp of what might be happening elsewhere in a confusing situation. The BEF was to become expert practitioners at this type of warfare over the next few weeks; alas, an expertise that was considerably damaged in that same period.

On the German side it was a day of order and counter-order and, in consequence, 52nd Reserve Division was unable to attack at all that day, having spent many hours simply trying to get into position. Despite all the problems, every effort was made to put together a meaningful attack on Langemarck and so maintain the pressure on the British defenders. Interrupted in the midst of a morning orders group by shelling, Oberst von Gilsa, commander of Reserve Infantry Regiment 235, simply drew his sword, ordered the advance and his regiment set off from Poelcappelle Station for Langemarck, drums beating. Gilsa fell, shot dead, shortly afterwards and command devolved on Major Bredt. This attack, too, soon petered out, as 'Unteroffizier B' later explained:

> Once more we received orders to attack. My heart was still beating within me, my courage did not fail me and I was able to summon up the strength and resolution that was urgently necessary ... In large masses, the Feldgrauen moved out of their trenches and launched forward. Who could differentiate between those knocked involuntarily to the ground and those who just wanted to take a short breather, prior to continuing? The rows thinned out, becoming less regular.
>
> Here and there whole sections, or single individuals, could be seen dashing forward and all in the same position – half ducked down, head stretched forward. They threw themselves down into cover, sprang up and rushed forward with a speed which had often been missing during the period of training... Then we received our own orders. The next five to ten minutes were absolutely dreadful. There could be no such thing as fire of that density. No longer did I look backwards to the right or the left. Where were my men, my section? Killed, wounded? I simply cannot say. I did not feel the bullet which grazed me and later sent me to the rear. I could see that my hand was bleeding, but it did not incommode me in any way. Anyway there was no good lying there: forward and forward again. We covered a long bound across a bare, wide meadow, which had literally been ploughed up by shells and was criss-crossed by heavy small arms fire, then I saw a trench to my front. Assessing quickly where I might find a space, I plunged, half dazed, into cover. I found myself in exactly the same spot I had been on Wednesday [21 October] and where I had lain and waited for evening.
>
> Before I could think straight or do anything, I had to get my breath back. What marvellous protection the knapsack, that much maligned modern instrument of torture, can offer! As mentioned, we were crammed together under the heaviest artillery fire imaginable, seeking protection in this shallow, narrow trench. Our knapsacks were thereby forced upwards and, naturally, provided protection from above. What a state the mess tins were in afterwards! There were seven holes in them, two from a rifle bullet, the remainder caused by shrapnel. How would it have played out for me, had I considered my equipment a nuisance and left it behind?

During the evening of 22 October Reserve Infantry Regiment 237 consolidated its positions to the south of Poelcappelle and west of Passchendaele. On its left were located Reserve Infantry Regiment 240, Reserve Jäger Battalion 24 and half of Reserve Infantry Regiment 238. The remaining elements of Reserve Infantry Regiment 238 occupied Broodseinde and Reserve Infantry Regiment 239 was moved to divisional reserve.

Mandel Chateau, Passchendaele, in pre war days, although in fact some distance to the east of the village. It served a variety of purposes for the German army.

Chapter Five

23 October 1914

Despite disappointment over the ground gained on 22 October, the overall Fourth Army assessment was that the forces involved in the contact battle for Langemarck still had sufficient fighting power to make feasible a further attempt on 23 October. Throughout the night strenuous efforts were made to dump artillery ammunition on the gun lines then, once it became light, the bombardment of the village and surrounding area began once more. Reserve Infantry Regiment 239, which had been in reserve for the past twenty four hours, was marched forward to add weight to the renewed assault by 51st Reserve Division. The division decided to deploy it, together with a number of batteries of Reserve Field Artillery Regiment 52, off to the right and under command of General von Wechmar, who also directed the remains of Reserve Infantry Regiment 239 and Reserve Jäger Battalion 23.

51st Reserve Division's attack on Langemarck, 23 October.

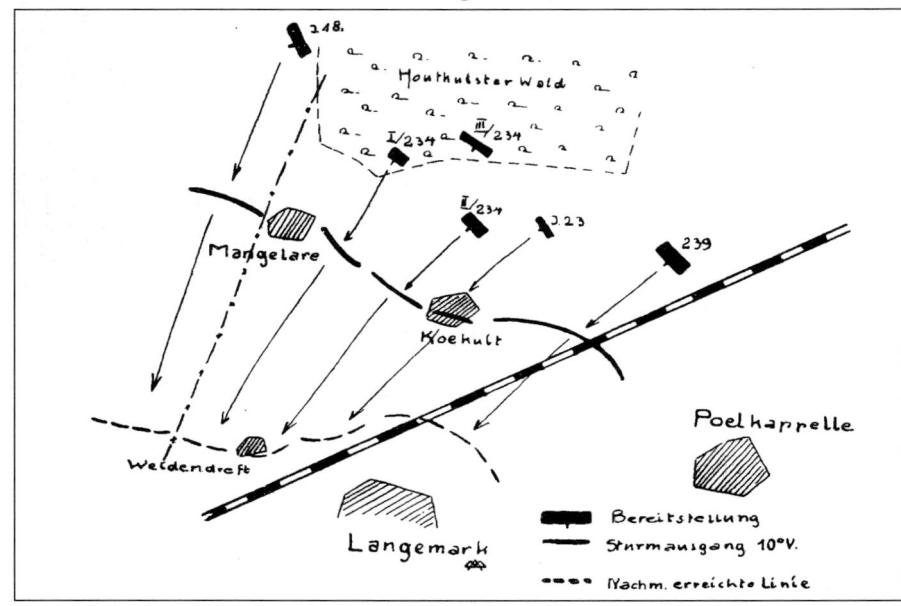

Whilst these forces were manoeuvring into position, the allies mounted a series of small scale night attacks which made matters difficult. However, this 'Detachment Wechmar' eventually reached its forward assembly areas, though not in time to set out under the cover of darkness. Its axis of advance was the Langemarck – Boesinghe railway and the objective was the Ypres Canal. The plan, possibly somewhat ambitious, had been for 46th Reserve Division, on the left flank of XXIII Reserve Corps, and Detachment Wechmar, on the right of XXVI Reserve Corps, to move simultaneously and coordinate their actions. The fact that Detachment Wechmar could not move until after dawn meant that the opportunity to develop synergy was lost. 46th Reserve Division duly began its attack at the appointed time, but the late arrival on the start line of XXVI Reserve Corps of Wechmar's forces enabled the British artillery to concentrate its fire initially against 46th Reserve Division and then switch it to meet Detachment Wechmar. The British infantry battalions were also able to provide mutual support and the combination prevented the attack from succeeding.

46th Reserve Division, its right flank anchored on Bixschoote, was quickly drawn into desperate fighting that absorbed its entire strength. There were some gains. A group composed of men of Reserve Jäger Battalion 18 and some from Reserve Infantry Regiment 213, under the command of Major von Loesen, attacked and captured Bixschoote mill, together with 150 British soldiers; and sub units of Reserve Infantry Regiments 209 and 211 of 45th Reserve Division were involved in hand to hand bayonet fighting just outside the town.

Beyond the Kortebeek, Reserve Infantry Regiments 214, 215 and 216 of 46th Reserve Division found themselves also involved in a desperate fight at close range. Frequently they attempted to get forward against volley fire at ranges of less than fifty metres, suffering appalling casualties in the process. Despite this the regiments carried on with attack after attack, even when the chances of breakthrough were reduced to nothing. Some idea of the price paid by these inexperienced troops comes from the simple fact that Reserve Infantry Regiment 215 was rapidly reduced from twelve strong rifle companies to only four weak composite companies. The other

Oberst von Wedel, commander Reserve Infantry Regiment 209.

formations were similarly reduced; barely an officer was left on his feet. Nevertheless, the attacks continued well into the afternoon, the surviving unteroffiziers and gefreiters stepping into the gaps left by the death or wounding of their seniors. In one or two places the St Jans Beek was crossed. Some British soldiers were captured, there were seizures of equipment, but the attack was over. The regiments were being reduced to mere husks by the obstinate British defence and, as it went dark, there were further losses when the assaulting troop became silhouetted against the fires of burning buildings and offered easy targets for the British infantry.

Faced by mounting losses, the survivors of Reserve Infantry Regiment 213 and Reserve Jäger Battalion 18 attempted to withdraw, but hardly any of them succeeded; the blazing windmill at Bixschoote turned night into day. Altogether the regiments had lost more than two thirds of their manpower on the west bank of St Jans Beek. At the first sign of a British counter-attack, the senior German officers on the spot decided to abandon these untenable gains and they led all who could still walk back across the Kortebeek to relative safety. The entire battlefield was strewn with the dead and dying, whilst those of the wounded who could still move spent a painful night attempting to get back to their own lines.

2nd Division

Eight kilometres away, the right flank, south west of Zonnebeke, continued to be held by the **Irish Guards**. They had a relatively quiet morning; though enemy machine gun fire became considerably more pronounced throughout the day. An attempt was made to probe the German defences of Zonnebeke when Lieutenant Alexander (to become a significant military commander of the Second World War, as well as Minister of Defence in the 1950s) led a platoon into the village and towards the church, but had to retire in the face of the opposition. In the afternoon there was considerable shelling with shrapnel; a German infantry attack was beaten off with comparative ease. On their left, 2/Coldstream took fairly heavy casualties during the day, losing their second in command, Major Markham, to a mortal wound as well as six killed, ten missing and two wounded.

In the evening, at about 5 pm, the French *17th Division* launched an attack through the Irish Guards'

Major Ronald Markham, second in command, 2/Coldstream Guards, killed 25 October 1914. A casualty of the early days of the war, he is among a number who was brought home for burial by his family (to Sysonby, in Leicestershire); it was not long before this practice was banned and there were only very few exceptions.

The brickyards near Zonnebeke, west of the village; note the church spire to the left of the large chimney.

lines, fought their way into the village but not much further and then, at 9 pm, relieved the battalion, which was moved south to the brickyards at Zillebeke, where they arrived at 2 am.

2/Grenadier Guards retained their rather precarious hold:

> *The trenches, composed of isolated holes which held two or three men apiece, were exposed from the left to enfilade fire, but there the Battalion had to remain for two days. They suffered many casualties. While making his way down the firing line, Captain Maitland was forced to walk a great deal in the open, and was wounded in the head by a sniper, who succeeded in hitting several other men.*

Lieutenant F Miller, the other officer casualty, was killed by a shell; Captain ED Ridley described the incident and sequel of Maitland's wounding:

> *Turned out early after a cold, but quiet, night ... Enemy suddenly appeared 1400 yards to front and started to entrench. Fired a few shots at them to get range. Sniper about 500 yards off began to take us on. He was a good shot. Mark* [Maitland] *came along and eventually sat on back of trench. I had got him to take his cap off so as not to draw fire when he was suddenly hit by the sniper on the right side of head above ear. He bled a bit, groaned, but*

Taken in a dugout on the Aisne, Lieutenant Miller is in the centre of the photograph. Major Lord Bernard Gordon Lennox (right) was killed on 10 November (buried in Zillebeke Churchyard) and Lieutenant Dowling (left) survived the war.

> *suddenly was quite all right. I tied up his head and advised him to return to remain in trench but he would not, and ran back to Coy HQ and eventually to Bn HQ and hospital. The sniper then gave it us hot, fired every time we showed an ear. I think he was a sportsman and did not fire at Mark when he saw he was wounded. Eventually I had to go out to stop the expenditure of ammunition. Got out by crawling and went to Sergeant Fremlin's trench where the sniping was not so bad. From there to Stock's from where I could get at the whole line.*

As the day drew in, the Battalion were interested observers of the French attack by General Moussy's *33 Brigade*.

> [We] *watched the French attack Passchendaele with much interest. Though the attack was met with a heavy artillery and rifle fire, and made but little progress, the personal gallantry of General Moussy himself and his staff, who exposed themselves freely while close up to the front trenches, made a great impression on all the officers and men of the 2nd Battalion.*

Major Jeffreys, of the Grenadiers, fluent in French, was attached temporarily as a liaison officer and commented on Moussy and his staff:

> *He* [Moussy] *received me very kindly and told me to come along with him. He had two staff officers with him – both very smart,*

> *especially one (a cavalryman) in a light blue tunic with silver lace and red breeches. He seemed to have no Headquarters, as we understand them, to which reports could go, but he walked about amongst his troops with the two staff officers and seemed more like an umpire at a Field Day than a commander of attacking troops.*

The advance stalled, but Jeffreys had to admire Moussy's élan, written in rather more blunt language than the diplomatic tone of the regimental history:

> *General Moussy went forward and and stood at the cross-roads* [later known as Kansas Cross] *on the Zonnebeke–Langemarck road, a most unhealthy spot, as it was being shelled and a machine gun from the direction of Passchendaele was firing straight down the Wieltje Road. However, he showed not the slightest sign of fear and nor did his two staff officers, who laughed and joked at the bursting shells. I think these two, at any rate, were determined to show me that they didn't care and I (though inwardly hating it) was equally determined to show them that I did not care either. There was a good ditch with a bank towards the enemy along the Zonnebeke road, and in it was Gilbert Follett* [who went on to command his battalion but was killed in September 1918 whilst commanding 3 Guards Brigade] *and his Company of Coldstream. He said to me, 'Why don't you get in here with us?' I asked the General if he wouldn't get into the ditch, and after at first demurring, he did get into it, followed by the other three of us. I was very glad to get there. [...]*
>
> *I liked him and admired his gallantry, but could not make out how he thought he was commanding! He did the work of a regimental officer, had no communications; received few, if any, reports, and on the rare occasions when he sent any reports, he sent a staff officer with a verbal message.*

The Grenadiers were relieved by the French between 10 and 11 pm, withdrew a couple of miles and had some hours of rest and then, on the 24th, at 5.30 am moved to form a reserve for 6 Brigade. On the right, 3/Coldstream was not particularly affected by the major German attacks of the late afternoon and evening over on their left; it suffered casualties of fourteen wounded. It withdrew in the evening, along with the other battalions of the Brigade, and arrived at Zillebeke between 3 and 4 am. Sandwiched in between 3/Coldstream and 2/Worcesters were two companies of 2/Connaughts, C and D, which had been in the line since the advance stalled on the 21st. The battalion suffered casualties of nine killed and twenty wounded, mainly to heavy shelling – and of these casualties, most were amongst C Company, on the right. Along with the rest of the division, 5 Brigade was relieved by the French at about 10 pm and moved to a rest area known at this stage of the war as 'Halte', to the east of Ypres.

5 Brigade
2/Worcesters faced a new day under a real battering from shell fire:

> *Next morning the bombardment increased to a storm of shell fire. That third day of battle proved the most trying day that the Battalion had yet experienced. Officers and men were worn out with lack of sleep, and crouched in the battered trenches, dazed and stunned by the concussion of bursting shells. But the fighting spirit of the troops was unimpaired, and Private CE Lively in particular earned general admiration by the fearless way in which he carried messages across the open despite the bombardment.*

For his work that day, Lively was awarded the DCM – and went on to be commissioned. The nature of his actions which led to the award illustrates one of the bigger problems faced by the defenders during these days. Because the defence line was so unsophisticated, often unconnected slit trenches or rifle pits, there were significant casualties amongst platoon and company officers as they went from trench to trench as part of their duties; the wounding of Captain Maitland, 2/Grenadiers, is a good example of this. Further casualties were caused by the complete lack of communication trenches, making resupply very precarious and which was largely restricted to the essentials during daylight hours – ie ammunition. Food supplies were extremely limited, even at night, and most of it was cold – not wonderful news when the conditions were as one might expect for an October in northern Europe. Messengers faced particular hazards, as urgent communications had to be brought by runner who had to move above ground for much of the time – as well as having the added problem of locating the correct rifle pit. Finally, medical evacuation was also made more difficult: usually there was no acceptably secure way to evacuate the wounded from the line until darkness set in. The regimental history continues:

> *On the left of the Brigade front the great shells blew the British trenches to pieces and at dusk the enemy's infantry again*

attacked. But the battalions of the 5th Brigade were still unbeaten and once more before their musketry the attack withered away. That last attack apparently exhausted the enemy's strength; no further onslaught was attempted and the ensuing night was fairly quiet.

5 Brigade, as noted previously, was also relieved by the French that night.

The bulk of the Brigade was relieved by French troops at 11 pm [the relief of the Division was conducted from left to right], but 2/Worcesters were left to the last, to cover the withdrawal of the British guns, and did not leave their trenches until dawn the next morning. Shrapnel and rifle fire made the relief difficult, but eventually it was completed and the French troops had taken over. In the dim light of dawn the Battalion assembled behind the line and tramped off to rest, a column of utterly weary men, unwashed, unshaven and caked with mud. Through St Julien and Wieltje they plodded, through St Jean and thence to that 'Halte' east of Ypres, where the railway crosses the Menin Road – the place which afterwards the whole Army was to call 'Hell-fire Corner'. There the rest of 5 Brigade were found lying in bivouac. The Battalion arrived at the bivouac lines at 8 am, cheered by the prospect of rest and food. They were told that they might expect three days rest; but that rest was destined actually to last twenty minutes. Breakfasts were not yet ready when urgent orders came to move forward at once.

2/Ox & Bucks once more seemed to take the brunt of the attack on 2nd Division's front. Colonel Davies's diary gives a full account:

In the afternoon they shelled both the farm and the trenches. A trench just west of the main road, where Baines was in command, was smashed in by HE shells, but the men luckily suffered little harm. They were ordered to retire about 50 yards, until the shelling subsided, and re-occupy the trench if the German infantry attacked.

At 5.30 pm an attack was made by the enemy – this time by a larger force than on last evening. They attacked chiefly on the east of the main road, coming on in very thick lines, and in places got close up to our trenches, but our men were absolutely cool and steady, and fired well. The attack appearing to be more formidable than that of yesterday, I reinforced with every man, until the firing was as full as it could be. I also succeeded in getting up ammunition, and after the repulse of the attack every man was again well supplied. Our men in the culvert again did great execution.

The result of the attack was as before; some Germans got very close, but in the end they turned and ran back behind the next hedge, 150 yards off. Here they remained for some time, with a good deal of shouting, which appeared to come from officers trying to get their men on again. Anyhow no further assault was made and they retired to their own trenches. Our casualties were two men killed and five wounded; [Captain, C Company] Ponsonby and [Second Lieutenant, A Company] Humfrey were also wounded.

Both these two officers were subsequently killed – Humfrey in May and Posonby in September 1915. Captain Dillon, in his letter to his sister previously quoted, wrote rather more graphically of the events of the day:

In my section, about 200 yards, I had about 150 men, and just where I was myself was the thinnest portion. The night came on rather misty and dark, and I thought several times of asking for reinforcements, but I collected a lot off rifles off the dead, loaded them and put them along the parapet instead. All of a sudden about a dozen shells came down, and almost simultaneously two machine guns and a tremendous rifle fire opened on us. It was a most unholy din. The shells ripped open the parapet and trees came crashing down. However, I was well under ground, and did not care much, but presently the guns stopped, and I knew then that we were in for it. I had to look over the top for about ten minutes, however, under their infernal maxims, before I saw what I was looking for. It came with a suddenness that was the most starting thing I have ever known. The firing stopped, and I had been straining my eyes so that for a moment I could not believe them, but, fortunately, I did not hesitate long. A great grey mass of humanity was charging straight on to us not fifty yards off... Everybody's nerves were pretty well on edge, as I had warned them what to expect, and as I fired my rifle the rest went off more or less simultaneously.

One saw the great mass of Germans quiver. In reality some fell, some fell over them and others came on. I have never shot so much in such a short time: it could not have been more than a few seconds and they were down. Suddenly one man – I expect an officer – jumped up and came on. I fired and missed, seized the next rifle, and dropped him a few yards off. Then the whole lot came on again, and it was the most critical moment of my life. Twenty yards more and they would have been over us in thousands, but our fire must have been fearful, and at the very last moment they did the most foolish thing they could possibly have done. Some of the leading men turned to the left for some reason, and they all followed like a great flock of sheep. We did not lose much time, I can give you my oath. My right hand is one huge bruise from banging the bolt up and down. I don't think one could have missed at the distance, and just for one or two minutes we poured the ammunition into them in boxfuls. My rifles were red hot at the finish, I know, and that was the end of the battle for me.

The firing died down, and out of the darkness a great moaning came. Men with their legs and arms off trying to crawl away; others, who could not move, gasping out their last moments with the cold night wind biting into their broken bodies, and the lurid red glare of a farmhouse showing up clumps of grey devils killed by the men on my left further down. A weird, awful scene! Some of them would raise themselves on one arm or crawl a little distance, silhouetted as black as ink against the red glow of the fire ...

... There are not many of the original lot left now. I am the only captain and the rest subalterns. It fills me with a great rage. I know I have got to stop my bullet some time, and it is merely a question of where it hits one, whether it is dead or wounded. ... [The] whole thing is an outrage on civilization. The whole of this beautiful country is devastated – broken houses, broken bodies, blood, filth and ruin everywhere!

At about 11 pm, 23rd, we were told that some French troops were to relieve us, and that we were to go off to another part of the line. I was the first to be relieved [A was the right hand company], and started off. I got a good shelling on my way, but no damage. We got assembled at about 4.30 am, and I learnt who

Lieutenant C Murphy, Ox & Bucks, killed 21 October. ... *not badly wounded and made comfortable close to a haystack till a stretcher arrived, when another bullet him in the head...* He has no known grave.

Lieutenant G Turbutt, Ox & Bucks, killed 21 October; buried in Poelcapelle British Cemetery. His immortal claim to fame is that he found the Bodleian Library's original folio edition of Shakespeare in his family library, and was instrumental in restoring it to Oxford.

The whole of this country is devastated – broken houses, broken bodies, blood, filth and ruin everywhere! (A) The shattered village of Poelcappelle, winter 1914; (B) The ruins of Poelcappelle Chateau.

the dead were – Harden, Murphy, Marshall, Turbitt and Filleul. We have now lost twenty officers, and we only started with 26.

This was hardly the sort of letter to calm the nerves of his sister at home; or, indeed, the readers of the *Oxford Times*, which published the letter on 21 November. Captain Henry Dillon had been in the army for fourteen years when he fought at Langemarck. He had seen service in South Africa, in West Africa and Northern Nigeria. He was awarded the DSO in June 1915, for distinguished conduct in the field. He went on to command the 6th (Service) Battalion, but was forced to take on less onerous duties, commanding the Corps Reinforcement Depot from 13 July 1917 until invalided home, dying there, in Spelsbury, Oxfordshire, in January 1918.

Extraordinarily enough, on 23 October the battalion only lost two officers wounded and two other ranks killed and five wounded; overall, during the three days it was in the line, the battalion, according to the regimental chronicle, suffered the very considerable casualties of five officers killed, five wounded; sixty one other ranks killed and 146 wounded or missing (almost certainly all killed or wounded); the great majority of these casualties were suffered on the first day, 21 October. The CWGC records seventy four men of the Battalion as being killed between 20 and 23 October, of whom twenty one have a headstone or a special memorial in a cemetery; the remainder have their names engraved on the walls of the Menin Gate.

Between the Ox & Bucks and the right of 1st Division were 2/HLI. It has a limited War Diary (which is true of many, indeed most, unit war diaries in these days) and a not completely satisfactory regimental history; during the fighting it lost two officers wounded and 117 other ranks casualties, of whom just over twenty were killed. Most of these men were lost on 21 October – the War Diary notes on that day that fourteen other ranks were killed, eighty were wounded and eight were missing. Although the history entries are short and perhaps a little given over to purple prose, it does make two interesting points – the first about the difficulties of supplying the line and the other about fire control.

Behind the line the transport wagons rumbled to and fro through Ypres all night long; the drivers coaxing their uneasy, gallant horses closer to the sound of the guns. The fatiguemen crawled out of the trenches and went back to meet those unloading the limbers behind the company headquarters, carrying back seven-pound tins of bully-beef and boxes of ammunition through the darkness, while the guns roared, the shells burst and hails of bullets cracked round their heads. *In the trenches there was no wild 'brassing-of'. All fire-orders were scrupulously given, and as scrupulously obeyed—'half right! two hundred! enemy in front! two rounds ! fire! repeat! repeat! repeat! stop!' By exactly the same method used by the 71st* [which became 1/HLI] *to stop seven cavalry charges on its square at Waterloo, so, a century later, the 74th* [which became 2/HLI] *stopped the Landwehr before Ypres. It was not as easy as it sounds. It is a method which calls for superlative training, iron nerves, and a spirit which enables a man to keep going until he drops unconscious with fatigue.*

What is clear is that it was 2/Ox & Bucks that took almost all the weight of the German attack on the evening of the 23rd, as illustrated by the various regimental accounts from 5 Brigade.

On this front, to the east of Langemarck, the German army had an extremely trying day. It had proved impossible before 9.00 am for General von Wechmar's formations to attack. His skirmishing lines then moved quickly to arrive at the Kortebeek, some 1,500 metres from Langemarck. Here they came under very heavy fire and were forced into cover, where they tried to dig in - never an easy matter in such circumstances. allied machine gun and shrapnel fire caused increasing casualties for several hours until the line began to crumble. Near panic set in. The move to the rear of small numbers of individuals accelerated rapidly, until entire skirmishing lines were racing for the rear.

Their attack a complete flop, they were finally rallied on the line of the old positions by Poelcappelle Station. 51st Reserve Division then directed that that line was to be held at all costs.

As has been mentioned in the British accounts of the day's fighting, this setback was not limited to the divisional right flank. The centre also failed and retreated to Poelcappelle. 46th Reserve Division found it impossible to retain its furthest point of advance and it, too, pulled back. There can be no doubting the collective sacrificial courage of these formations; some rifle companies had losses of more than ninety percent of their strength. The whole battlefield was strewn with corpses, but it had all been in vain. As night fell on 23 October, the few gains made that day were lost, as were all those of the costly recent days of battle. Although their own losses had also been high, the allies had won an important tactical victory. The Germans assessed that for the time being a further advance in this sector would be impossible so, leaving the wreckage that had once been Langemarck to burn out, the German front line was established from the southern side of Mangelaere – Poelcappelle Station – Poelcappelle – Broodseinde Crossroads.

1st Division

This slightly unreal situation extended to 1/SWB, the right battalion of 1st Division. Despite the fact that the great weight of two attacks were taking place less than a thousand yards from its right front and rather closer on its left, it seemed to have little impact on the battalion. The CWGC records only two men killed on 22 October and one on 23 October, despite the fact that the positions were regularly shelled and came under small arms fire. To the rear, however, Langemarck was systematically being destroyed; battalion headquarters, discretion being the better part of valour, were removed from a house in the village to an open field.

Although the line had been thickened up considerably on the western flank of 1st Division, prior to the launching of a counter attack to recover the lost ground around Kortekeer Cabaret, the same could not be said of the situation to the immediate north of Langemarck. There was a gap of about 400 yards between 1/Welch and 1/Coldstream, a consequence of the previous day's events at the cabaret, when 1/Coldstream had had to close the gap on its left, between their positions and those of the Camerons. This was a deficiency that was to some extent remedied by Major Pritchard of 26 Field Company RE under orders from the CRE (Commander Royal Engineers) of 1st Division, Lieutenant Colonel Schreiber. The solution was to dig a strong, deep traversed trench, with a low barricade in front of it, during the night 22/23 October, across the road that runs north from Langemarck, at a point on the road in the area of today's large German cemetery. Another was then constructed to its left front; and the two were connected by a defensible communication trench. All that was now required was manpower to hold the position, which came at about 4.30 am (although the regimental history says 2.30 am) from two platoons of A Company, under Captain Robert Rising, of 1/Glosters, in reserve at Varna Farm. Nos 4 (right of road) and 3 (across the road) Platoons (Hippisley and Baxter respectively) covered the gap between 2/Welch and 1/Coldstream; the field of fire was good except for the length of the Koortebeek in front, which had steep banks some five feet deep.

The Germans maintained heavy artillery fire on Langemarck from early morning. From about 7.30 am they advanced from the direction of Koekuit along the road, under the cover of increased shelling on the village and the British positions, and then spread along the banks of the Kortebeek, particularly on the British left. At 9 am, under cover

Second Lieutenant HE Hippisley, Glosters, killed 23 October; he has no known grave.

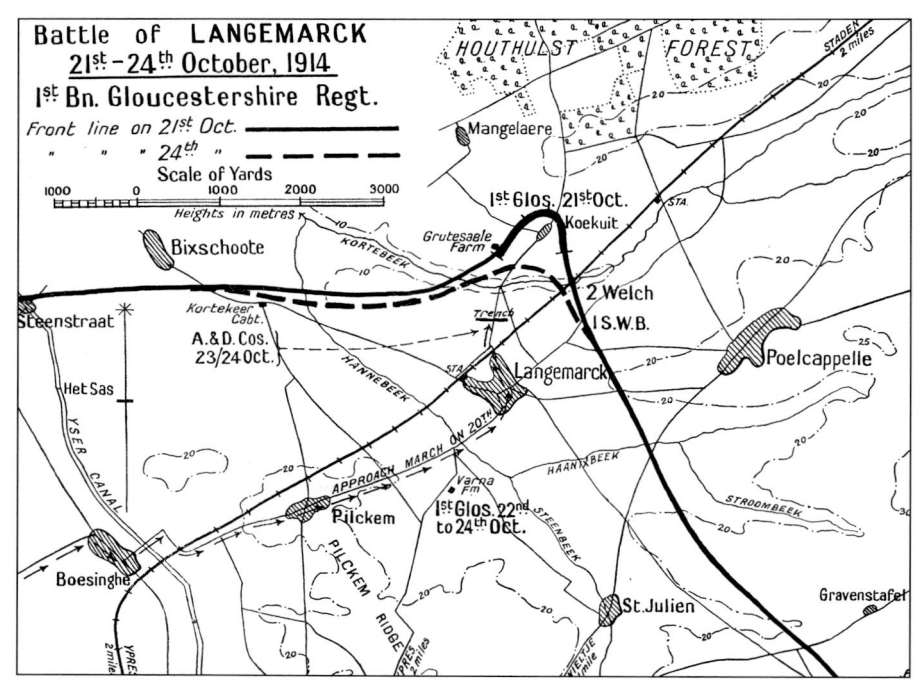

1/Glosters, 21 – 24 October.

of the smoke from a burning farm and haystacks on the British side of the stream, they advanced on the British left; at the same time they also tried advancing down the road 'led by a man carrying a flag'. This latter party was soon halted, the flag bearer being shot down in the process. However, under supporting fire from a machine gun – soon put out of action – troops on the British left made their way to within a hundred yards of the British position, crawling through a root field and began to create a firing line prior to an all out assault.

Thus far the German tactics had worked reasonably well; they had identified a weak area in the British line, the connection between 1/Coldstream and the Glosters. Rising managed to pull No 15 Platoon (Yalland) from D Company, which had come up to support 2/Welch on the right; he used them to reinforce his left.

The Germans used the ground to get themselves into a position where they could attack the Coldstream in flank and rear; the latter fell back in reasonable order some two hundred yards and took up a new position in a turnip field. They were helped to do this by the Glosters, who in the meantime were facing several large scale assaults on their part of the line; and also had to cope with the exposed left flank that the Coldstream withdrawal had created.

It will be recalled that 1/Coldstream were minus a company (No 3), which had got pulled into the fighting in the immediate vicinity of Kortekeer Cabaret. No 2 Company was on the left, in a position that had been sited in the dark and left one trench in particular in a vulnerable position. The Germans made good use of the ground and covering artillery fire and smoke, and managed to take the trench in enfilade; its loss having a knock on effect on the rest of the Company's position, so that it had to fall back. The original line was restored by a counter attack in the evening, with the assistance not only of the Glosters but also of a company of 2/KRRC, which was acting as a reserve for this part of 1st Division's line.

By 1 pm the attacks had died down considerably; 'the enemy began to attempt a withdrawal which, under pursuing artillery fire, soon became a disorderly rout. By 3.30 pm all that remained of the attack was persistent shelling.' The average number of rounds fired by the Glosters during 23 October was reported to be 500. The casualties on the day (as stated in the regimental history) were three officers – two killed (Hippisley and Yelland) and one wounded; and fifty one other ranks of whom fifteen were killed, nearly all of whom came from A or D Companies.

The attack beaten off, the two companies of Glosters remained holding the line until withdrawn, along with the rest of 1st Division, on the night of 24/25 October, when the battalion went into bivouacs near Bellewaarde Farm (Hooge).

The only offensive action taken by I Corps on 23 October was the attack to restore the line around Kortekeer Cabaret. The troops available to Brigadier General Bulfin (2 Brigade) and their disposition were: 1/Northamptons between 1/Black Watch and 1/Camerons; whilst 1/Queen's were behind the centre of the Camerons' position and 2/KRRC was on the left of it. 1/Loyals and 2/South Staffs were in reserve nearby. The Loyals' history gives a succinct outline of the plan:

> *At 5 pm on the 22nd the Battalion was ordered to move up from Boesinghe to St Jean, which was reached at 8 pm; but very shortly afterwards fresh orders came to hand for a further advance, this time to Pilckem, which was reached just after dawn on the 23rd. Here, while the men lay down and took what rest they could, Major General* [sic] *Bulfin assembled commanding officers and issued orders as follows: the Northamptonshire, 2/KRRC and 1/Camerons were to remain in occupation of the trenches that they were holding; 1/Queen's, lent from 3 Brigade, was to attack over open ground to the right*

of the Pilckem road, whilst 1/Loyals was to work through the more enclosed country to the left of the road and attack the trenches to the west of the line, these two battalions then pushing home the assault on the line simultaneously.

Lieutenant Hyndson of the Loyals published an account of the early months of war, *From Mons to the First Battle of Ypres*:

23 October: Shortly after daybreak the firing increases in volume directly to our front, and a good many stray bullets fall among us, but though there is an unpleasant 'zip' about them as they strike the turnip leaves, no one is hit. Soon after 9 am the officers are sent for by the Colonel and he addresses us as follows:

'[…] We are to attack and recapture the lost trench, and will be supported by 2/South Staffords from 6 Brigade. A, B and C companies are to lead, and D Company is to be in reserve under my direct orders. The machine guns will support the attack from the best possible position. ... [The] attack will begin in half an hour from now.'

The British Official History gives some clarification of these orders. The ground on the right required an advance of a thousand yards over open ground. 1/Queen's primary role was to attract the attention of the Germans whilst the Loyals on the left used the closer country, more enclosed and undulating, to get within 150 yards of the Germans' position. The Queen's were to move through the Northamptons and the Loyals through the Camerons; 2/KRRC would provide what supporting fire they could to safeguard the Loyals' left flank. In addition a substantial number of guns were made available – thirty of them from three RFA batteries, positioned between Pilckem and Het Sas, and some heavy guns, from 26 Battery RGA, the latter of which fired on the enemy's approach roads to the position.
The BOH states:

[The] *advance in the heavy mist of the early morning* [in fact it was not all that early – 10.45 am] *at first made good progress, although the battalions were unacquainted with the ground, and the positions from which to start had to be found in the dark. The North Lancashire were eventually checked by some wire erected by the enemy during the night, and two companies of the South Staffordshire were sent up to reinforce; but so well was the movement timed that the whole front of attack arrived almost simultaneously within a couple of hundred yards of the Germans.*

The Loyals moved forward with C Company on the right and A on the left, with the other two companies in support. Ernest Hamilton, in his *The First Seven Divisions*, wrote of the Loyals' attack:

> *In this order they advanced to within 300 yards of the trenches where they began to come under a very heavy shell fire. Major Carter decided to charge at once with the bayonet, and he sent a message to this effect to the KRR[C] on his left, asking them to advance with him. This, however, they were unable to do, and Major Carter accordingly decided to attack alone. Captain Henderson, with the machine gun section, pushed forward to a very advanced position on the left, from which he was able to get a clear field of fire for his guns, and the Battalion formed up for the attack. Captain Crane's and Captain Prince's companies were in the first line; the other two were in support. The order to fix bayonets was given; a bugle sounded the charge, and with loud cheers the Battalion dashed forward, and in less than ten minutes had carried the trenches and cleared them of the enemy.*

Lieutenant Hyndson gives a somewhat breathless account, none the worse for that, of his company's part in the attack:

> *... At 10.45, having explained all we know to the men, we deploy and advance. My company* [although not stated, this is almost certainly B Company] *is on the right, and we almost immediately come under long distance rifle fire, so I order the men in my platoon to open out to four paces interval, and on we go.*
>
> *Soon the Hun shooting becomes more accurate, with the result that several men are shot. Therefore I call a halt, and search Bixchoote* [sic] *through my glasses. Yes, there, just in front of the houses nearest to us, some eight hundred yards away, are the enemy trenches, although the occupants are invisible. We must get closer, so I invite the sections to advance, but now only one at a time, covered by those awaiting their turn, whom I order to fire at the German trenches and houses, which are obviously also occupied by the enemy. On we go, gradually working forward by rushes, which decrease in length as we get nearer and nearer. At every rush a few men fall, but we can do nothing for them. ...*
>
> *Soon we work up to within two hundred and fifty yards of the*

enemy trenches, where we find the survivors of the Cameron Highlanders, who are still full of fight and have been supporting our advance manfully. They are partly covered by some shallow trenches which they have been able to dig during the previous night, and we dump ourselves amongst them, thankful to get shelter from the bullets. We can now occasionally catch sight of the Huns, whose firing has become less accurate...

    We are now close to the 'Bosche' trenches and must pause to wear down his nerves until he dare not show a hair before we can complete the attack. We commence to fire for all we are worth at selected portions of their position. Little by little we get the upper hand, but the slightest attempt on our part to work forward is met by angry bursts of fire. About this time, Miller made a gallant attempt to gain ground, but unfortunately both he and the men who were with him were shot down, and the command of the company descends to me again. I notice the Germans dodging past a gap in the hedge some 250 yards to my front, and order a section to fire at them as they slip past. Remembering their snap shooting practice in peace time on the range, the men enter into this task with zest, and many of the flitting figures are seen to fall. We afterwards found twenty or thirty dead Germans in this area. A red house in front also gives us considerable trouble, as several riflemen are in occupation who bravely continue to shoot at us, but eventually the garrison cease fire, and we afterwards found only dead and dying men inside. ... And so the fighting goes on until about 1 pm, when the firing from the enemy trenches almost dies down. The time has now come to put the finishing touches to the battle, and we work forward in small groups until only 200 yards separate us from the enemy.

    From this point of vantage the whole regiment rises up and with rousing cheers, which must have put fear into the hearts of the Germans, we surge forward with fixed bayonets and charge. ... On we dash, yelling with all our might, passing over the front German trench we bayonet the surviving defenders and pass on to the reserve trenches. Here we expect to meet stout resistance, but the Germans have had enough and suddenly the glorious sight of masses of grey coated men standing to surrender meets our gaze. ...

Captain E Miller, Loyals, killed in action 23 October and is buried in Poelcappelle British Cemetery. Aged 36 when he died, he had been married less than a year.

Isolated bodies of Germans continue to resist and must be rounded up; one particularly brave man, established on the top of a windmill, continues to fire and refuses to surrender, so we have to set fire to the building, but in spite of all this he goes on firing until the building collapses and its brave defender perishes in the flames. I go on past a house flying the Red Cross flag when suddenly an awful thing happens. From the rear a screaming noise, followed in rapid succession by others with resounding crashes, as one after another shells land amongst us. What has happened? In a second it is only too clear. Our guns have mistaken us for retreating Germans, as we are now well ahead of the remainder of the battalion. For a moment we pause, and then I shout to the men to get back to the house flying the Red Cross flag. Back we run, with the exception of a few men who are knocked out, and we get out of the danger zone. On reaching the house, what a sight meets my gaze! The whole place is crammed with German dead, dying and wounded, all lying together on the floor, packed tightly as sardines. Finding one or two unwounded Germans hiding amongst the others, I stationed a guard by each exit, and proceeded to make a search. The result is a bag of twenty men and, as the shelling has died down, I proceed to report to headquarters.

British artillery fire 'obliged the Battalion to evacuate the captured trenches for a time', but they were re-occupied and held all that night, and in the morning they were linked with those of the Highlanders on the right and the Rifles on the left. On 23 and 24 October the Loyals suffered two officers killed (Miller and Kingsley) and four wounded. Captain E Miller was an officer in the Special Reserve and had only joined the battalion on 17 October. 178 other ranks were casualties, of whom – according to the CWGC records – thirty-nine were killed. All but the two officers (buried at Poelcapelle British Cemetery] are commemorated on the Menin Gate.

It is interesting to read the account of **1/Queen's**, showing how the same battle and the same principal events can be seen so differently by different observers. Their history, quoting an officer who was there, says:

Second Lieutenant G Kingsley, Loyals, killed in action 23 October and buried in Poelcappelle British Cemetery. He had only been commissioned in the June of 1914.

At 10.15 am they started on our trenches with Black Marias and Coalboxes [German howitzer shells, used indifferently of 150 – 210 mm calibre, emitting black smoke on detonation and sometimes also referred to as Jack Johnsons]. *A Company was on the right of the* [Pilckem] *road, and D Company on the left, and we advanced in four lines, reaching our* [old?] *front line trenches about 50 yards short of the Inn, without many casualties; most of the enemy's shrapnel passed harmlessly over our heads, and our own artillery were doing very good work. Sergeant Monk and a platoon of D Company did the actual rushing of the Inn and released some eighty-odd 'Jocks', prisoners who came skipping out of the Inn in great delight.* [In fact there were just under sixty prisoners.] *Sergeant Monk obtained a DCM for this eventually. D Company was then ordered to the next ridge, about 400 yards north of the Inn, and A Company was directed to hold the line of the Inn-Langemarck road in support of D Company.*

At 5.30 pm, when it was getting pretty dark, there was a sudden burst of rifle fire in front, and after a few minutes' pause we saw a column of men in fours approaching from our right front, all dressed in khaki and shouting in English. They seemed to be making so much noise, shouting and blowing bugles, that I got suspicious, and with the help of glasses made out that they were Germans. Many of them had on helmets, and only a few of the leading men were wearing putties. I gave the order for rapid fire, and evidently it came on the Germans as a complete surprise; they stood for about a minute, and we could see them dropping like sheep as we blazed into them. They all then lay down, but we could still pick them off in turn on the ground. ... We stopped another counter-attack about half an hour later and had no trouble after that. At about midnight Captain Stanley Creek rejoined with about forty of D Company; he had been cut off by the same party of Germans who had come around his right flank, and the only way he could rejoin us was by leading his men into the enemy's lines and make a detour, which eventually brought him in on the 2nd Brigade front. Eight hundred prisoners were taken to-day, but our casualties were pretty heavy: Lieutenant MD Williams killed [Cement House Cemetery XIX A 16], *Captains HNA Hunter and CBM Hodgson* [subsequently killed in 1918] *and Lieutenants JB Hayes and FRW Hunt wounded, sixteen men killed, thirty wounded and eighty nine missing.*

The night passed quietly, but there was a good deal of shelling by the enemy on the 24th, while in the evening he attempted two *attacks, but was repelled, then at 11 o'clock at night the Battalion was relieved, 15 men at a time, by French troops, the operation being successfully carried out despite the fact that the opposing lines were no more than 100 yards apart.*

The *Annals of the **King's Royal Rifle Corps*** gives another account of 23 October; this time it is the Queen's who get omitted, the Northants get a starring role and their casualty figures suggest that they had a rather hotter time of things than the BOH account would suggest.

On October 23 the 2nd Battalion advanced to the attack of the lost trenches at 6 am. The two leading companies pushed on till they reached the old support trenches, where they were held up, having pretty heavy casualties in the advance and from shelling after they had been held up. The Germans shelling their own front line trenches, a good many of the occupants bolted and offered a good target to the riflemen, who got some thirty of them as they ran. About 2 pm General Bulfin ordered the Northants to attack the German left flank, but the attempt was unsuccessful. The North Lancashire were then sent in and, working further round to the flank, were completely successful, driving out of the trenches the Germans, who, bolting across the open, gave a splendid opportunity to our leading platoons and machine guns. They left some 300 or 400 killed and wounded on the ground. D Company and part of C Company pressed on with the North Lancashire and occupied the lost trenches. D Company alone took 130 prisoners. The losses of the Battalion in the fight were thirty six killed and about sixty wounded [including two officers].

Only one of these men has a known grave: Rifleman William Knight is buried in Cement House, VIIA.E.9.

1/Camerons were not directly involved in the morning attack, but were keen, if perhaps inaccurate on occasion, observers:

While the KRRC worked round the German right, and had some very stiff cross country fighting in doing so, a company of the Queen's attacked and recaptured the inn in brilliant style, thereby securing many German prisoners, and at the same time recovering a lot of wounded [no able bodied prisoners, then?] *Camerons who had been missing the previous night, including Second Lieutenant Huskie. ... About midday, after a fire fight of some hours' duration, a general advance was made all along the line which swept the*

Germans out of their positions, and during the afternoon enabled the British troops to reoccupy their old trenches of yesterday. During this advance the remains of the Camerons got somewhat mixed up with other regiments, but two sections of A Company found themselves in the trenches which had been dug by Lieutenant McCall's in the field between A Company's left and the brickyard.

The extent of the enemy's losses became apparent by this operation, the whole area of the fighting being marked with dead Germans and littered with items of clothing and equipment. Here and there, however, the 79th tartan could be seen amongst the dead. When the enemy recovered from their rout, they began their old tactics of sniping the British troops in their trenches, and after the German artillery joined in and made their occupation very costly. It was therefore decided, again very wisely, to withdraw to the straight trench south of the inn, and this operation was carried out at dusk, hastened by renewed activity on the part of the enemy, who lost little time in reoccupying the inn.

All was not quiet during the night of 23/24 October; **1/Black Watch**, on the right of the morning's attack, noted:

Situation map, the evening of 23 October.

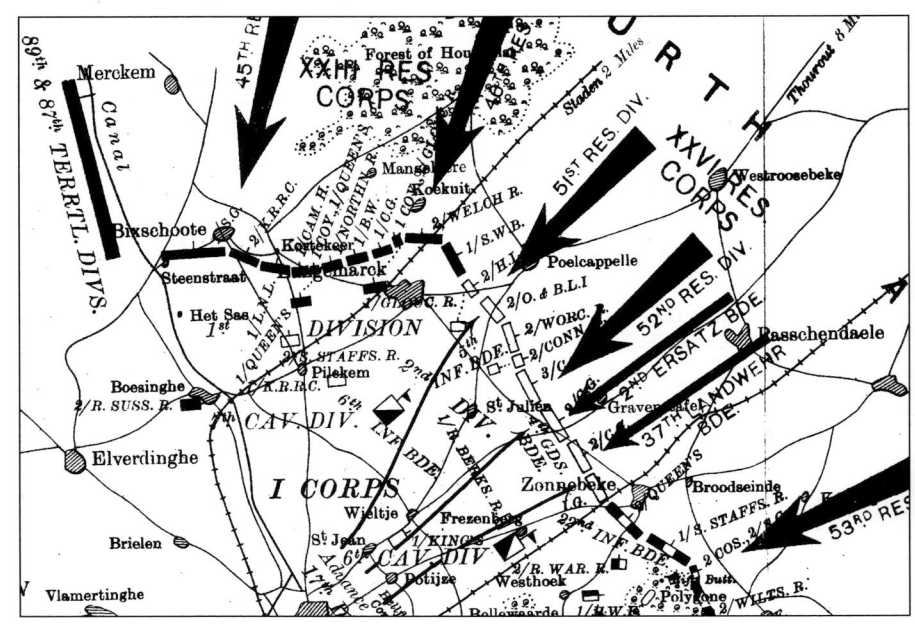

In the evening [23rd] the rest of the Battalion moved up to Remi Farm [north of the Langemarck road], and established connextion [sic] with the Coldstream Guards on the right, so that by midnight the position was restored and reorganized. Another attack was made on the Cabaret this night, the Germans advancing in mass formation, singing 'Die Wacht am Rhein' and 'Heil dir im Siegerkranz'; they were beaten off, but all through the 24th heavy attacks were made on the Camerons, and on D Company on the left of the Battalion. Captain Urquhart [the sole Great War casualty buried in Boesinge Churchyard] *and Lieutenant Bowes-Lyon* [the late Queen Mother's cousin] *were killed on the 24th and Lieutenant KG Macrae badly wounded. ... At 5 am on the 25th French territorials relieved the Battalion, which had been constantly engaged for two days and two nights. There was no opportunity for rest...*

Lieutenant C Bowes Lyon, Black Watch, killed 23 October and buried in New Irish Farm. Cousin to the future Queen Mother, he had survived the sinking of the ship bringing him home from an engineering appointment in India in May 1914 and being wounded twice prior to being killed.

Including the two officers, seventeen men of 1/Black Watch were killed between 23 and 25 October. Interestingly enough, Bowes-Lyon was buried alongside Urquhart in Boesinge Churchyard but, for whatever reason, is now interred in New Irish Farm, XXX D 11.

Withdrawn from the firing line on the morning of the 24th, relieved by 1/Queen's, **the Camerons**:

...went into support south of the inn. There they were still under unaimed fire, both rifle and artillery, but the conditions were mild in comparison to the previous three days' nerve wracking experience. Nobody had washed since leaving Hazebrouck on the 20th, and there was no chance yet to break the spell. Meals, too, were difficult of attainment, as the mess cart had been temporarily in the hands of the Germans at the inn, and the officers could be seen sitting behind a haystack eating fids [sic – presumably chunks or slices] *of meat with their fingers. The men were disposed in ditches and what cover could be found; they were all dead tired and preferred sleep to safety. At 8 pm the order came to stand by, which put an end to further recreation, but a welcome change occurred very early on the morning of Sunday the 25th when the troops of the 1st and 2nd Brigades were relieved by the French.*

The history records losses for this period in front of Kortekeer Cabaret as being, 'approximately 76 killed and died of wounds and 4 wounded'; the CWGC records would suggest that these figures are accurate. Three officers were killed or died of wounds (one of whom was the medical officer – a disproportionate number of such officers were casualties in I Corp's battle between 20 and 25 October – for example, besides Chisnall, the Camerons' Medical Officer, the MOs of 3/Coldstream, 1/Northamptons and 1/Worcesters were also killed); six were 'severely' wounded; four were 'wounded; one was 'slightly' wounded and one was 'invalided', a total of fifteen officers out of the twenty four who had marched out of Poperinghe on 21 October.

The BOH makes an unusual observation about the postscript to the successful attack. Once the various units were established in the recaptured line:

Two medical officers killed or fatally wounded on 23 October and in the same action, near Korteker Cabaret: Lieutenant G Chisnall (attached Camerons), who died of wounds on 24 October and is buried in Cement House VIIA.E.10; and Captain MJ Lochrin (attached Northamptons), who has no known grave.

> *Such a feeling of hilarity, however, prevailed, that it was only with the greatest difficulty that some of the men could be restrained from collecting souvenirs and persuaded of the necessity of preparing against enemy counter attacks.*

Over on the extreme left of I Corps, holding the line to the canal at Steenstraat and to the rear of Bixschoote, 1/Scots Guards seemingly had a much calmer couple of day than the rest of the Division. Its history notes that C Company supported the attack to recover the lost ground of 22 October, and then:

> *A German attack on the left of the Scots Guards at about 1 pm was repulsed with heavy loss. Otherwise there was nothing very remarkable on this day, or the 24th, except the usual heavy shelling and a great deal of sniping.*

They moved out of their trenches at midnight on the 24th, relieved by the French.

The BOH concludes its narrative of the affair at the Korketeer Cabaret with a bittersweet commentary:

On examining the ground, General Bulfin came to the same conclusion as Colonel MacEwen had done on the previous night: that the line near the road in rear was the best one, and he withdrew the troops from the Korketeer salient and occupied for the night the new Cameron trenches just south of the Langemarck-Bixschoote road. The British had greatly increased their confidence in themselves by their successful counter attack and greatly alarmed the enemy, but otherwise the result of the operation had been waste of energy and unnecessary loss of life. The casualties of the 1st Division on this day were 1,344; those of the XXIII Reserve Corps which attacked it must have been very considerably heavier.

In a number of ways this criticism is unusually harsh for the BOH – and in great part inaccurate. Whilst there was a withdrawal near the Cabaret itself, the indications are that other parts of the salient that were captured were retained by 1st Division, according to whether they improved the position of the line or not. The German attacks on the northern and north eastern flanks of 1st Division had nothing to do with the counter attack and were a separate initiative by the Germans – at the very least, the assault on the Kortekeer Cabaret salient must have forced them to readjust their ideas. This is especially true if what the populist German history, *Ypres 1914*, has to say about the British attack is even remotely true: it described it as a prepared attempt by large reinforcements 'to break through our line and roll up the part of the front lying to the north of it as far as the sea'. Finally, whilst Edmonds states that 1,344 casualties were incurred on 23 October, this simply is false – as is made clear a few pages later in the BOH, when it states: [1st Division] 'had suffered fourteen hundred casualties, mainly in the 1st and 3rd Brigades, during its <u>four days'</u> fighting'; a time period that fits much better with reported casualties in the various regimental histories.

With the replacement of the men of I Corps by French troops, the BEF's part in the actions around Langemarck came to an end during First Ypres. French formations now took on I Corps' original plan, the attempt to envelop the German right flank. After some initial success, their attacks too became bogged down, pushing the Salient a little further to the east. On the left, the Belgian and French forces continued to fend off the German assaults on the Yser in very bitter fighting; only after the locks at Nieuport were opened on 28 October and the sea, released gradually over a few days, inundated much of the territory between there and Dixmude, did that position become relatively secure. Yet the fighting here on 10 November threatened to be almost as serious

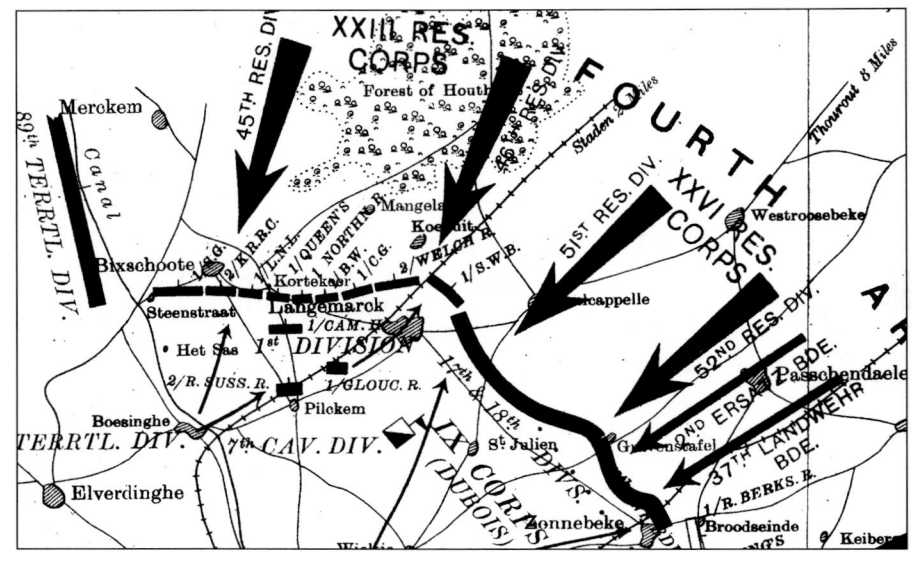

Situation map, on the evening of 24 October.

and as significant as that which took place along the Menin Road the following day; it was a serious error not to launch the attacks on the same day, as originally planned.

2nd Division sidestepped to the right and became heavily involved in the defence of Polygon Wood, though a brigade was also sent to the area of Zillebeke, to provide support to that part of the line; 7th Division narrowed its front, giving over some of its left flank to 2nd Division and 1st Division was withdrawn to reserve positions just east of Ypres; but there was to be no respite for it. The plan, indeed, was for the French to engage in an offensive, using the substantial forces that Joffre was building up, and for the BEF formations towards the north of the line to participate in such an attack. The Germans had other ideas.

So ended the first attempt by the Germans to capture Langemarck. The formations committed to the operation had behaved with courage and tenacity, but the task was beyond them. Ill prepared and inadequately supported throughout, they had been poorly commanded and they paid an appalling price, which no post-war huffing and puffing about the 'Spirit of Langemarck' could erase.

Chapter Six

24–31 October 1914

There was complete chaos around Langemarck on 24 October. Dead and dying soldiers lay all over the battlefield. Very few German officers had survived the fighting of the past few days. As a result the surviving parties had no leadership to turn to for guidance or orders. The dismal remnants of the shattered rifle companies of Reserve Infantry Regiments 233, 234, 235 and 239 were hopelessly intermingled and were occupying shell scrapes and rudimentary trenches between Poelcappelle and Mangelaere. There was no overall plan for the defence, nor could there be one until order was restored. Oberst von Gilsa of Reserve Infantry Regiment 235 had been killed and Oberst Wilhelmi of Reserve Infantry Regiment 236 severely wounded, so the first priority was to replace the two of them.

Oberst Wilhemi, Commander Reserve Infantry Regiment 236; seriously wounded 24 October.

That afternoon Major Grimm, a battalion commander of Reserve Infantry Regiment 233, was directed to assume command of Reserve Infantry Regiment 236, who described the situation which confronted him thus:

> *The night was well advanced before we were able to set off for the 236th. Our guide became disorientated so, instead of arriving where the regimental staff was located, we found ourselves out front in amongst the battle trenches. Profiting from the error, I immediately familiarised myself with the layout of the position and met up with a number of the men. The first impressions were not promising. There was an air of great nervousness in the trenches. Despite a lack of evidence, there was a general assumption that the enemy was going to attack and, throughout the night, a huge amount of ammunition was wasted shooting at shadows. No sooner would this be stopped in one place than it began again elsewhere.*
>
> *When I toured the entire position in the early dawn, I found*

that it was occupied by members of five regiments. As well as the 236th, there were men from the 233rd, 234th, 235th and 239th. A lack of junior leadership had made it impossible to sort out the situation. With the aid of the battalion commanders it gradually became possible to organise and develop the position. However, it was, for example, necessary for me personally to accompany them around the forward trenches in order to ensure that bread and other rations had been correctly distributed and to check that the sections were gradually being reorganised. At that time there was a generally careless air.

In some places the lack of food caused by a breakdown in the system of rationing was beginning to have a serious effect on morale. Reserve Infantry Regiment 233 had made an effort to organise carrying parties and get food forward, but within Reserve Infantry Regiment 235, which had suffered particularly severely and where the command structure was extremely precarious at this time, a couple of days spent eating raw turnips had led to a deterioration in battlefield discipline. The regimental history notes:

Despite heavy enemy shellfire on Poelcappelle, the field kitchens moved there during the occasional pauses in firing. Naturally, there was no possibility of organising the orderly collection of rations. Because of the fact that during the previous few days the men had been existing on raw beets, two to three men from the forward sections, and sometimes more, raced to the rear to grab some food from the nearest field kitchen. This endangered the positions very much ...

Luckily there were no enemy attacks and soon matters improved as more commanders were posted in. Oberst von Wunsch assumed command of Reserve Infantry Regiment 235 on 25 October (though he himself fell ill and had to be replaced two days later) then, on 26 October, the remnants of Reserve Infantry Regiments 234, 235 and 236 were concentrated into a 'Group Poelcappelle' under command of Oberstleutnant von Busse. There was still no question of these battered formations mounting attacks, but their poorly constructed trenches offered little protection and they continued to lose men to artillery fire. The situation was much the same in the sector of 46th Reserve Division, just to the west of Reserve Infantry Regiment 234. Its regiments, too, had been fully occupied during the days following the Langemarck disaster with the need to reorganise and restore their combat effectiveness. The pressure and strain on all concerned comes through strongly in this letter, written at the time by Offizierstellvertreter Franke of 12th Company.

> *Within the past five minutes, 10th Company has suffered one man killed and two wounded. There are two or three trench lines to our front, but bullets still keep cracking over our heads. Naturally, there are shells and shrapnel rounds as well, which at any moment could come crashing down into our little room, which resembles a kitchen. Last night we had to turn out five times because the enemy was either attacking, or at least bringing down heavy fire. Once again, only those in the very front line were permitted to fire. The remainder spent the night with their weapons unloaded and their bayonets fixed, so that they would not be able to fire on the comrades out to the front by mistake. It makes everybody extremely nervous, but the main thing is that it helps to keep things calm.*
>
> *The enemy airmen must obviously be reporting accurately because, as soon as they have returned home, artillery fire comes down. Our men have learned to take cover and keep still until the aeroplanes have departed. The fact that I am still alive is a special mercy and one of God's miracles, for which I cannot give sufficient thanks. What have I done to deserve it? May God continue to help me! ... I have not seen my batman for four days; it is said that he has been wounded. What's that? – a shell has just landed a mere twenty paces to our front without damaging us and now another has come down a bit more to the right and further forward. What is the next one going to do? May God be with us!*

The French army, having assumed responsibility for the Langemarck sector, remained mostly on the defensive and spent the next few days improving their positions. As some sort of order was restored by the German army, it became possible to move the hardest hit regiments into reserve briefly, but the remainder were warned to be ready to prepare for yet another all out effort to capture Langemarck on 30 October. It is difficult at this remove to know how much faith the higher echelons of the chain of command had in this particular operation but, because the so-called Army Group Fabeck was about to attempt to break through south of Ypres that same day, it was important to maintain pressure all along the front, in case the Allies should consider transferring additional forces south to help block this new threat. Although the intention was for 51st Reserve Division to attack alongside 46th Reserve Division, its few remaining troops had been concentrated into 'Group Poelcappelle', which had very little fighting potential left, so instead its role was restricted to active (but not very effective) patrolling and holding its positions, so as to provide a firm shoulder for a thrust southwards by 46th Reserve Division. 45th Reserve Division, meanwhile, was to renew the attack on Bixschoote.

Although the corps order for 30 October was issued early the previous day, the divisional orders did not arrive at some of the forward regiments in sufficient time. The plan was to launch the attack at 6.30 am. 45th Reserve Division was ordered to assault Bixschoote, 46th Reserve Division the line Bixschoote (exclusive) – Kortekeer Cabaret – Weidendrift and 51st Reserve Division Langemarck itself. Similar efforts were being made up and down the Fourth Army front, though with what expectation is hard to say. None of the histories of Reserve Infantry Regiments 234, 235 and 236 - 'Group Poelcappelle', the only remaining fighting troops of 51st Reserve Division - make mention of this attack so, even if the attempt was made, the attack clearly did not make significant progress forward of the start line. The personal diary of Kriegsfreiwilliger Emil Pouplier of 4th Company Reserve Infantry Regiment 234 does, however, mention an ill-fated attack conducted on 31 October. This must represent the last operation by troops of 51st Reserve Division before it was relieved.

Today was supposed to lead to a decision. An attack on a broad front was intended to advance our lines at long last. A few men from each section went back into the village to knock together some assault ladders, so that we could climb out of the trenches quicker. We were linked up with 46th Reserve Division on our right ... The order ran through the trenches and we made final adjustments to our equipment then, a moment later, the company commander bawled 'Go!' We sprang like cats up the ladders and out of the trenches. Left and right our comrades had also climbed over the parapets and we set off slowly, rifles tucked under our arms, in widely extended lines. There was an eerie silence. Not a shot was fired and our artillery did not fire one single shell. That was something quite extraordinary: an assault without artillery preparation? We looked questioningly at one another.

Off to the left in a field of hops as we advanced we saw a great many dead men lying around – blackened, bloated corpses ... We were amazed that there was still no enemy fire. Quietly, in orderly lines, we continued to move forward slowly. We had covered about five hundred metres when the dance finally began.

From Langemarck itself; from positions left and right of it; from the fields all around came the sound of gunfire then, in front of us, behind us, in front of us once more and behind us yet again, shells crashed down, exploding with great roars and sending pillars of earth and dust flying as high as houses into the sky. We raced to take cover, but we were so close to the exploding shells that showers of earth kept being thrown over us, so we were pinned down for some time.

Hissing and roaring, this 'blessing' poured down over us. We could do absolutely nothing. We could not fire; we could not see a thing; we just lay there in a field on a forward slope as though we were on a presentation tray. The shells crept ever closer and everywhere they were striking home. Our men were running backwards and forwards, trying to avoid the places where the fire was hottest. It was a crazy form of chaos. It was impossible to hold out. In ragged groups we ran in all directions seeking cover, any cover, anywhere ... The cannonade continued with undiminished intensity, accompanied by the crack of small arms fire. Many, many of our men, dead and wounded, lay strewn around the open fields as far back as the hop poles. There was no way forward; there could be no way forward, the fire was too intense and the enemy infantry had such clear targets that they could have picked us all off one by one. They had us on a presentation platter. The men could not be kept in line. The platoon commander gave the order, 'Back to the start line!' Zig-zagging back and forth, running to avoid incoming shells, we made our way back individually. We could hear bullets striking the ground and the artillery fire harried us all the way. Once more we passed the hop field with its black corpses, now joined by many of our comrades ...

This was simply another disaster to add to all those that had gone before. Survivors and the walking wounded made their way back throughout a night, whose silence was broken by the harrowing groans of the helpless wounded and the shouts of men trying to alert their comrades not to fire at them as they attempted to re-enter the positions. As Pouplier also remarked, 'We could not credit that we had been ordered to assault in broad daylight, without artillery preparation' – but they had been and all they could do was take care of the wounded and try to minimise further casualties.

Meanwhile, four to five kilometres to the west, the battered remnants of 46th Reserve Division had made yet another attempt to capture Bixschoote. The battlefield situation was complicated. The front line trace was indistinct and complex. In consequence, when the attack began both regiments of 89 Reserve Infantry Brigade - Reserve Infantry Regiments 211 and 212 - were forced to sit impotently and wait whilst Reserve Infantry Regiments 209 and 210 of 90 Reserve Infantry Brigade attempted to push forward until they drew level. This caused particular difficulties for Reserve Infantry Regiment 212, whose front line formed a bulge, several hundred metres forward of the general line. Because of this a certain amount of redeployment of units from 89 Reserve Infantry Brigade took place, the aim being to strengthen the other brigade and assist it to make swift progress. However, the attendant manoeuvres were observed by the French defenders, who were placed on high alert and who also launched minor pre-emptive attacks of their own.

Generalleutnant Wasielewski, Commander 90 Reserve Infantry Brigade.

However, 90 Reserve Infantry Brigade was able to attack immediately the preliminary fire lifted at 6.30 am, but it was soon in serious trouble. When the fire lifted, it triggered a massive defensive fire plan by the allied gunners. The forward trenches were kept under fire and other guns raked the whole of No Man's Land systematically and ceaselessly. Despite this some troops from Reserve Infantry Regiment 210 achieved a small bridgehead on the far bank of the Markejevaert, one of numerous canalised streams. There they joined together with men of Reserve Infantry Regiment 212, but their combined strength did not even equate to one weak rifle company. At that point the advance stalled. French machine guns prevented further movement by engaging the attackers with heavy enfilade fire and they brought up reserves which were spotted forming up and threatening the right flank of Reserve Infantry Regiment 210. In response, all less one platoon, which had been given the task of maintaining contact with Reserve Infantry Regiment 212, were pulled back and the regiment was redeployed to face the new threat though, in the event, nothing came of it.

Despite the unpromising situation, it was decided at about 9.00 am to start the attacks of Reserve Infantry Regiments 211 and 212. That of Reserve Infantry Regiment 212 barely got across the start line. The moment the advance was spotted such heavy observed gun fire was brought down on it that any thought of attacking was abandoned and the leading troops began digging in where they were. Despite this there were many casualties which had been incurred to no useful purpose whatsoever. The attack on Bixschoote by Reserve Infantry Regiment

211, with elements of Reserve Infantry Regiments 209 and 216 in support, enjoyed brief success. Their achievement in managing to advance despite an appalling weight of defensive fire was remarkable, but French pressure meant that the village had to be abandoned the following night and all the losses had been for nothing.

Apart from one company commander, Hauptmann Brauchitsch, commanding the 2nd Battalion, was the only officer still on his feet and, in the words of the regimental history, 'His battalion had been totally decimated and so was disbanded'. Brauchitsch then assumed command of 3rd Battalion the following day when its commanding officer, Major Birkenstock, was medically evacuated. In all, the battles around Bixschoote cost the regiment twenty four officers and 674 men. It was a very high price to have paid for an operation designed to do little more than provide a diversion to cover attacks elsewhere and one which achieved nothing more than the gain of a few useless metres of ground.

46th Reserve Division, reinforced by Reserve Jäger Battalion 18, also attacked that day, their sector lying between that of 45th and 51st Reserve Divisions. The day before it had been reorganised into two brigades to improve command and control. 92 Reserve Infantry Brigade was created from Reserve Infantry Regiments 214 and 216 plus Reserve Jäger Battalion 18, whilst Reserve Infantry Regiments 213 and 215

46th Reserve Division's attack on Langemarck, 30 October.

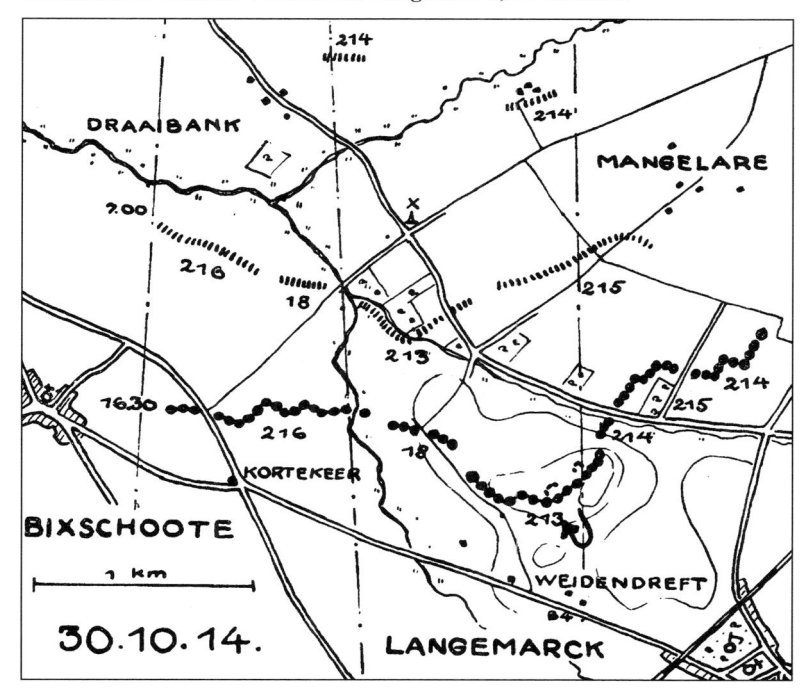

formed 91 Reserve Infantry. On 30 October the division attacked with all four regiments in one great wave. Little is known about Reserve Infantry Regiment 216, because it has no history, but that of Reserve Jäger Battalion 18 indicates that it attacked towards the south, leaving Bixschoote to the east. Reserve Infantry Regiment 213 assaulted Weidendrift frontally, so the Jägers were obliged to move further southwest than envisaged. Reserve Infantry Regiment 215, for its part, did not even receive its orders until 3.00 am 30 October, so it was unable to plan or prepare systematically.

Despite this, the regiment made the start line on time and initially pressed on quite rapidly, with the scattered French troops north of the Broenbeek withdrawing quickly in front of them. A bayonet charge got them in amongst the positions of the 96th Regiment of the Line and fifty prisoners were taken. It was not long, however, before their situation deteriorated. They were occupying a salient in the French lines, Reserve Infantry Regiment 234 barely advanced and the companies of Reserve Infantry Regiment 213 were thwarted every time they tried to get forward. This was hardly surprising; the Reserve Infantry Regiment 213 mission was tough. Its left hand companies had to get across the Kortebeek, which at that point ran at an acute angle to the direction of the attack, and the companies also faced having to negotiate the Draaibank – Langemarck road, which also ran away at an acute angle. This meant that as soon as the operation began it was highly likely that the two thrusts would splinter and separate and that control would be very problematic. The geography did not help either. The approaches to the Kortebeek were swampy and Weidendrift was located on high ground covered by a lattice work of ditches, fences and hedges, whose defensive potential had been maximised by the French. As a result the attackers faced a series of machine guns built into strong points and a multi-layered defence.

To add to their problems, the men were physically exhausted and emotionally drained after ten days of continuous fighting. Their losses, especially amongst their officers, had been severe and they had had to go without food repeatedly due to breakdowns in their administrative system. However, the attack had to be conducted. Just after 6.00 am their guns opened up but such was the incompetence of their crews that almost all the shells dropped short, in some cases very close to the start lines. The French defenders could not have been given a clearer alarm signal and almost immediately defensive fire missions were being fired, together with harassing fire on routes to the rear. There was a significant number of casualties before the attack even jumped off then, once the advance began, the fully alert defence caused havoc and brought the attack to a standstill in short order. On the left it never got across the

Draaibank – Langemarck road, whilst those heading for Weidendrift itself were soon forced into cover and prevented from moving.

The regimental commander, Oberst Ottmer, was hit and seriously wounded in the chest near to the mill southeast of Draaibank. Major von Loesen, commanding officer 1st Battalion, stepped into the breach and the attack continued throughout the day. Reserves were deployed but it was nearly 3.00 pm before small groups from Reserve Infantry Regiments 213 and 209 got close to the French positions and they could do no more. When it went dark, the survivors began to dig in at the furthest points of advance. Despite a further sacrificial effort, they had made little progress and the French still held Weidendrift (in the fields to the east of the present German cemetery). Nobody had crossed the Bixschoote – Langemarck road and French heroics had ensured that Langemarck was still out of German reach. The German offensive on this sector of the front had now lost all its momentum. Hauptmann von Hammerstein, 5th Company Reserve Infantry Regiment 213, later noted:

> *We were in an unenviable position – right up against an enemy in overwhelming strength. However, after the experience of the past few days we could be reasonably sure that the old French territorials and colonial troops would not attack. We, too, were too weak to launch another assault. For the time being, it was just a matter of holding on as best we could.*

French situation map, Langemarck, 31 October.

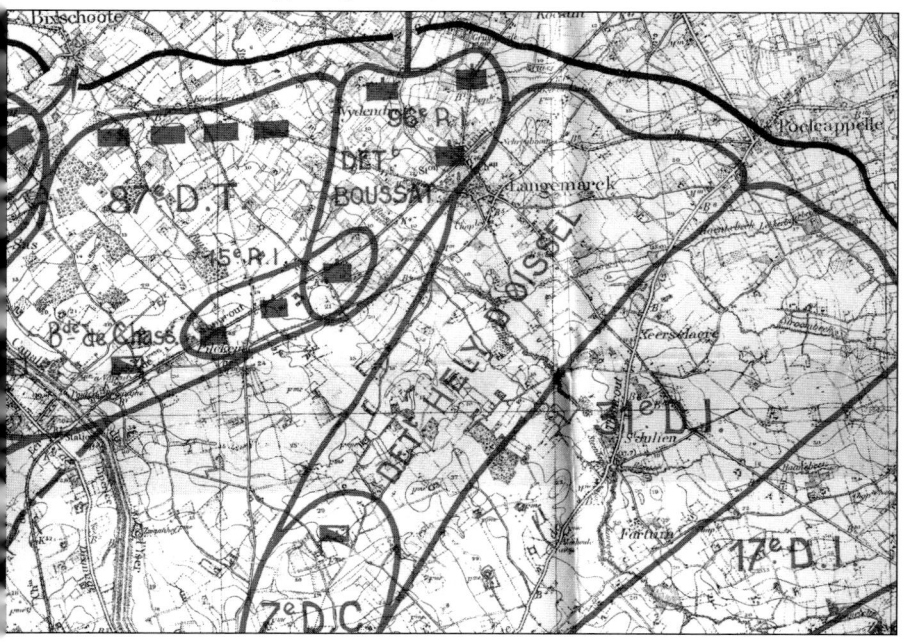

By early November, the Allies were fighting hard to maintain their defences along the general line Bixschoote – Langemarck – Gheluvelt – Hollebeke and so deny a breakthrough to the Fourth Army. For the time being the reserve corps were a spent force, but it was still considered essential to capture Langemarck, despite the rapidly strengthening defensive position. The Belgian flooding of the polders near the coast, begun at high water on 28 October and taking a couple of days to take effect, prevented further German advances, also meant that substantial German forces were now available for redeployment. To that end light screening forces were left to observe the inundations, whilst other formations of III Reserve Corps, primarily 5th and 6th Reserve Divisions, were moved south, along with 44th Reserve Division. The moves complete, a concerted effort was made to deploy all three divisions in line, with a view to driving the French defenders out of Langemarck. So much for the plan. In the event minor counter-attacks by the French led to a further wearing down of the German troops and the occasional temporary crisis, so co-ordinated action proved to be elusively difficult, because the fresh formations found themselves having to relieve other

Generalleutnant von Dorrer, Commander 44th Reserve Division. He was killed in action at Verdun on 1 April 1916.

forces in the line and attempting to orientate themselves and identify the precise enemy locations to their front. This was far from easy in the flat terrain.

The men of Reserve Infantry Regiment 48 of 5th Reserve Division tried on arrival to discover information about their opponents, but that same day, during the afternoon, Hauptmann Moeller, commanding 9th Company, had to report, 'There is nothing to be seen of the enemy, but if we as much as show the point of a helmet we bring down a torrent of fire, including machine gun fire, on ourselves.' At least note was taken of this and 9 Reserve Infantry Brigade cancelled a planned attack due to French alertness, determination to resist and lack of hard intelligence. The same restraint was not demonstrated by the neighbouring 10 Reserve Brigade. Reserve Infantry Regiment 52 advanced a total of 150 metres after a series of attacks without adequate fire support. All momentum was lost and the casualties continued to mount with little to show for them.

The 6th Reserve Division experience was broadly similar. Its orders for the relief in the line were:

> *12 Reserve Infantry Brigade is to relieve 51st Reserve Division and occupy its positions: right flank on the Staden – Langemarck railway line where it crosses the Kortebeek; left flank approximately by the Haanixbeek (one kilometre southwest of Poelcappelle). The inter-regimental boundary is to be where the northern Poelcappelle – Langemarck track bends to the southwest for the first time. Reserve Infantry Regiment 35, because its strength is weaker, is to occupy the right hand sector, whilst Reserve Infantry Regiment 26 moves into the left hand sector. The relief of 51st Reserve Division is to be complete by 6.00 am.*

The relief was in fact achieved by 5.00 am and the units of 51st Reserve Division headed for the rear, glad to be away from the uncomfortably weak trenches which they had been occupying for several days.

Chapter Seven

1–9 November 1914

The ground where the trenches were located was low lying so, not only were they overlooked in a number of instances by the French positions, they already contained about twenty centimetres of stagnant water, which the rainy weather was making deeper by the day. The clay was so clinging that it frequently sucked the boots off the wearer's feet. Reserve Infantry Regiment 35 likened the place to 'an Eldorado for frogs' and Hauptmann Bartsch, commanding its 3rd Battalion, stated that the whole position was like, 'pea soup on top of a base of *Syndetikon*' [a fish-based household glue]. Due to a lack of timber it was almost impossible to provide much needed overhead cover against shrapnel fire, so not only were the troops forced to endure unspeakably bad conditions, they were also vulnerable to harassing fire, snipers and machine guns. To add to the miserable surroundings was the sight and stink of hundreds of rotting, unburied corpses. Despite all these dispiriting circumstances, orders arrived, directing that yet another attack on Langemarck was to be organised on 3 November, to form part of a more general assault from Dixmude to the Ypres – Menin road.

The plan called for 5th and 44th Reserve Divisions to move up during the night 2/3 November until they were level with 6th Reserve Division, then all three divisions were to advance simultaneously. Almost inevitably there were difficulties. Elements of 44th Reserve Division got lost, arrived on the start line late and discovered that they were wrongly deployed in rear of 5th Reserve Division. As a result the relief of 46th Reserve Division was delayed. Furthermore, XXIII Reserve Corps, which was meant to be involved, did not attack at all; and 45th Reserve Division became so involved in a defensive battle of its own that it could not take part until the afternoon. The plan was over complex and it unravelled under pressure. 45th Reserve Division made some small progress, 5th Reserve Division advanced a few hundred metres in the first rush but

Oberst von Basedow, Commander Infantry Regiment 212.

then, following earlier orders, moved into cover until 44th Reserve Division came up on its left.

Pressure from above ensured that another attack was launched and some German units closed right up to the French positions. To the south, XXVI Reserve Corps found it impossible to make any progress due to heavy artillery fire and XXVII Reserve Corps did little better on the approaches to Veldhoek. All along the line there were many German casualties on 3 November A combination of poor work by the guns, the exhausted state of the troops and determined defence caused the attacks to stall and there seemed little chance of any improvement in the near future. Despite this fact yet another repetition of the attack on Langemarck and west to the Yser was ordered for 4 November. Increasingly effective and reinforced French artillery and small arms fire meant that all these attacks failed completely.

Despite this further setback, there was another attack in this area on a three divisional frontage on 5 November. This time 44th and 46th Reserve Divisions, together with 5th Reserve Division, were to attack Langemarck and Kortekeer Cabaret simultaneously. It was another extremely difficult day of hard fighting. The after action report of 2nd Company Reserve Infantry Regiment 52 describes vividly, but in purple prose, the difficulties encountered as they tried to move towards the slightly higher ground to the south of the Kortebeek.

On the morning of 5 November as dawn was breaking, we received a whispered order, 'Make ready, we are going to attack!' Silently we crept along the communication trenches towards the front line; however, before we reached that point, led by Feldwebel Schröder, we launched up out of the trench and, with loud shouts of Hurra! we threw ourselves at the enemy. Countless bullets cracked past our ears, but nothing could put us off. Over there a comrade would be falling silently, mortally wounded; here another would be moaning with pain, but nobody could or should have helped. 'Onwards, ever onwards' was the cry. 'Up and at the enemy!' We were threatened with death and destruction from a nearby copse, where a machine gun was firing away from one corner.

Swiftly sizing up the situation and seizing the moment, our feldwebel raced towards this target. With great courage he stormed forwards through a hail of bullets, spotting that the crew was laying the machine gun on us. Quickly, before that could happen, Schröder was on them, swinging his sword through the air and bringing it down on the gunner. His skull smashed, the men collapsed and a second cut dealt with the other man. Shouting Hurra! our feldwebel seized the machine gun. It was the work of a few moments and he was oblivious to the bullets. That, however, was not sufficient and we pushed on into the wood, which was teeming with Frenchmen. With Feldwebel Schröder leading us on, we continued the advance, where the blood-drenched sword saw further action. On we went through the undergrowth until the opposition was mown down or captured. On several occasions we saw our feldwebel surrounded by Frenchmen, but he thwarted their bayonet thrusts with deadly slashes of his sword. So it continued until the wood was cleared and the enemy had taken to their heels. We called a halt in the next trench, where the heroic act of our feldwebel was discussed by everyone.

Aware that artillery support had been poor during the previous days, this time a major effort was made to get the guns right forward, so that they could not only neutralise the infantry positions and key points, but also engage in counter-battery work. Reserve Field Artillery Regiment 44 was deployed in a typically aggressive way that day. It was responsible for the neutralisation of the bridges at Het Sas and Steenstraat, together with the French artillery nearby. Having been occupied in that way throughout the morning, when the attacking infantry had closed to about fifty metres of the Bixschoote – Langemarck road, with Reserve Infantry Regiment 48 making progress towards Kortekeer Cabaret, the decision was taken to move 1st and 6th Batteries forward across St Jans Beek, and gallop 5th Battery and part of 7th Battery forward to bring direct fire down on Kortekeer Cabaret. This was done, but so close was the range that the German infantry had to be withdrawn 150 metres in order to be out of the danger area. All this resulted in some progress being made, but a breakthrough remained as elusive as ever.

Still determined to do everything possible to bring operations in Flanders to a victorious conclusion, Falkenhayn's staff identified formations from elsewhere along the Western Front which could be redeployed north. One such was 9th Reserve Division of V Reserve Corps, sent from the Verdun area to reinforce III Reserve corps. It was occupying forward assembly areas by 8 November, but although all ranks were ready to do their duty to the limit of their ability, it is nevertheless evident that many had little faith that they would be able to achieve success where there had been so much previous failure. The adjutant of Reserve Infantry Regiment 19, Oberleutnant von Schauroth, later had this to say about their prospects:

Headquarters XXVI Reserve Corps (Commander, General der Infanterie Freiherr von Hügel) was located in Westroosebeke. The information that filtered out concerning the previous battles dampened spirits considerably. It appeared that the newly arrived regiments of 9th Reserve Division were to make the eighth attempt at an assault which had already failed seven times. When we then met up with the remnants of the young regiments we heard about the utter lack of success of their operations. Amongst the very few surviving officers there was an air of deepest depression. Our morale then sank to zero.

Whatever the state of morale amongst the reinforcements, the decision was to continue the offensive and, late on 9 November 1914, the Commander Fourth Army, Duke Albrecht of Württemberg, issued a special Order of the Day

The enemy, who are still defending their current positions obstinately, are to be thrown back on 10 November by means of a general attack, launched by Fourth and Sixth Armies, which will envelop them. Every man of Fourth Army is to be aware that the very highest standards are expected of him during this attack.

In the event, only Fourth Army launched a major attack on 10 November.

Chapter Eight

The End of the Battle

The attack of 10 November was the one which started the myth of Langemarck. The Supreme Army Headquarters communiqué that evening made the most of the minor successes of the day and specifically referred to the singing of the National Anthem on the battlefield. It reads in part.

> *We made good progress yesterday along the Yser. Dixmude was assaulted. More than 500 prisoners and nine machine guns fell into our hands. To the south our troops pressed on over the canal. To the west of Langemarck* [the men of] *some of our young regiments charged forward towards the first line of French trenches, singing Deutschland, Deutschland über alles, and captured them. About 2,000 Frenchmen of the infantry of the line and six machine guns were captured. To the south of Ypres we drove the enemy out of St Elooi, a place that has been bitterly fought over for several days. About 1,000 prisoners and six machine guns came into our possession there.*

Not mentioned, glossed over completely, is the fact the battles around Langemarck and Bixschoote on 10 November were complete, bloody failures for the German army. The casualty count was enormous, nothing

Situation map, pm 10 November.

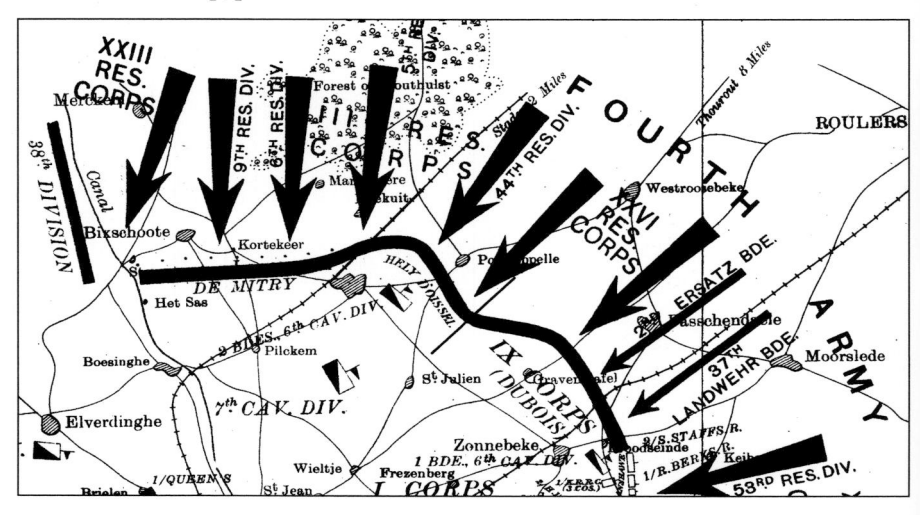

was achieved and the hope of achieving a crossing of the Yser and a breakthrough north of Ypres finally died. Schauroth once more:

> *An increasing number of reports from the front line indicated that an assault in the prevailing conditions offered no prospect of success. All attempts to convince higher authority of the hopelessness of a frontal assault through the morass of the Flanders clay, in the face of complete lack of clarity regarding enemy, ground or even our own positions and to dissuade them from sticking to their plans failed totally. The order to attack early on 10 November was confirmed; it was fated to run its course.*

Flanked on its right by 6th Reserve Division and with 51st Reserve Division to its left, the regiments of 9th Reserve Division were to attack Langemarck from a start line west of Poelkappelle. There was no specific H Hour. The regiments were to be in position and were to advance the moment the barrage lifted onto the rear areas. We have little detail about the role of Reserve Infantry Regiment 6, which advanced west of the Poelcappelle – Kerselaar road, because its history was never written, but Reserve Infantry Regiment 19, advancing to its left, experienced a day of appalling casualties for no return. The preliminary gun fire did not neutralise the French defences at all, so the moment that its 1st and 2nd Battalions began their attacks, each with three companies forward, they were met by an extraordinary weight of enemy fire. Amazing to relate, although 1st Battalion recalled later that French shells buzzed around the assaulting troops, the forward companies of these battalions managed to get right up to the French positions and some survivors even pressed on into the depth positions.

Oberst Smalian, Commander Reserve Infantry Regiment 19.

The cost was enormous. Some companies simply withered away, trapped in front of uncut barbed wire with no means to pass it. Every officer involved was killed or wounded, with the sole exception of Landwehr Leutnant Dreyer of 2nd Company, who later left this description of events:

> *By now it was 6.30 am and completely light. Suddenly the air was filled with a howling sound and the crash of an impact. A*

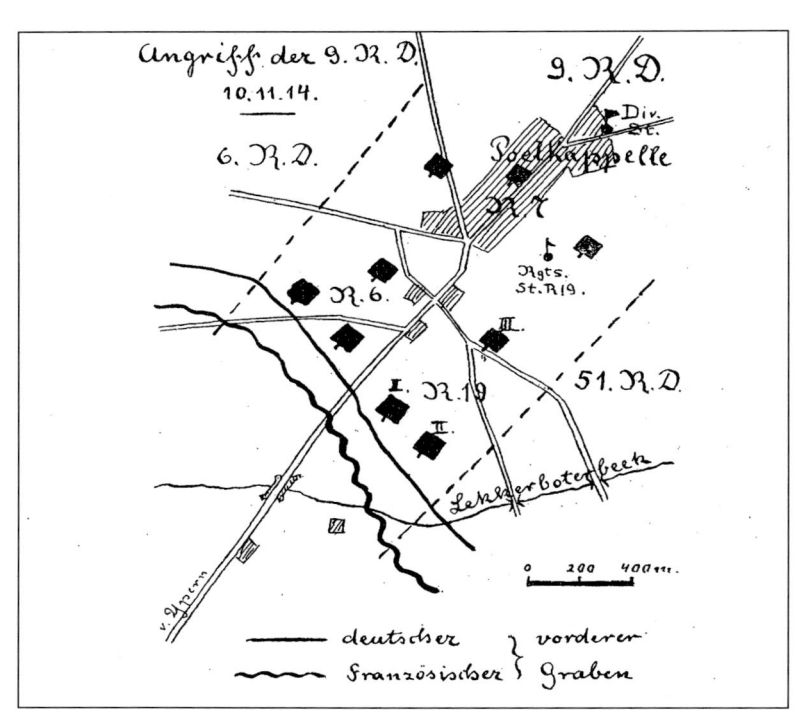

Situation map of 9th Reserve Division, 10 November.

great cloud of dark smoke shot up over the poplar trees alongside the road by which we were lying. Shell splinters whistled past our ears and branches crashed down from the trees. Sergeant Heise was taking cover with a section on the far side of the road. Suddenly another shell crashed down. The shells of our own artillery landed in front, behind and beside us; some smashed down in the trenches, killing the men there.

I caused the remainder of the company, approximately twenty five men, to take cover under the bridge, there to await the end of this lengthy shelling. I then despatched a gefreiter back along the line of the stream. He returned to report that the French trenches were all occupied. So, together with remnants of the company, I was sitting in a mousetrap. Something had to be done. Towards 10.00 am I had [the men] *occupy the edge of the road and opened fire against the French, who were withdrawing from their rear trenches. Wherever red trousers appeared, they were blasted – and always with good effect. My men were displaying outstanding calm and cold blooded control as they fired and observed. We continued to fire until about 2.00 pm. Finally we could hold out no longer, because we were under heavy fire from the flanks and rear, so we took cover in a French trench which was about one hundred metres to the rear and which offered more protection. About thirty men came with me and the rest of 1st Company arrived after dark.*

On the right flank, where 2nd Battalion was deployed, there was less resistance and it was possible to break into the defensive system and overrun two lines of trenches. Here, too, however, most of the troops were stopped by barbed wire in front of the third line and suffered accordingly. 5th Company, out on the left flank, also had to contend with thigh high water in the Lekkerboterbeek, 150 metres from their objective. They managed to cross, though their commander, Hauptmann Grüttner, was killed and the remainder were then hit by German field guns firing short as they moved towards the enemy trenches. Seven out of nine officers of 6th and 7th Companies who took part in the attack were killed. 8th Company, in reserve, was never committed but Offizierstellvertreter Baltz, located in a forward trench, observed the entire bloody failure.

As the company moved up through the communication trenches we were not all in very high spirits. We had seen nothing of the promised powerful artillery bombardment. Holding our breath, we lay in wait. Suddenly the first waves made ready to climb out of the trenches. From the sector to our right came the sound of rapid rifle and machine gun fire. Immediately the assault force set out in our sector as well, though it was also under heavy small arms fire that dominated it. Just as we were pushing forward to the place from which the assault had been mounted, there to stick it out and wait for the order to advance, shells coming from our rear impacted in endless succession immediately in front of our trenches. No Man's Land was strewn with dead and wounded. Individual wounded men crawled back to our trenches. There was nothing else to be seen of the once proud three companies. It was simply dreadful.

During this catastrophic day for 9th Reserve Division, Reserve Infantry Regiment 19 suffered casualties of twenty four officers and 213 other ranks killed in action. This indicates clearly how much the junior officers tried to inspire their men to get forward. Five officers and 293 other ranks were also wounded and two officers and 590 other ranks were missing. Some of this last category were captured but the greatest number were killed. This appalling outcome was the direct result of sending men into action against determined and well deployed defenders with inadequate preparation, time for reconnaissance or proper fire support.

One member of Reserve Infantry Regiment 19, who took part that day, later summarised the attack as follows:

> *Amongst the men, the order to attack did not raise the slightest bit of enthusiasm, in complete contrast to similar situations previously. There was general amazement that such an order could have been issued when there was absolutely no information about terrain or enemy. At daybreak I looked out from our trenches over the battlefield. My heart sank within me when I saw that the ground in front of the enemy positions was covered with field grey, whilst the whole area was strewn with our men, lying dead individually or in twos and threes. Confronted by this sight, which I shall never forget, the involuntary thought came into my head, 'Was this really necessary?' Here the commanders had launched something with no consideration for the consequences: they had simply sent entire regiments - the best men – to their deaths. Could they ever provide a justification for this entirely foreseeable bloodbath?*

This view was later endorsed by Oberleutnant von Shauroth, adjutant of Reserve Infantry Regiment 19, in this lament for his fallen comrades.

> *Hundreds of our finest men gave their lives for something which was completely hopeless. It is indicative of the spirit of 1914, however, that the sacrificial courage displayed enabled the attack to be driven into the depths of the enemy position. That was the tragedy of Poelcappelle: each participant, imbued with a highly developed sense of duty, tried his sacrificial best, even though he was convinced of its hopelessness right from the start. The men of Poelcappelle did not go to their deaths through any sense of bravado; rather the deeds and performance of Reserve Infantry Regiment 19 bore the stamp of the old inherited Prussian sense of duty and faithfulness unto death.*

The Reserve Infantry Regiment 6 assault also failed. At that, the divisional commander committed his reserve, Reserve Infantry Regiment 7, in a vain attempt to regain the initiative. By now it was broad daylight, so an advance across open ground was impossible. Instead the attackers exploited every covered approach, but many did not even get as far as the communication trenches leading forward. Some small groups did

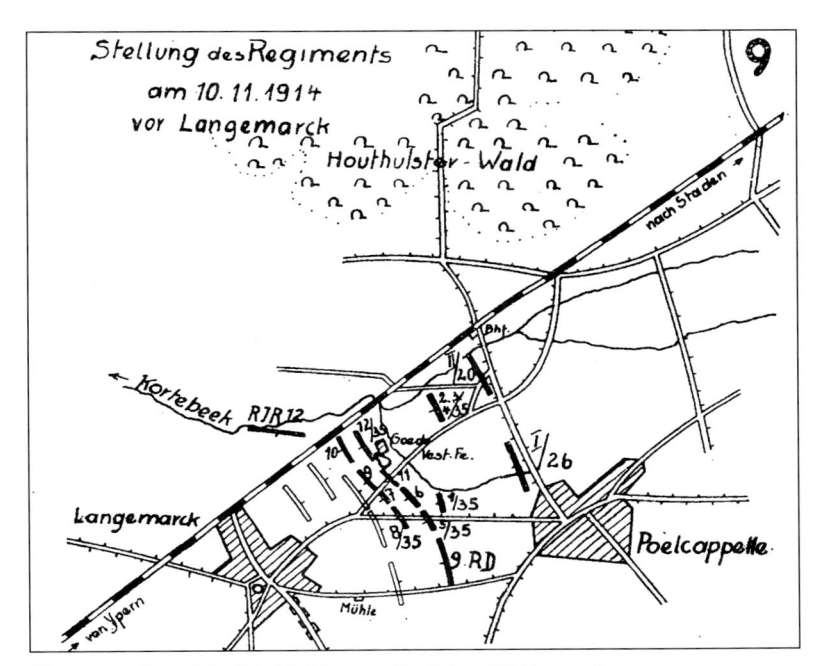

Situation Map RIR 35, 6th Reserve Division, 10 November.

eventually reach the front line, but they too were pinned down there, attracting heavy fire every time they tried to get forward. Very soon every available trench or shell hole was full of dead and dying men and all movement became impossible. It was, nevertheless, hoped that an advance by 51st Reserve Division, scheduled to begin at 6.30 am, would improve matters, but it was completely unsuccessful as well, many sub units spending the entire day pinned down under fire. It must be remembered, naturally, that these newly formed units of 51st Reserve Division had been in action near Langemarck since 20 October without relief and were effectively fought out, despite having received the first drafts of reinforcements. By 1 November, Reserve Infantry Regiment 235 had already lost seventy percent of its strength but was still in the line and unrelieved. This was typical of the other regiments of 101 Reserve Infantry Brigade. So, in response to orders to attack, all that could be done was to amalgamate the survivors of Reserve Infantry Regiments 234 and 235, together with those of Reserve Jäger Battalion 23, under the Brigade Commander, Oberstleutnant von Busse, then to send them into action.

That said, it seems evident that Headquarters 51st Reserve Division was inadequately briefed on the situation, if the preamble to its orders for the following day are anything to go by.

> Tomorrow morning a general assault is to be launched against the enemy opposite us, who are to be attacked and thrown back. The Army Commander expects the attack to be pressed home with the utmost determination. Every man is to be made aware that he is expected to give of his best and to close with the enemy come what may. The infantry attack is to begin tomorrow at 6.30 am. Oberstleutnant von Busse is to command the attack within divisional boundaries. All his currently available troops are subordinated to him for the attack, together with the battalion of Reserve Infantry Regiment 235, which I have been holding in reserve.

Maintaining the same air of confidence, 101 Reserve Infantry Brigade directed that

> 1. The men are to be briefed about the high importance attached to the success of this attack. Every effort is to be made to make sure that they are fully keyed up to succeed.
>
> 2. In the right hand sector, the attack will be mounted by Reserve Jäger Battalion 23 and 2nd Battalion Infantry Regiment 235, led by Major von Mengersen. In support, from 5.00 am tomorrow morning, will be 3rd Battalion Reserve Infantry Regiment 235. This battalion is to be deployed so as to be able to reinforce the right flank of Reserve Infantry Regiment 234 if necessary. The left sector will be the responsibility of Reserve Infantry Regiment 234, led by Major Krumbiegel-Möllmann.
>
> 3. During the advance, contact is to be maintained to the right, so that the attack is co-ordinated with Reserve Infantry Regiment 19.
>
> 4. As soon as possible after the start of the assault, our forward trenches are to be occupied by supporting troops in order to guard against counter-actions. Similarly, until the success of the attack is certain, machine guns are to remain in their [current] positions.
>
> 5. If the forward trench is captured, it is initially to be occupied and developed for defence. Only then is the advance to be continued in conjunction with neighbouring units. There will be pauses in the artillery fire. These are to be used for reconnaissance and to enable engineers to work. All successes are to be reported.
>
>   Signed: von Busse.

During the night a party of forty sappers from Reserve Pionier Company 51 arrived, bringing supplies of temporary bridges with them. The equipment and specialists were then dispersed among the five leading companies and tasked with bridging any gaps and dealing with barbed wire as and when it was encountered. The attack was to be preceded by an artillery fire plan but once more, as so often at that time, this achieved less than nothing because it failed to neutralise the defence and simply alerted it. To add further to the difficulties, H Hour had been set for 6.30 am. By then it was daylight, so the enemy, comprising men of the British 2nd Division in some places and French troops elsewhere, were able to bring lacerating aimed fire down as soon as the attack began. In this area No Man's Land was no more than one hundred metres wide, but not one member of the assault force crossed it; each separate attempt was utterly destroyed and in the meantime the depth positions also came under heavy harassing fire. During the morning 3rd Battalion Reserve Infantry Regiment 234 lost 150 men and others fell in an equally hopeless attempt during the afternoon. This day saw the very last attack on this sector for the time being. The Corps Commander included in his orders for 11 November instructions that 'Brigade von Busse', on 11 November [was] to take, 'every opportunity to damage the enemy to the front and to gain ground in coordination with 9th [Reserve] Division'. However a response was completely out of the question for these exhausted troops and they were withdrawn a short time later.

Their relief came none too soon, as Offizierstellvertreter Baltz 8th Company Reserve Infantry Regiment 19, makes clear.

The long hours up until we were relieved were torture. Our morale was at rock bottom. The men were very nervous; the sentries were constantly opening fire, without being able to make out any sort of target, until they were finally calmed down. The condition of the forward trenches was the cause of great concern. In stretches they were completely indefensible. The firing steps had slid down into the mud in places, so it was impossible to see out, never mind to open fire effectively. Once it went dark there was a constant procession of wounded crawling back one by one. It was also possible, despite constant small arms fire, to bring in several of the wounded who were lying forward of our trenches, unable to move. In the end we were so exhausted that we were able to sleep standing up, with our heads leant against the damp wall of the trench. At long last relief arrived.

Out to the right of 9th Reserve Division on 10 November, the situation was every bit as bad. Hardly any troops of 6th Reserve Division even moved forward from their trenches. Quite apart from anything else, the bad weather and awful conditions in the trenches had taken a severe toll on the troops. Several key personnel had been medically evacuated and there was general concern, despite generous issues of rum and red wine, that the cold, wet weather was badly affecting the health of the men of the Division. Already the previous day, Reserve Infantry Regiment 26 had been withdrawn from the line, to be replaced by Reserve Infantry Regiment 6 of 9th Reserve Division. Regardless of the physical condition of the troops, III Reserve Corps was left with no choice but to issue orders for a resumption of the assault for 10 November. In this area the plan was for 3rd Battalion Reserve Infantry Regiment 35 to be left in reserve, initially because it was positioned too far back and there was a chance that an attack by it might endanger Reserve Infantry Regiment 12 to its right. However, 2nd Battalion Reserve Infantry Regiment 35, with 1st Battalion following up in depth, was directed to assault at the same time as Reserve Infantry Regiment 6.

In the event, when the 5.00 am H Hour, arrived, the German front line was being bombarded so heavily that there was no question of starting the attack. Out to the right Reserve Infantry Regiment 12 had made a minor advance and it proved possible to make a little progress. On the left flank, however, Reserve Infantry Regiment 6 made one attempt to get forward, but suffered such high casualties that it had no choice but to pull back once more. This in turn prevented 2nd Battalion Reserve Infantry Regiment 35 from attacking. There was also a feeling that there might be an enemy counter-attack on this sector, so all available reserves were deployed forward as a precaution.

As night fell on 10 November the result in this part of the front had been exceedingly meagre. The German advance in recent days had seen their positions pushed forward to the edge of Langemarck and Bixschoote, but the attackers and their supporting arms were too worn down after their exertions to be able to make any meaningful impression on the French defences, which became stronger and more resistant every day. It had proved almost impossible in the short term to change this situation, because what few reserves or uncommitted forces were still available tended to be pushed forward piecemeal to prop up the lines where they were especially weak. One example of this comes from Reserve Infantry Regiment 24 of 6th Reserve Division. Despite earlier heavy losses, on 10 November it was able to bring together a usable force by combining 9th and 10th Companies and what was left of the Machine Gun Company. They were then despatched to reinforce

Reserve Infantry Regiment 48, which was actually part of 9 Reserve Brigade of 5th Reserve Division. Even though their contribution was necessarily small, it was urgently required, as this description of the conditions by Oberst von Kleist, Commander Reserve Infantry Regiment 48, shows.

> The terrain around Weidendrift was covered in a labyrinth of trenches. Opposite the right flank, at a distance of 120 metres, were the enemy positions, which they seemed to be reinforcing. On the left flank, opposite the 'farmhouse group', the distance was more like eighty metres. For over eight days my men had been hanging on in holes in the ground lined with a bit of straw and only a stretched groundsheet as shelter from the rain. They had to obtain their water by digging holes a little deeper in the bases of the trenches. Fetching rations from the field kitchens, which were located some two and a half kilometres away as the crow flew, was an awful experience. The ration carrying parties were forced to stick to certain paths, where the mud was still knee deep and where they were affected by both the 'evening blessing' and the constant harassing fire. The return journey lasted about four hours and reduced them to a terrible state when they eventually returned to the forward positions, worn out and carrying food which had gone cold.

As has been described, there was an all out attack west of Langemarck on 10 November and this was intended to be supplemented by yet another assault by the formations withdrawn earlier from west of the Yser and moved south to maintain the pressure on Langemarck from the north. General von Beselar, the Corps Commander, directed that,

> The enemy are to be driven back against the canal by a thrust to the south by the reinforced III Reserve Corps. Without waiting for further orders, the attack is to begin promptly at 5.30 am. Weapons are to be unloaded.

Two hours before H Hour it was already apparent that the attack was not going to enjoy surprise. By 3.00 am allied defensive fire was coming down so heavily that Major Hauß of Reserve Infantry Regiment 48 was unsure if any sort of attack would be feasible. In an attempt to generate more supporting fire, he directed 3rd Battalion Reserve Infantry Regiment 48 and Reserve Jäger Battalion 3 to remain under cover in their front line trenches; then to fire in support of the movement of their neighbours. For the time being, 2nd Battalion was pinned down in its trenches and unable to move but once 44th Reserve Division out on their right began to advance at 9.30 am, Major Hauß sent out an amended attack order.

> *3rd and 12th Companies, commanded by Reserve Leutnant Graeff, are to launch an attack astride the northern Bixschoote – Langemarck track against the northernmost extremity of the enemy position. Hauptmann Mathieu, to whom these companies are subordinated, is to follow up with his three companies and further press home the attack as necessary. As soon as the enemy salient is driven in and on my order, 3rd Battalion Reserve Infantry Regiment 48 and Reserve Jäger Battalion 3, under Hauptmann Rohrbeck, is to advance against the area Kortekeer* [Cabaret] *crossroads windmill 250 metres to the west of the crossroads.*

The plan was for 2nd Battalion to begin its own advance once measurable progress had been made elsewhere and, to that end, artillery forward observation officers came to the frontline and adjusted fire onto Kortekeer Cabaret. Time passed and one of the company commanders, unwilling to wait any longer, led his men forward at 11.15 am. Two companies from Reserve Infantry Regiment 24 were sent to stiffen the attack and, with their assistance, Hauptmann Mathieu managed to get his attack going forward by mid afternoon and captured Kortekeer from the north. This was a significant success against the former point of maximum resistance. Major Hauß was then able to order his 1st Battalion, together with Reserve Jäger Battalion 3 and the surviving of 1st Battalion Reserve Infantry Regiment 24, to press the attack frontally. A short bombardment of the enemy positions began at 2.55 pm, the lines of infantry shook out and the attack was soon underway.

The attack was something of a disappointment. Inevitably a number of enemy positions and weapons had survived the shell fire and they were quickly into action. A pair of machine guns posed a particular threat, though good work by Bavarian Foot Artillery Battalion 2 silenced them both. This enabled the attackers to get forward and secure the Bixschoote – Langemarck road as far as a point 200 metres east of Kortekeer Mill. There was also a minor French withdrawal from hasty positions south of the road and troops from Reserve Infantry Regiment 48 moved forward to occupy the place once it was dark. This attack marked the high water mark of the German advance on this sector and there the lines stabilised.

What was left of 44th Reserve Division attacked on the extreme right, with its flank company moving down the east bank of the Yser. Reserve

Infantry Regiment 205 and Reserve Jäger Battalion 16 operated on the right flank, with Reserve Infantry Regiment 206 to their left. Of course it was the deeds of these particular regiments which featured in the Supreme Army Headquarters communiqué of 11 November. The history of Reserve Infantry Regiment 205 was not published until 1937 and long before then the Langemarck myth was firmly entrenched in German life. One result is that aspects of this history are questionable and it includes even more extravagant language than usual. The 44th Reserve Division's objective was the capture of crossing points over the Ypres Canal and, to that end, it was the task of Reserve Infantry Regiment 205 and Reserve Jäger Battalion 16 to advance as far south as Steenstraat and Het Sas. This was a highly ambitious operation, but everything possible was done to facilitate it, with work continuing throughout the night to get the jumping off trenches as far forward as possible and to position mortars and ammunition to assist in the preliminary bombardment.

However, the assault itself was designed to rely on surprise, so there was no firing on this part of the front until 5.35 am, which was H Hour + five minutes and it turned out that the defenders were on full alert when the attack began. A heavy neutralising concentration of fire would have been helpful. As it was the French were ready for action when the attackers set off at 5.30 am. They brought down a storm of fire and the result was effectively a massacre of 1st Battalion, whose last two remaining officers were killed, together with many of their men. Oberst Freiherr von Schleinitz, the regimental commander, could only report, 'Attack carried out. 1st Battalion destroyed, with the exception of the regimental commander, the adjutant and a few men.' The brigade commander, Generalleutnant von Dieringshofen, despatched about half a platoon forward to reinforce and they added their strength to that of the survivors, who were back on their original start line. Assessing that the German situation was extremely vulnerable, the French commander decided on an immediate counter-attack. He would have done better to have considered his options for a longer period, because 2nd Battalion Reserve Infantry Regiment 205 was still occupying its starting position, slightly ahead of 1st Battalion. This meant that the French were subjected to intense flanking fire which splintered and stalled the attack. Hauptman Klos then charged with his leading companies, took numerous prisoners, threw the French back off their positions then pursued them into the depth of the French lines. Gefreiter Lewerenz of 5th Company Reserve Infantry Regiment 205 describes what happened next.

> *We had gone quite a long distance when I, together with several comrades, spotted a number of Frenchmen running into a house. We pursued them and fired into the house, then we dashed over and gathered by one of the walls. Shots were then fired from the house and one comrade was killed. There were twelve to fifteen of us. I leapt over to the door of the house and put several bullets through it. We then heard shouts coming from inside. We had a prisoner with us who could speak German, so we sent him inside with instructions to tell the occupants to surrender. The prisoner emerged from a window, saying that they did not want to. This was followed by firing from the window, the cellar and the ground floor. We could not think of anything other than to smoke them out. Some comrades stayed to keep watch, while others went to get some straw. This was set alight then thrown through the window. The Frenchmen then tried to make a bolt for it as a group, but our shots drove them back. Gradually the flame and smoke in the building became too much and the occupants came out one by one without their weapons. There were fifteen of them and we took them prisoner. Whilst some of us escorted them to the rear I, together with the remainder, pushed on until we reached our new position and began to dig in.*

The Reserve Infantry Regiment 205 men had in fact reached a French depth position which was too strong for them to tackle. Furthermore they were now being subject to fire from every French gun within range. The only possible response was to dig in and try to hold firm where they were, just short of Steenstraat, some 400 metres from the canal. Their situation was verging on the desperate. The commander, Oberst Freiherr von Schleinitz, having been wounded in the neck, was helped to the rear by his adjutant, Leutnant Freiherr von Wachtmeister, who then went to report the situation to the brigade commander. Unaware that Hauptmann Klos, commanding officer 2nd Battalion, was still in action, the brigade commander told Wachtmeister, to gather up every man he could find and return to the front to take charge of all the remaining personnel. Despite the fact that they had captured fourteen French officers, 1,154 other ranks and five machine guns, his men were near to collapse and total exhaustion after nine days and nights in the front line. On the way forward, the regimental history claims that the following improbable incident occurred:

> *During the march forward through the thick, sticky mud, it was necessary to call a halt for a short breather in the ruins of*

Bixschoote. One man discovered a piano in a half-collapsed building. Freiherr von Wachtmeister had it brought out. One man who could play it sat down and began to play a folk melody. Too uninspiring for men on the verge of exhaustion! Then came a dance tune, which brought life back to tired limbs! Military marches. Hey, that was the stuff to lift the spirits! Then, when the commander gave the signal to continue the march, came the only piece that could truly match the glory of this great day. Singing, Deutschland, Deutschland über alles, they set off for the front line trenches.

Thus do myth and legend become entrenched fact. However, the chances of this story being true are vanishingly small. The remaining 44th Reserve Division reserves gradually reached the front line, but they were so few in number that all they could do was bolster the lines of Reserve Infantry Regiments 205 and 206 and Reserve Jäger Battalion 16. The last Jägers had managed to profit from the progress made by 2nd Battalion Reserve Infantry Regiment 205, but then became snarled up in woods south of Bixschoote. Reserve Infantry Regiment 208, in reserve since 7 November, having been reduced through casualties from 3,000 to an appalling 270 all ranks, nevertheless provided a composite company under Leutnant Seevers, which took part in the follow up towards the evening and it finally dug in about 500 metres north of Steenstraat. There were no other readily available reinforcements so the advance in this sector also made no more progress.

With the advance stalled, the first priority was to establish a defensible line of trenches, but this was far from straightforward. Because none of the units of 5th Reserve Division had got much beyond the Langemarck – Kortekeer Cabaret salient left when the 44th Reserve Division operations also halted, it meant that the forward troops were at great risk of counter-attack. All the men in the front line remained on full alert throughout the night then, the following day, the French defenders did indeed attempt unsuccessfully to drive them out. Nevertheless, the entire area was under continuous artillery bombardment which, when combined with the awful physical conditions, made the final forty eight hours that these severely depleted units were kept in the line a terrible trial. The situation in the neighbouring 5th Reserve Division sector was much the same. Casualties and the numbers medically evacuated continued to climb and it was only possible by dint of combing out every spare man throughout the III Reserve Corps area that it was possible to hold on at all. One of those unfortunate enough to have lived through these final hours later described how,

Langemarck after its capture in spring 1915; note the ruins of the church in the distance.

The forward position of Reserve Infantry Regiment 239 near Langemarck in the winter of 1914/15. Recognisable trench warfare had well and truly arrived in the Salient.

It rained heavily during the night. The platoons were unable to get any food, because it was impossible to link up with the vehicles ... The platoons had to attempt to obtain some sort of cover from enemy fire in a half-dug French trench, which offered a flank to the French, was full of mud and water and was equipped with no dugouts or other shelter. We fed ourselves from tinned rations which we took from the bodies of dead British and French soldiers who were lying around. We could not do any work on the trench by day, because the French maintained a rapid rate of fire on it. This was particularly marked at midday each day, when we were also shelled. The battle continued unabated through 13 November, when it rained all day and throughout 14 November as well.

The trenches became ever muddier. It was impossible to arrange weather protection and bundles of straw were soaked through in a very short time. Rationing was extremely difficult to arrange. A combination of artillery fire and the bottomless mud meant that the field kitchens could get no more than half way to the positions from their locations in Houthulst Wood. As a result, it took the carrying parties one hour each way, so the food was cold when it arrived in the trenches. It was completely impossible to warm it up; there was not a single dry item of combustible

Forward positions of 51st Reserve Division, 1914/15.

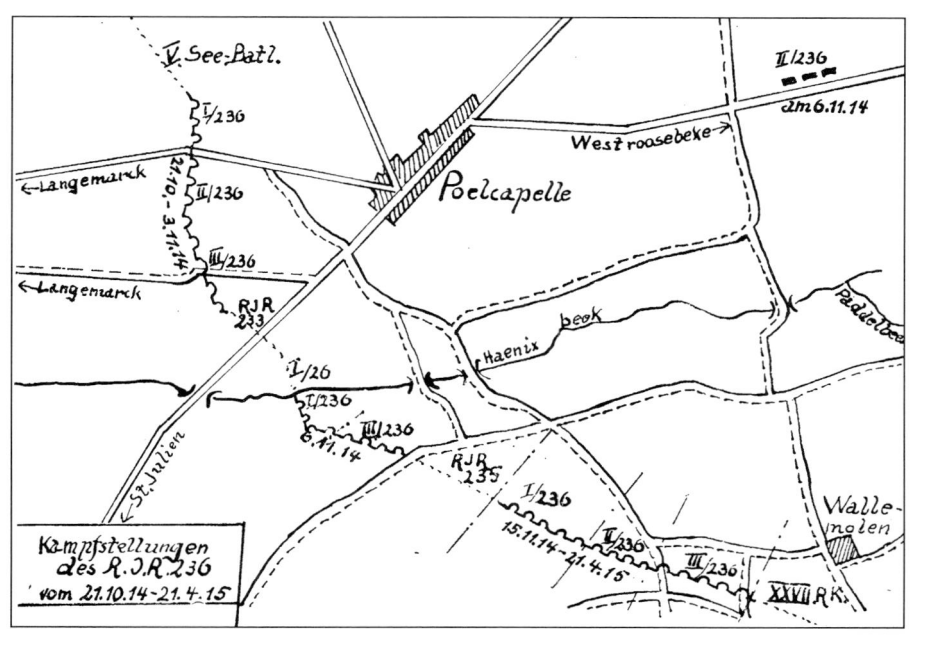

material, so the health and strength of the men began seriously to be reduced. Morale was at a very low ebb, especially following the assaults, which had achieved nothing and of which there seemed to be no end in sight.

At dawn each morning, the battle, which had faded somewhat during the night, increased once more in intensity. One day our artillery fired six heavy shells short, landing them in our trenches and forcing us back. Once the error was corrected we regained our old positions. About seventy five Frenchmen, followed a little while later by an officer, came along one of the communication trenches which led to the enemy position, surrendered to us and were moved back to the rear. The French artillery fired on this group, killing and wounding several Frenchmen. At long last, at midday on 16 November, orders arrived stating that all the formations of III Reserve Corps were to be relieved by VIII Corps in an operation which was to be completed by 11.00 pm.

The relief which greeted this order must have been immense. It marked the end of the German attempt to break through the allied line north of Ypres and there the lines solidified throughout the winter, until the assaults supported by the release of chlorine gas the following April saw the ruined village of Langemarck finally fall into German hands.

General Advice for Tourers

Traditionally this has been a different section at the beginning of each of the *Battleground Europe* books; in future it will be much less full. The series is some twenty years old. British motorists nowadays generally have far more experience of driving abroad and all that entails. The almost universal availability of the internet and good web sites (with improved search engines), from tourist office level down to individual gites, means that details about differing types of accommodation and other useful information is both readily available and up to date. A number of web sites, such as that of the Western Front Association, the Great War Forum and the Long Long Trail also provide tips or one can ask questions on line that usually provide very helpful responses. A further development in recent years is the website of the Commonwealth War Graves Commission (www.cwgc.org), with considerably enhanced capabilities, which enables people to discover a wealth of information about burials by name, by regiment and by date, so that there is no need for the cemetery section to be as full as in the past.

Some general pointers include:
• Ensure that your car insurance is fully valid (this particularly applies to comprehensive insurance); that you take out appropriate personal insurance and that you have your European Health Insurance Card. Bear in mind that, although the arrangement is reciprocal – there might, nevertheless, be charges in both Belgium and France that are not applicable under the NHS.

• Ensure that your vehicle is equipped with all the mandatory items: spare light bulbs; fluorescent vests for driver and all passengers (best to have them in the car rather than in the boot); breathalyzers (France – though the law is in a somewhat chaotic state as this book goes to press); warning triangles; small fire extinguishers; etc., etc. Rules change, so it would be as well to check on the AA website or equivalent for the most recent regulations. Similarly, keep up to date with regulations for the transportation of animals from the UK and back; if you are bringing a pet, the Euroshuttle is the least stressful method to get across the Channel.

• It is advisable to have your passport with you, as the Franco-Belgian frontier is never far away. Although it is extremely rare to be asked for identification, it can happen.

• The drink drive limit is substantially less than that in the UK.

Langemark 1914 Tours

For ease of navigation the modern Flemish form of the place names is used throughout this section; if there is any doubt about a place name in the text (where we have usually followed the usage of the original sources) and its modern equivalent, the former is also given at first use. Note that there are radar traps and speed cameras all over the place in West Flanders, so it is prudent scrupulously to observe all speed limits; the motorway maximum is 120 kph in Belgium and many villages and towns have areas with a 30 kph limit, especially near schools, churches and hospitals. 'Sleeping policemen' are common and can have quite a vicious bump.

A few key points:

These tours we regard as car/bike tours unless specifically stated otherwise. However, some, or parts, of them are short enough to be walked by the fit and the committed. Any tour of a battlefield on foot leads to a better appreciation of the ground, but time and other factors often makes this impracticable. Not one of the tours in its entirety (and most not at all) is practicable for a bus – a minibus is probably the maximum sized vehicle and even then, with the bigger ones, there are likely to be issues. Before using any large vehicle for a tour, therefore, we strongly urge that a reconnaissance be carried out.

In 1914 both sides were operating from very small scale maps – often 1:100,000; for example, positions are often reported in terms such as a 'quarter of an inch under the 'o' of Veldhoek'. The BOH and other sketch maps are good general indicators, but a certain amount of tactical military wisdom will indicate where particular positions were likely to have been.

The majority of these tours will take even regular battlefield visitors to areas that may well be new to them, covering parts of the Salient that were to see very little of the BEF after 1914 except in the later stages of the Battle of Third Ypres and from late September 1918.

Many of these tours are over minor roads – often passable by two passing cars only with difficulty. Obviously, cars should not block roads and entrances to farms and the like; nor should drivers move far from their car if use is made of the passing places (that are a feature of some of the roads) as a stopping/viewing area.

The time of year of your tour is important; the tours are generally in rich agricultural areas, which brings advantages and disadvantages. There are many small, narrow roads, with minimal road signs; there are often deep ditches running alongside (hazardous especially in the winter, but also in any slippery conditions); and maize is grown widely, a problem not faced by the armies in the autumn of 1914, meaning that views are often blocked and some roads seem to be passing through a small Amazonian jungle, with zero visibility on either side of the road.

On balance, the best touring periods are likely to be March-April and May; and mid August to early September. However, wheat is not nearly as prevalent as on the Somme, for example, so that June and July might also be practicable. The winter months, from December, will find the fields more or less clear of obstructing growth, but the negative side includes the greater risks on the roads themselves, the shorter daylight hours and of course adverse weather conditions and the cold.

With the approach of the centenary, we understand that there will be – or are under consideration - some changes in facilities; for example, new car parking at Polygon Wood, at its north eastern end (near the two CWGC cemeteries there) and near Black Watch Corner. Major expansion work has been undertaken at the Passchendaele Museum in Zonnebeke (though parking is limited).

The Belgian authorities seem to have a particular way of dealing with road closures relating to utilities or perhaps road improvements or refurbishment. The overwhelming tendency is to block off a road completely. For example, whilst preparing these tours in October 2012: the Menin Road was blocked at Geluveld (a diversion for only smaller vehicles took you through the village); the Menin Gate was blocked to traffic; Beselare was blocked to heavy vehicles, with a circuitous diversion for the rest; the Dixmuide to Ypres road was blocked for several kilometres of its length; the road past the Zonnebeke Musuem was closed; Messines has been effectively cut off, we were told, for some eighteen months, at the time of writing; and so on.

We strongly recommend that you try and lay your hands on at least the modern 1:50,000 maps that cover these tours; and a satnav set on 'view map' was invaluable during our touring. Alas, these smaller scale maps are not very readily available, in our experience; *In Flanders Fields* usually has some at 1:25,000 and 1:50,000, but it cannot be guaranteed that they will have them. The relevant 1:50,000 maps for this book are **IEPER 27-28-36** and **ROESELARE 19-20**. These should be adequate. Google Earth's capabilities are also helpful for planning the visit.

The maps used to illustrate the routes are contemporary to the Great War and should be adequate as the road systems in the area have changed little; where a new road is used this will be roughly indicated.

The focus of this book is Langemarck 1914; inevitably the routes will take you past numerous memorials and cemeteries relating to other periods of the war. Generally speaking we do not talk about these, unless we are using them to assist with the navigation. As regards museums, there are several in the Salient and we mention them where applicable. Some have a philosophy that they wish to put across, some simply house exhibits (some better labeled than others), some have trenches; each has its merits and all are worthy of a visit.

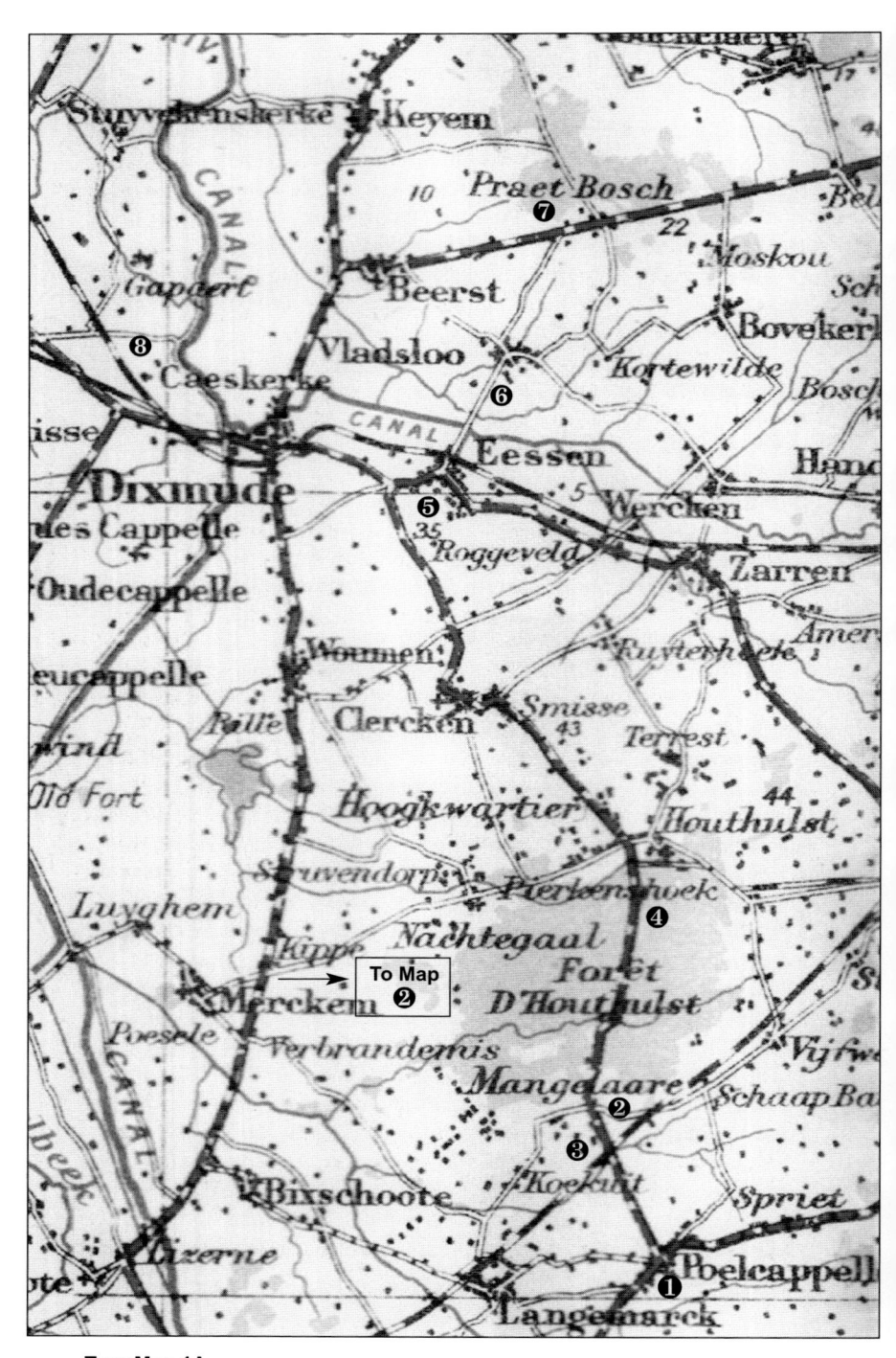

Tour Map 1A.

Tour One:

A Car Tour

Poelkapelle - Poelkapelle Station - Houthulst Wood - Klerken - Vladslo - Diksmuide - Trench of Death - Kippe - Draaibank - St Jans Beek - Mangelaar – Koekuit (Madonna) - Broenbeek - Weidendrift - Langemark German Cemetery

Depending on how long is spent at, for example, Vladslo German Cemetery or the Trench of Death, allow four hours.
See maps also on pages 41, 44, 57 and 78

This tour begins, for convenience, in the centre of Poelkapelle **(1)**; plentiful parking is available there, in particular in front of the church. It is always useful to have a good look at the spires of the churches, as these become useful distant marker points during the battlefield tours. At the central roundabout, with the distinctive 'stork' memorial to French fighter ace Georges Guynemer, take the turning to Houthulst and Diksmuide and proceed for about two kilometres, looking to the left (west) as you do so, across terrain across which the Germans advanced and over which there was heavy fighting for much of late October and November 1914. This will bring you to the site of **(2) Poelkapelle Railway Station** (now gone). There is space to park immediately on the further side of the line (the rails have been ripped out), on the right

View towards Langemark from near the old railway line.

Poelkapelle Station (as was) on the right, with the Staden line now converted for use by pedestrians and cyclists.

Koekuit

View towards Madonna (note distinctive church tower, with copper roof) and southwards, including what was known as Koekuit in 1914.

hand side of the road. The line is used as a cycle track in this area. Walk south west along the track until it emerges into open countryside **(3)**; from here there are excellent views over the area where part of the German 51st Reserve Division launched its attack on Langemark (to the south west) and Koekuit (to the north west) on 21 October; there were numerous attacks of varying ferocity across the same ground over the subsequent three weeks or so.

Return to your vehicle and head north towards Houthulst. At a roundabout, follow the sign to **Houthulst Belgian Military Cemetery**. Houthulst Wood (much reduced in size from the area it covered in 1914) begins where the road kinks first right, then left and is used today by, amongst others, the military *démineurs*, who deal with unexploded ordnance recovered from the battlefields. From 1914 it was in use by the Germans as a rest area and trains were placed within it to provide rudimentary but very effective shelter. The Belgian cemetery **(4)** is on the

The Belgian cemetery at Houthulst Forest.

158

Madonna church

right of the road and unmistakable; there is sufficient parking for a coach beside it. This cemetery, laid out in a star design in 1923, contains 1,723 graves of Belgian soldiers, 493 of whom are unknown. There are also 146 French graves and eighty one belonging to Italian soldiers who died in German captivity. The overwhelming number of Belgian burials date from the offensive of late September 1918 but, in the case of that of *Luitenant Victor Callemeyn* 10th Regiment of the Line, Block F1 Grave 1379, killed manning a forward position near Langemarck on 29 April 1918, there is a strong link with 1914. Callemeyn, who was born in Kortrijk on 20 February 1895 and who was a minor poet, enlisted into the Belgian army the day after the German army marched into Belgium. Rushed to the front, together with many other inexperienced young soldiers, he was wounded the first time he went into action near Dendermonde. Recovered and later commissioned in the field, he was awarded the Knight's Cross of the Order of Leopold for bravery and also held the War Cross, the Liberation Medal and the Belgian Commemorative Medal. One interesting feature is that graves of totally unknown Belgian soldiers are inscribed in both French and Flemish but where the man was known to be a Flamand or a Walloon only the relevant language is used on the headstone.

The graves of Italian servicemen who died in German captivity.

Continue north towards Houthulst. Many of the attacks on Langemark and Bikschote developed north to south across the ground to the left of the road, once the attempts to storm Langemark directly from the east stalled. Carry on through Houthulst on a very straight road towards Klerken, which gains height quite rapidly as it approaches that place. It is worth finding a **good view point near and south of Klerken**, because its elevation makes surveying the battlefield to the south rewarding. Coming out of Klerken there is a left turn to Woumen and right to Diksmuide. Take the Diksmuide route then head right at a major junction signposted Roeselare as far as Esen; stop **(5)** by the very obvious **church** by a road junction – you will be heading for Vladslo.

In October 1914 **Esen** was an important outpost of the defence of the critically important route to Diksmuide. During the evening of 20 October, men of Reserve Infantry Regiment 201 and Reserve Jäger Battalion 15 arrived there, having crossed the Handzame canal one kilometre to the north and swung westwards. Firing broke out and a pitched battle, some of it involving panicky shooting and clashes between groups of German soldiers, ensued. This led in turn to a very dubious incident when houses were burned down and a group of Belgians, suspected of being *franctireurs*, were burnt to death in the **church** by the jägers, enraged to find that it was locked and barred. The adjutant of Reserve Infantry Regiment 201, Leutnant von Frantzius, wrote later,

> About 6.30 pm I was standing in front of our regimental headquarters, which had been established in a house near the church when, all of a sudden, the church clock struck 7.00 pm. I immediately reached for my watch and said, 'That is odd; it is only just 6.30 pm'. At that precise moment, a wild exchange of fire began. Hauptmann von Bonin and I immediately searched our house and found a uniform jacket which had been taken off and dropped on the floor. In the meantime the men, roused by the burst of firing, were in an excitable state and it is entirely possible that some may have loosed off their weapons at random.
>
> Further searching of the houses led to the discovery of enemy ammunition in various places. There was no doubt that an ambush by franctireurs had been attempted. In consequence, the regimental commander ordered the houses to be burnt down as a punishment. The bright light thus produced also prevented renewed ambushes from occurring.

This was quite a bloody affair; over forty five people appear to have been executed or burnt to death – including one who was very badly beaten up and then shot; whilst some 250 of the inhabitants were deported.

From Esen turn left by the rebuilt church and head to Vladslo. Stop **(6)** by **the church in Vladslo** to examine the very interesting memorial to soldiers and civilians of the village and several relevant burials in the churchyard. From Vladslo turn left, signposted Beerst, then a short distance later turn right along a minor road, the Gentweg. This twists and

The memorial chapel at Vladslo, with a number of photographs of civilian and military casualties of the war, as well as memorial plaques. There are interesting, related burials in the adjoining cemetery.

turns north northeast to meet a major road in about two kilometres. Turn right and continue until you reach a prominent junction, after several hundred metres, where you turn left, onto Houtlandstraat, signposted Leke 5 and the German cemetery. This is to be found several hundred metres or so on the left **(7)**; there is limited parking for light vehicles outside the cemetery, it would be more awkward to park a coach.

Today the **cemetery at Vladslo** houses the remains of 25,644 soldiers, whose bodies were concentrated in the 1950s from smaller cemeteries all over northwest Flanders. In contrast to Langemark, almost all those buried here are identified by name. It was originally laid out during the Great War and some of its noted oak trees are more than one hundred years old. The dominating feature of the cemetery is the famous

The German cemetery at Vladslo.

'The Grieving Parents.'

'The Grieving Parents' in their original location, a few kilometres away, in the German cemetery at Esen-Roggeveld.

sculpture *Das trauende Eltenpaar* (The Grieving Parents), which was carved out of Belgian granite and originally placed in position in a military cemetery near Esen in 1932, before being moved here in 1956. Originally conceived by the sculptor Käthe Kollwitz in December 1914 as a lasting memorial to her young son Peter, who was killed in October 1914 while serving with Reserve Infantry Regiment 207 (at the time buried near Esen, transferred here after the Second World War), it took her almost twenty emotionally charged years to complete. During that time, she broadened the scope of the project, dropping the figure of her son, which originally was to have been flanked by the parents so that, although the direct family link was always maintained, gradually she came to see her work as a representation of all parents who had suffered the loss of a son in the war.

The sculptress, Käthe Kollwitz.

On 11 August 1915 she began work on the anniversary of the day that Peter had left home. 'Today', she wrote, 'I worked on his head for the first time. I was in tears.' By 1925 she planned that, 'The mother should be kneeling, her arms outstretched, overlooking all her sons. The father should also be kneeling.' She first paid a visit to Flanders the following year, finalising the placement of the figures and changing her mind about their posture. As created, the sculpture we see today shows the mother kneeling, head bowed, totally bereft and unable to conceal her grief, whilst her husband, choking back tears, his arms folded tightly around his body, stares out over the mass of graves, his face a study in sadness mingled with pride. On the day all was complete Käthe Kollwitz and her husband spent a long time at their son's grave in the small cemetery at Roggeveld, then moved to the figures. 'I stood in front of her', she wrote later, 'saw myself in her face, wept and stroked her cheek gently.'

Peter Kollwitz

Her thanks for this fine sculpture was to be condemned by the Nazis and expelled from the Prussian Academy of Arts, but her work has outlived them and is deserving of your close consideration during your visit as you walk to the graves of this representative group of men killed nearby in the autumn of 1914. The cemetery register tends not to be available here, due to constant theft or vandalism, so you need to be aware that the block number appears on each of the horizontally laid head stones and that Block 1, where a great many 1914 burials are located, is diagonally left of the entrance and Block 3 is just forward of the Grieving Parents.

> Leutnant Kurt Solveen Reserve Infantry Regiment 48 KIA west of the Yser October . Block 1 Grave 66.

Offizierstellvertreter Karl Freudenberg 4th Company Reserve Infantry Regiment 204 KIA Diksmuide 25 October. Block 1 Grave 1423

Kriegsfreiwilliger Karl Hübner 2nd Company Reserve Infantry Regiment 202 KIA Schudderbeurs 20 October. Block 1 Grave 1838.

Major Karl Freiherr [Baron] von Eynatten Reserve Infantry Regiment 48 KIA west of the Yser 1 November. Block 1 Grave 2316.

Gefreiter Oswald Anke 1st Company Reserve Infantry Regiment 204 Born Chemnitz 26 January 1896. KIA Diksmuide 1 November. Block 3 Grave 176.

Leutnant Hans Becker Reserve Infantry Regiment 248 KIA west of the Yser 23 October. Block 3 Grave 204.

Musketier Peter Kollwitz Reserve Infantry Regiment 207, son of Käthe Kollwitz who sculpted the 'Grieving Parents'. Born Berlin 6 February 1892 KIA near Diksmuide on 23 October. Block 3 Grave 29.

PETER KOLLWITZ MUSKETIER 23.10.1914

Wehrmann Albert Kasten Machine Gun Company Reserve Infantry Regiment 208. KIA west of the Yser 24 October. Block 3 Grave 39.

Oberleutnant Bruno Költz 3rd Company Reserve Infantry Regiment 202 KIA 30 October west of the Yser. Block 1 Grave 981.

Major Otto von Kietzell 3rd Battalion Reserve Infantry Regiment 204 Born Neisse 27 January 1874. KIA Diksmuide 25 October. Block 3 Grave 398.

Kriegsfreiwilliger Berthold Schmidt 10th Company Reserve Infantry Regiment 204 Born Berlin 9 August 1893 KIA Diksmuide 25 October. Block 3 Grave 762.

Major von Treskow Reserve Infantry Regiment 205 KIA west of the Yser 30 October . Block 3 Grave 179

Sanitäts-Unteroffizier Max Schulze 12th Company Reserve Infantry Regiment 234 KIA near Wallemolen 5 November. Block 5 Grave 742.

Some original headstones, originating from cemeteries that were transferred here, are scattered along the boundaries of the cemetery; of particular interest is that to two brothers, killed within a few days of each other, located by the right hand boundary hedge as you enter the cemetery.

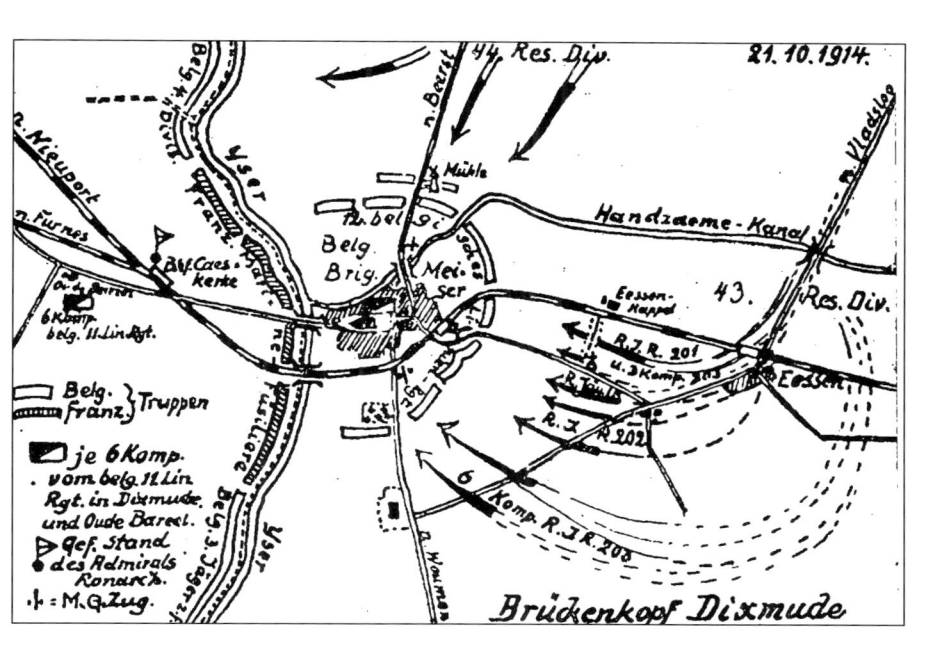

Return to the major road and turn right, signposted Diksmuide 7. Pass through Beerst, from where attacks on Diksmuide from the north were launched, then turn left onto the N369. Note the views over the water meadows to the right, showing how open the approaches to the Ijzer canal were. Continue into Diksmuide to a crossroads and turn right onto the N 35, signed Ieper, Veurne and Nieuwpoort. Go straight on at traffic lights towards Veurne. On the left, just by the bridge over the canal, is the hotel Sint Jan, which is on the site of the **Minoterie**, a tall flour mill where there was heavy fighting. Immediately after the bridge turn right along the line

Diksmuide Station under fire.

A view over a section of the Trench of Death.

French marines brought up to play their part in the defence of the Yser Line.

Belgian cyclist troops; it may look like a bizarre form of transport to our eyes, but it was very effective in getting men moved around in 1914.

Admirals Ronarc'h and Lacaze present medals to *Fusiliers-Marins*.

The cost of war.

of the canal, signposted Stuivekenskerke. There are good views over the water meadows and forward left to where the area of inundation began. Continue about two kilometers to the **(8) Trench of Death** preserved trenches. Admission to the site and associated museum is free and you should allow approximately one hour for the visit. It is worth spending some time here, if only to consider the tremendous efforts made by the Germans to reach the resolute Franco-Belgian defences in this area in a series of actions that endured for several days until the inundations (of which there is a map on the upper floor) came into full effect by the end of October halted German efforts north and some distance to the south. It is open from 1st April - 15th November from 1000 to 1700 each day. There is a café nearby.

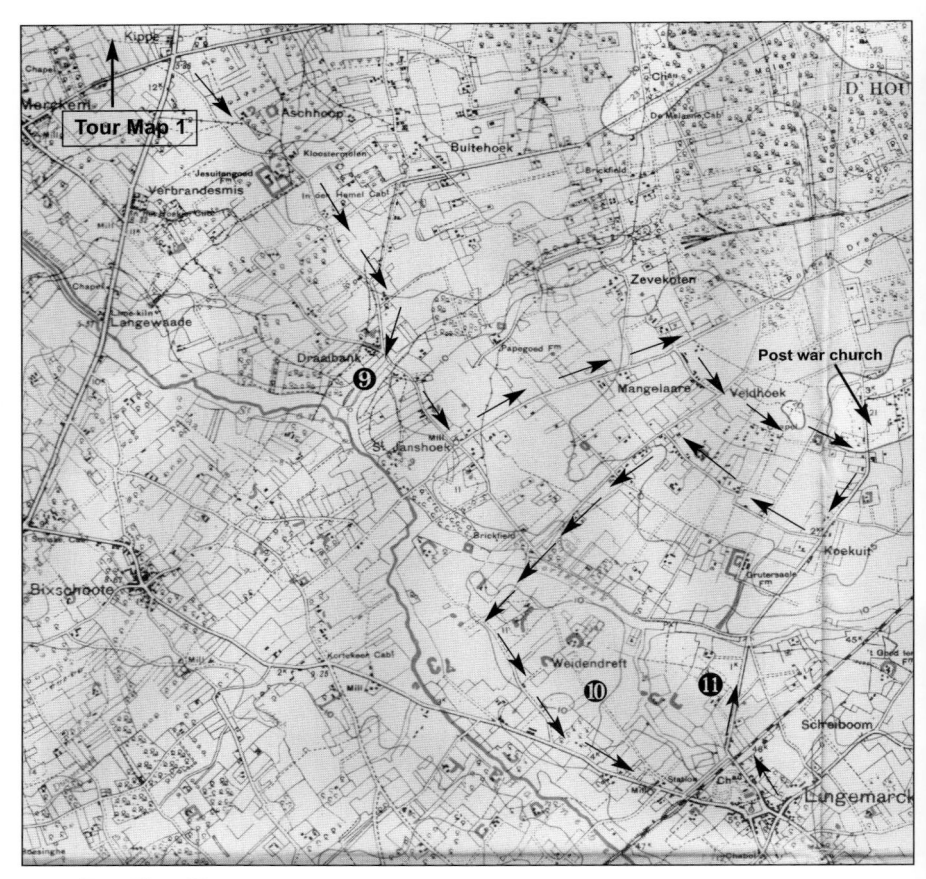

Tour Map 1B.

Retrace your route to the centre of Diksmuide, then turn right on the N369 signposted Ieper and Merkem. Remain on the main road, driving south through Woumen, from which place several attacks on Diksmuide from the south began, to Kippe (**switch to Tour Map 1B**). From Kippe, just beyond a major crossroads with traffic lights, take the turning on the left, currently by a furniture shop onto Kloosterstraat, a road restricted to 3.5 tonnes or less, so unsuitable for any vehicle larger than a minibus, which will take you to Draaibank. You will see a sign 'Boskant' just after the turn.

Good views of Bikschote church are to be had on the right as you approach **Draaibank** (about two and a half kilometres from Kippe), the houses of which are obviously located on ground higher than the surrounding area. It was this elevation that made the hamlet tactically important. At the end of Kloosterstraat turn left at a T junction onto Groenestraat. There is a tall chimney **(9)** about a hundred metres to the right of the correct road. This is a useful position indicator when viewing the battlefield from further south, especially around Kortekeer Cabaret. There are excellent views towards Bikschote from this higher ground. It was near here, in a small copse, that Oberleutnant Ernst 'Papa' Grimsehl, commander 8th Company Reserve Infantry Regiment 213, was killed during a major battle against the French defenders on 30 October. Aged fifty three, Grimsehl had been a well known physicist and headmaster of a technical school in Hamburg before the war. He was one of the oldest casualties amongst the forward troops on either side, had already been awarded the Iron Cross Second Class for gallantry and was widely mourned. One of his platoon commanders, *Vizefeldwebel Robert Thiemann* later described his passing.

> *Calmly, Oberleutnant Grimsehl advanced into battle with my platoon (3rd). In a copse to the east of the Draaibank – Langemark road at about midday I met up with him again, when he called me over and I took cover next to him. Our wood was under a dreadful weight of enemy fire, especially from the artillery which was showering us with shells. Many a brave comrade already lay there on the ground, dead or wounded. I had just left him for a few moments to go to the aid of a wounded man nearby when I was wounded myself, as was he. I crawled over to him and found that he had a wound to his left hand which I bandaged up. This would be about one minute after the shell landed. He had also been wounded in the head by a rifle bullet, which caused his death. Even as I treated him, I could see that death was approaching. Without giving any sign of pain, or even opening his eyes, our good and courageous leader left us. The day cost 8th Company considerable casualties, but those who survived felt as one with our honoured fallen ... During the evening of 30 October, before I went back to the dressing station, I once more sought out the place where he had met his fate and found him in exactly the same position, leaning back against a tree as though he was having a gentle nap. A rare and beautiful death brought an end to a life of many blessings. Honour his memory!"*

Turn left at a crossroads (Kruisstraat is written fairly high up on a building on the right at the crossroads junction) onto Pottestraat and head for Mangelare. Houthulst Wood can be seen slightly off to the left in the distance. It came much closer in 1914, its south western extremity within easy strolling distance of here. Continue for just under a mile up a hill past a number of houses to a right turn onto Mangelaarstraat. There is a sign 'Madonna' here, but you are still well to the west of that place. Continue on the same road (this was an original road until you come to a minor crossroads; the continuation is a post war cnstruction) through **Veldhoek**, which becomes Gistelhofstraat. Continue to a T junction and turn right past a pub - De Zon - on your left. The distinctive **Madonna church** with its pyramidal copper roof may be seen clearly from here over on the left. You will find no reference to Madonna in 1914, as it is a post war town, the church built in the 1930s. Presumably the place gets its name from the dedication of the church, in turn probably derived from a convent of the Sisters of Our Lady of Sorrows, which was here in 1914. You are now heading towards the area marked as **Koekuit** on modern maps, which seems to have been absorbed into Madonna.

After several hundred metres turn right onto Galgestraat, signposted 'Tea Room Te Lande' and 'Green House B&B'. Carry on along this road until you come to a T junction; turn left on to Mangelaarstraat and proceed for just over a kilometre. At a T junction turn right and then almost immediately left at a triangular junction with a chestnut tree in the centre, the road being a continuation of Mangelaarstraat. Cross the Broenbeek (known as the Kortebeek in 1914) and continue onto the ridge (there is a sharp left bend as you come towards the crest of the ridge), which is the area of **(10) Weidendrift**. The ground in this part of the tour is more fully covered in Tour 2 below. From the high ground there are good views of Bikschote to the right and Langemark to the left. This area is of crucial importance to the 1914 battles, because the Germans never secured positions up here; they were always beaten back, first by the British and later the French, notably in the fighting of 10 and 11 November. Langemark Church and the German cemetery become ever more clear from this area, which was the last piece of defensible high ground before the village. Turn left on Bikschotestraat, pass a white coloured light industrial installation just before Langemark. Continue on past the Fire Station (Brandweer) on your left and turn left on Maarkt. The area to the left, between the railway line and this road, in 1914 was largely occupied by Langemarck Chateau and its associated grounds. Keep the church on your right; then turn left onto Klerkenstraat, signposted Staden 11, Diksmuide 20. Cross the old railway and the tour ends at **(11) Langemark German Cemetery** car park. This cemetery is covered in the sequel to this volume, *Ypres 1914: The Menin Road*.

The battered remnants of Langemark Chateau in 1915.

Tour Two:

(Walk/Drive) Kortekeer Cabaret: 1st Division's left flank

We would strongly recommend that you re-read the relevant pages in Chapter 3 (pp 60-72), particularly Chapter 4 (pp 80-91) and Chapter 5 (pp 107-119) in order to get the full benefit from the exercise.

If you walk this route it is likely to take you the best part of a morning or afternoon, though you can cut it short at one or two points, evident from the map. It is a very rewarding walk, given the detail of the accompanying tour map.

Option: Walking Tour: *This begins at Point 2, the mill.*

This is an excellent tour in which to be able to put yourself into the position of both the attackers and defenders; although the ground is less close today, because of changes in agricultural practices and apart from one or two huge modern buildings, things have changed very little over a hundred years and so it allows the tourer to appreciate how the ground might have been used and to appreciate the problems of both defenders and attackers.

There are various options of length for this tour; however, we do recommend that the tourer does the longest one practicable to get a fuller idea of ground, of the undulations in it, for better understanding the positioning of the defenders and to appreciate the physical challenges facing the attackers. Be aware that walking the route will take the better part of half a day if followed fully.

See maps on pages 81 and 91.

This tour begins at **(1) Bikschote Church**, another one with a distinctive tower/spire arrangement. Heading in a southerly direction (keeping church and associated graveyard on your left) and then, a hundred yards or so beyond the church, take the right fork (Pilkemstraat), which will bring you to a restored mill, **(2) Beeuwsaert Molen**, which is located south of the

Beeuwsaert Mill, near to the spot where a similar one existed in 1914; it serves as a marker for the Camerons' left boundary.

171

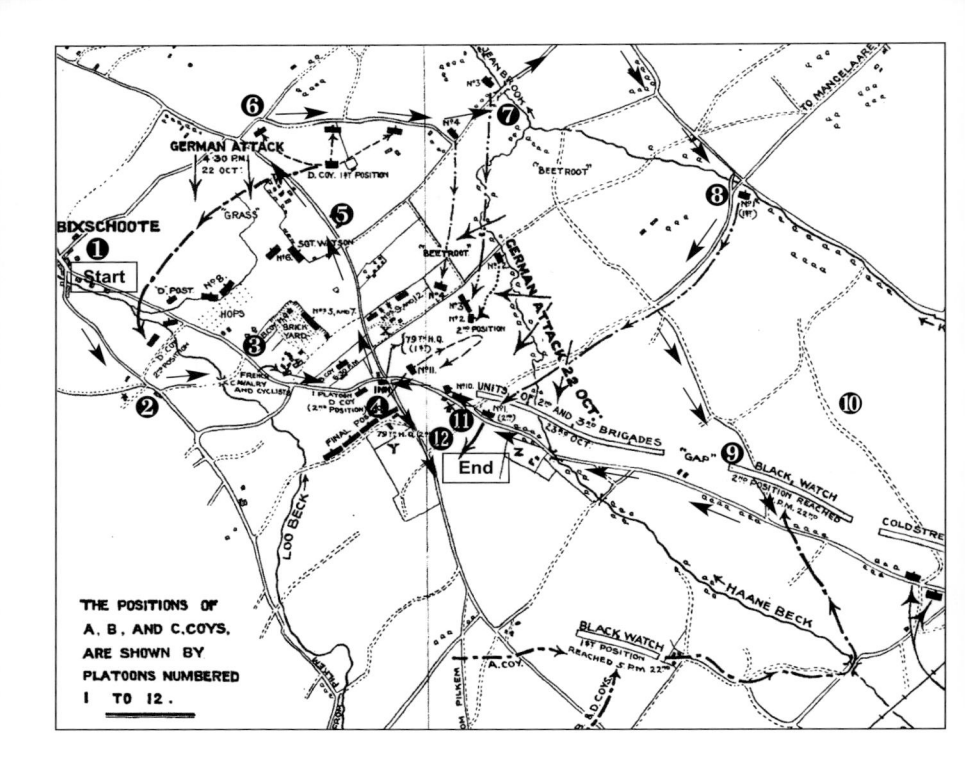

Bikschote - Langemark road and west of Kortekeer Cabaret. It is on raised ground, with good views back to Bikschote and in the direction of the Cabaret, indicated by tall poplars. The crossroads itself is not visible from the mill. There is ample parking by the renovated mill (but do keep clear of all entrances to the nearby farm), which can be visited on the first Sunday of the month. In fact the mill itself does not appear to be in exactly the same location as it was in 1914; and nor should it be confused with the mill that frequently appears in the narrative, which was situated on the Langemark road, to the south east of Kortekeer Cabaret.

The tour, which concentrates on the 22 October battlefield, though the same area was fought over repeatedly until mid November, is designed for both walkers and car drivers, but parts of this will inevitably diverge, as feet can go where car wheels cannot. The attempt to assault Langemark from the north that day with forces from 46th Reserve Division of XXIII Reserve Corps was a response to the failure of previous attacks to capture Langemark from the east. In fact there was such a high toll of casualties inflicted on the men of Reserve Infantry Regiments 213 and 215 in particular that the attack withered away in this area as well. Reserve Jäger Battalion 18, whose objective was Kortekeer Cabaret itself, commented that the day ended in a chaotic intermingling of all the divisional units. One participant, Musketier Scheidhauer of 8th Company Reserve Infantry Regiment 215, left a description of the events of the day which must have been absolutely typical of the experience of countless others.

> Never again did I experience so tough an assault as this one. Whistles blew to signal the start. A warrant officer was lying to my front. 'Herr Feldwebel, we must get going!' I pulled at his foot, but he lay there stiffly. He was dead. At the end of the next bound an Unteroffizier was lying down on the ground. I pulled at his clay covered boot. Stiff – dead. I shuddered all over. I raced diagonally across the road into the ditch on the right hand side. It seemed to me as though a woodpecker was pecking at the telegraph pole next to me; fine chippings of wood were falling on me. I then realised that I was lying in the beaten zone of a machine gun and its bullets were gradually felling the pole. Further forward a voice bawled, 'On your feet! Double march!' It was hard to make the decision to move. My rucksack was digging into my neck. Apathetically, I jogged slowly forward. Shot cows were bellowing in the fields. I ran with death at my throat and tore myself free of a wire fence as bullets whistled around me. Beads of nervous sweat stood out on my brow. Near a farm building I met up with an Offizierstellvertreter and about thirty men. Mentally and spiritually we were totally spent…

The Tour

[If the *walking route* is followed, it commences by walking back towards Bixschote from the mill, maybe fifty to a hundred metres, and then following the very distinctive field track (D Company's second position) to the main Langemark road; and then continuing the walk on the other side; note that this track that you will use did not exist in 1914. It passes in front of what was a hop field; this provided an obstacle of sorts, both physical and to observation, as hops climb on poles and wires, in addition to growing quite close together. From there it follows the car tour, though it can be abbreviated at various points.]

Looking back towards Bixschote (note particularly the church spire); the track which the walkers should take is indicated; it also marks the second position taken up by the bulk of D Company.

Bixschote

Start of Walking Tour

Track

Draaibank Wood   **Approximate site of the brickyard**

The road junction with the Langemarck road. In the right middle distance, approximately where the group of trees stand, is the location of the brick yard. In the far distance may be seen the small wood just to the east of Draaibank, through or near which Reserve Infantry Regiments 211 and 213 passed in making their attack.

Set off south and then east, towards the main Langemarck road, though noting the track to the north west along which the walkers will go, which marks the second position held by D Company of the Camerons.

Continue towards the main road and directly opposite the junction **(3)**, a couple of hundred metres into the field, is the site of the Brickyard, which has disappeared without evident trace, but whose associated buildings provided shelter for French cavalry and cycle infantry. It is the scene of Captain Orr's and companions' heroic, if futile, charge. Turn right on the main road and follow it to the crossroads that marks the cabaret **(4)** and where there was a pub in 1914. Take a sharp left turn here to the place where Sgt Watson's contingent was located **(5)**; there is space to get off the road, but be prepared to return to your vehicle at short notice to move it out of the way. A short walk west along a rough track (the one which walkers will have used) makes it easy to distinguish where the platoon positions must have been located, forward and on slightly higher ground.

On the track near Stop 5, in the area of Sergeant Watson's and No 6 Platoon's position. The windmill is clearly visible in the left distance and the housing associated with Bikschote, though the church is hidden.

The windmill   **Sgt Watson's and No. 6 Platoon's position**   **Bixschote**

Looking from the area of part of D Company's first position, with views across the valley of the St Jansbeek eastwards towards Mangelare and beyond. German attacks cae in from the right of the photograph at about 4.30 pm.

A view taken nearby towards Draaibank: the chimney stack and wood indicated.

Continue along the road past a farm, De Koppeldreve, which existed in some form back in 1914, until you reach a turning to the right marked by a low voltage overhead electricity cable. Take this turning and continue to where a cul de sac leads left **(6)**. Where an electricity sub transformer is located, one of the original D Company positions was in the field to the right of the road. There is room to stop in a light vehicle here. As you proceed along here, depending on the height of any crops, you can get views across to the north to the chimney stack that marks the area of Draaibank. Carry on eastwards and the second platoon position was between the road and the farm you passed earlier. The final position was just inside the field to the south of the road, more or less opposite a modern track leading away at an acute angle.

Arriving at a T junction, look left. In the field to the left was an initial position of No 4 Platoon. Turn left. Pause by St Jansbeek (St Jean's Brook) **(7)**. Number 3 Platoon was stationed in the field to the left of the road here. Cross the beek - a considerable obstacle to movement on foot - then look back to work out where the platoon must have been deployed. It is a good idea to note the steepness of the banks here; further to the south east and to Langemarck itself the banks are not so pronounced, but in 1914 they also provided a considerable obstacle to the attacking infantry there.

St Jansbeek from the bridge near which No 3 Platoon was originally positioned. Note the relatively deep banks of the stream. Langemark Church may be seen in the left distance

Continue up a hill past St Jans Kapel to the first junction on the right, by a house with a red roof. Turn right onto Beekstraat. There are long views here. At a mini roundabout, with a chestnut in the centre, turn right and cross the St Jansbeek once more. An outpost position was held near this junction **(8)** by No 1 Platoon. It clearly can only have been there to counter advancing enemy crossing the skyline and heading for the beek. This means that it (or the bulk of it) was almost certainly located on rising ground east of the road in a field with a modern red roofed farm house beyond it. From here there are good fields of fire and observation over a lengthy stretch of St Jansbeek. It is also quite evident from the German accounts that these outlying positions brought down a withering rate of fire on all attempts to get across St Jansbeek.

A view not far from Stop 8 of a farm on the Weidendrift ring contour, with the trees of the German cemetery at Langemark to its right. The position from where this picture is taken is more or less that held by the Black Watch on the night of 22 October.

Turn left at the next junction and proceed to a group of brownish buildings with cream or white coloured doors **(9)**, you are more or less in the 2nd Position of the Black Watch, though it is difficult to be precise. From this point look left to a farm with silos to its left and a large aluminium structure. The ring contour on which its stands is on the vital ground of Weidendrift **(10)**, which was fought over constantly for three weeks. The German cemetery at Langemark, surrounded by trees, can also be seen from here. At the main Bikschote - Langemark road turn right. Care - busy road!

The site of the mill, from the second floor of which the Black Watch machine gun was able to bring such effective – and for some time undisturbed – fire was to the south of this road near a modern wood which touches it **(11)** and by a new red roofed house and barn.

At Kortekeer Cabaret turn left and go past a large agricultural complex on your right; about a hundred metres beyond it there is space to park **(12)**. It was to this approximate area that the Camerons withdrew on 22 October. The track leading up to the modern wood gives an indicator, at its north western end, of the location of the mill.

A view near Stop 12, looking up the road to Kortekeer Cabaret crossroads; the buildings on the left of the road are behind the approximate position of the final position of the Camerons on the night of the 22nd, with the site of the battalion headquarters located amongst these buildings.

A view from near the same position of Draiibank Wood in the far distance and the approximate site of the mill, from which a Black Watch machine gun did so much damage.

Copse to west (400m) of Draaibank

Approximate location of the Mill on the Langemark Road

Tour Three:

Poelkapelle – Langemark: 1st Division's northern and eastern battlefield area

Given the occasional stop, allow two hours in a car.

Langemark - Koekuit - Hoge Roker - 't Goed ter Veste Farm - Schreiboom - Poelkapelle - east to Langemark then return to Langemark German Cemetery via site of White Mill.
See maps on pages 50, 57, 78, 94 and 108.

This tour is designed to familiarise you with the area east of Langemark. The route takes you along narrow roads (there are occasional passing bays on some of them), which are generally quiet but can be busy with agricultural vehicles. If leaving your vehicle it is essential that you park it in such a way that traffic can get past you.

This tour is ideal for a cyclist, but would be walkable (and worthwhile for the truly committed!) if the better part of a day is available. Again, it is an area where development has not impinged too extensively on the battlefield, although, *inter alia*, Poelkapelle has extended south and west since 1914 and there are post war industrial developments east and south east of Langemark.

Start at the car park of **Langemark German Cemetery**. Looking northwards you are viewing the ground across which the Germans advanced during the period covered by this book, most particularly on 23 October, but before and afterwards and through to the end of the battle. If the crops allow, you can get limited views to the west of the high ground of Weidendrift and of some of the bitter fighting involving both the Glosters and the Coldstream.

Turn left towards Koekuit.

Take the first left after exiting the cemetery and immediately after the beek, turn left, past the bunker used as a 34th Division memorial, followed by the first right; you will shortly arrive at an excellent view point on high ground near a farm on the left **(1 – just off the map)** – there is space to

View from Stop 1, looking across to the south east and south: Langemark to Weidendrift.

German cemetery | Langemark church

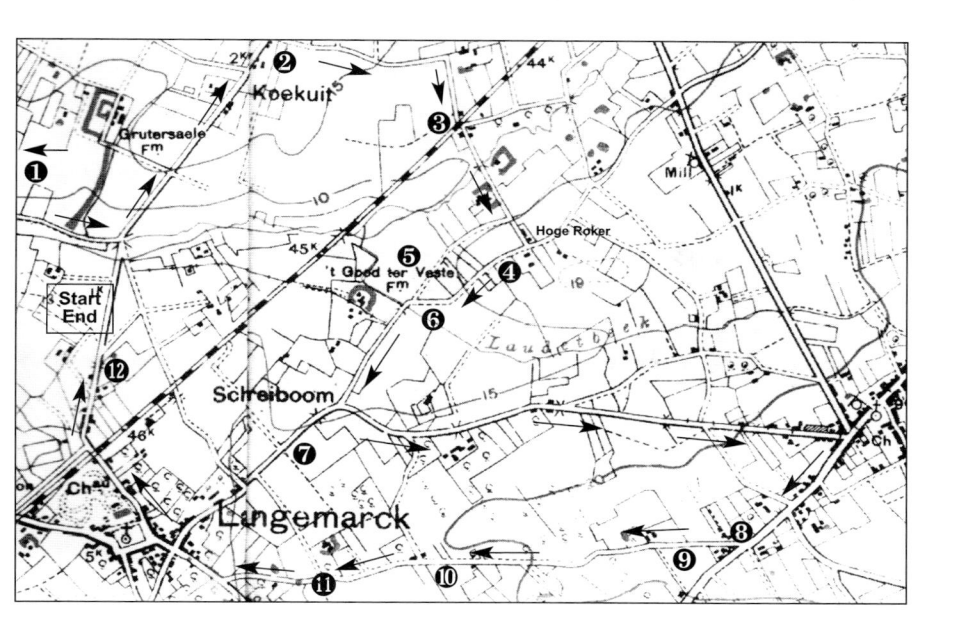

get off the road near the wide farm approach track. From here, on a clear day, it is possible to see the churches in Poelcapelle, Langemark and Bikschote; as well as providing a good view from the north over the much fought over Weidendrift. It also enables you to appreciate the nature of the slope coming down from the Mangelare/Madonna area towards the Broenbeek (the stream in the valley below, which joins with St Jansbeek) and Langemark.

See Map on page 108.

This position enables you to see something of the fighting of 1/Glosters on both 21 and 23 October; on 21 October, looking north, mainly to your right and the line running very close to where you are now standing; and to the south, on the 23rd, the defence of Langemark to the west of the Koekuit/Madonna road and the general direction of the location of the trench dug across it in the area adjacent, approximately, to the formal entrance to Langemark German Cemetery.

During the advance of 21 October, which it will be recalled involved a push towards Poelkapelle, it was anticipated that the French would be covering the left flank of 1st Division. This did not happen and the

Area of Weidendrift

Glosters were brought up to cover the left flank, finally taking positions in front of Koekuit (at about 10.30 am), thereby forming a distinct salient. From the high ground, in particular to the east of the hamlet, the Glosters were able to assist the Queens as they ran into the determined German assault from the area of Poelkapelle Station. There was also increasing pressure from Germans emerging from the area of Mangelare, to the north east, the Glosters' left flank. The position was held with some difficulty until the battalion was withdrawn to Varna Farm, south west of Langemark, at about midnight. The Glosters history notes that, just before leaving the position, two German *Einjahrige* soldiers from a Jager regiment were captured: 'these proved to be quite youngsters, with only two weeks' training'.

The line was brought back to just north of the Broenbeek (or Kortebeek in 1914), which at that time had banks which were about five feet high.

In the early hours of 23 October, Captain Rising (A Company) and a couple of platoons were brought up in support of 2/Welch. These men worked hard with Royal Engineers of 26 Field Company, who had already begun digging some field defences, including a trench across the road near the German cemetery. This provided good fields of fire except where the ground approached the valley bottom.

The German assault began at about 9 am: 'A party of [men] at the same time tried to advance down the road itself, led by a man carrying a flag. This man, whoever he was, was soon killed, and the remainder were driven back.' The threat now seemed to be most serious on the left flank, where the Germans had made use of the ditch system to get up on the Coldstream defenders. At some cost to the reinforcing Glosters, this attack was fended off.

Retrace your route to the Koekuit/Madonna road and turn left.

Carry on towards Koekuit, up the hill.

As you approach Koekuit you come to a 70 kph limit and a sign for a sharp turn to the right **(2)**. Take this road (Galgestraat) and head east. From this high ground, which marked the forward positions of the right flank of the Glosters on 21 October, there are excellent views towards Langemark on your right, Poelkapelle Church and the valley that saw such bitter fighting involving the Queen's. You might want to consult the sketch map on p. 57.

The road bears to the south and you cross the old Ieper - Roeselare railway at what became known as Namur Crossing **(3)**, where there is plaque, erected by a WFA Branch, referring to the VC action of Frederick Dancox on 9 October 1917. When the crops allow (maize or something similar completely block views in October), there are useful views along the railway line and the valley in which the Germans and the British clashed. Bear right at the fork in the road and dip down to cross the Broenbeek once more. The row of houses to the front is Hoge Roker. Turn right onto Schreiboomstraat at a T junction. Note the views

The old railway line heading west towards Langemark at what became known as Namur Crossing. There was heavy fighting on both sides of the line, some four hundred yards along it.

(approximately **4**) to the the north and south as they become clear from obstruction, the battleground for the right flank of 1st Division.

As you drop away from the hamlet it was on these slopes **(5)** that the British and German troops from Reserve Infantry Regiment 236 of 51st Reserve Division first clashed on 21 October. The Queen's held a line from approximately **(6)**, across the railway to the north; whilst D Company of the SWB held the line between this road and that to its south; these positions taken up by about 10 am, before the line was withdrawn back some five hundred yards towards Langemark by the end of the day. Drop down to cross the Landetbeek and 't Goed ter Veste Farm is half right.

Coming off the high ground of Hoge Roker to the west, with the furthest advance of the Queen's and the SWB, reached very soon after 1st Division began its advance on 21 October, approximately indicated. The bulk of 't Goed ter Veste Farm dominates the next rise.

't Goed ter Veste Farm

Approximate limit on Queen's advance

D Coy SWB 10 am

At the main Langemark - Poelkapelle road, turn left. This is a busy road - care! There is a light industrial plant on the right behind a green fence. The withdrawn line came back to about **7** on the night of the 21st.

As you proceed towards Poelkapelle there are broad views out to the left of the early Langemark battlefield, the battlefield of the SWB; the ridge line and Hoge Roker are also quite evident.

In Poelkapelle go right up to the roundabout where the Guynemer memorial stands with the tank memorial behind it and turn right onto Brugseweg, signposted Poperinge and Ieper. The abortive final assault of the German 9th Reserve Division on 10 November was conducted astride this section of road in the direction you are travelling. You shortly arrive at a filling station on your right that marks the furthest extent of the French outposts of Detachment Hely d'Oissel towards the end of the battle; and also of A Company of 1/SWB on 21 October, an area which was reached by about 10 am, the high water mark of 1st Division's advance in this area.

Turn right **(8)** just before it along Eeckhoutmolenstraat. There are wide views to the right along this road. Note how flat the terrain is and, although there are more houses than there were, the overall effect is similar one hundred years on. There are one or two wider stopping points **(9)** along this road. On the site of the White Mill **(10)** stands a house with a distinctive horse's head door knocker (it is on the right hand side of the house) and it is also marked by an isolated street lamp on a concrete

View towards Langemark taken from near Stop 9.

post on the left of the road. From here the first buildings in Langemark are 300 - 400 metres away. Polygon Wood can be seen on the horizon to your left as is the Totenmühle and Zonnebeke church.

As you enter Langemark – there is a road junction **(11)**, approximately the line held on the night of 21 October - continue straight on along the wider road through a relatively newly developed residential area as far as a T junction flanked with green bollards. Turn right onto Zonnebekestraat, which takes you to the traffic lights in the centre of Langemark; go straight ahead and return to the German cemetery car park, where this tour ends.

Optional Extra Leg. Near the entrance to the German cemetery **12**, take the very minor road on the right (but do not bother if the standing crops block any views); this is the area of the trench dug across the road and in the fields nearby there would have been some further trenches dug by Rising and his men; some (although one does not need to take away the idea that there was a great mass of defences) of those on the left flank were doubtless within the present cemetery boundaries. At the road junction turn left and on the main Staden road turn left again and return to the end point, the cemetery's car park, on the right.

Tour Four:

The 2nd Division Tour

Langemark German Cemetery - Vancouver Corner - Windmill - New Houses - Poelkapelle - Lekkerboterbeek - Vancouver Corner - Winnipeg - 's-Graventafel Ridge - New Zealand Memorial - Kansas Cross - Dochy Farm - Zonnebeke Station - Tyne Cot - Broodseinde Crossroads - 7th Division Memorial - Noordeinhoek - Polygon Wood - Zonnebeke - Former crossing point of Ieper - Roeselare Railway.
See maps on pages 50 and 57.

Allow two to three hours in a car; the museum, if visited, deserves at least ninety minutes.

Turn right out of the car park of Langemark German cemetery and head into the town. Go straight ahead at the traffic lights onto Zonnebekestraat.

As you leave the built up area (approximately at **1**), you will be close to where what was then called the Haanixbeek goes under the road. On the left was the battlefield of 1/SWB, though as the day progressed other battalions, or parts of battalions, were interposed into the line, elements of 2/HLI and 2/Connaught Rangers. To the right of the road was where the right flank of 2nd Division, 5 Brigade, was brought forward to prepare for its attack on 21 October, delayed by the late arrival of 1st Division.

At Vancouver Corner **(2)**, on the Poelkapelle road cross over and take the Zonnebeke road (also signposted to Dochy Farm New British Cemetery), leaving the Canadian memorial on your left. After a couple of hundred yards, take the first turning to the left, marked by a small shrine, leaving an extensive group of glass houses on your left. Head for the obvious windmill (Oude Steenakker Molen, sometimes known as the Death Mill) then bear left by the mill, leaving it on your right.

You will pass by the replacement building for Hubner Farm **(3)**. See if you can find a safe place to stop. Consult the map on p. 185. You are roughly in the centre of the area held by 2/Worcesters and it would be an appropriate point to re-read some of the descriptions of the fighting given here, for example from p. 49 ff and p. 100 ff, most especially that of

The 'Death Mill', situated to the rear of 2/Worcesters' position.

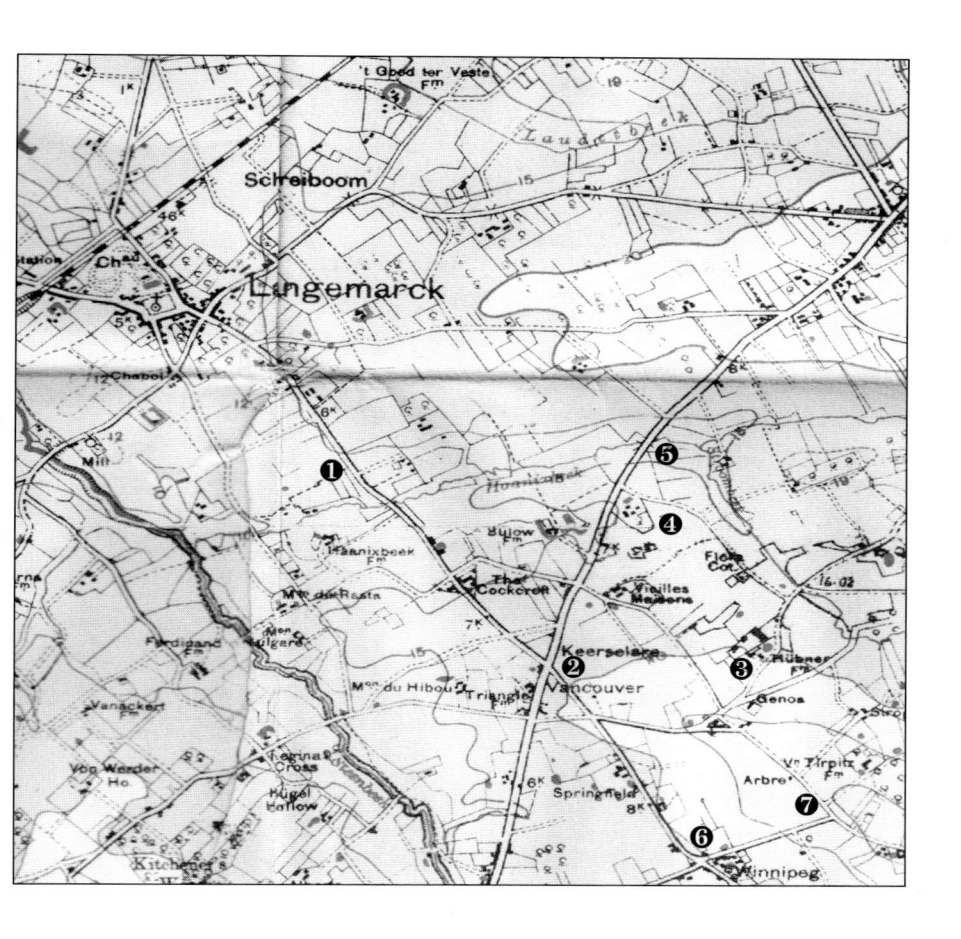

Captain Dillon. On the Worcesters' right the Connaught Rangers were brought up and on the left the Ox & Bucks, whose line extended across the Poelkapelle road. Beyond the Connaughts were 3/Coldstream of 4 Guards Brigade (though it must be recalled that units were brought in and out of the line throughout the fighting 21 – 24 October).

As you come down the rise take a turning to the left, Stroombeekstrat (if you cross the beek you have gone too far). This is very close to the forward positions of 5 Brigade. You pass a grey agricultural building on the right (useful views to the south, to give some dea of the problems the Germans faced as they moved forward to attack) and arrive at a group of houses **(4)** round three sides of a square and enclosed by a well-tended beech hedge. This is the site of New Houses, which served as battalion headquarters for the Ox & Bucks; the CO, Lieutenant Colonel Davies, kept an extraordinarily full diary, extracts from which on pp 101-105 should be read here. Continue to the major road junction. This is Brugseweg. Turn right and proceed towards Poelkapelle. Pause by the Lekkerboterbeek bridge **(5)** at the bottom of a dip in the road (the bridge

The Lekkerboterbeek, at this point marking the limit of 5 Brigade's advance.

is wide enough to allow you to stop here), where the close nature of the ground around Poelkapelle is obvious. This is just forward of the line, though some men were posted forward of here. Keeping in mind the heavy and fast moving traffic, it is useful to get across to the other side and to appreciate the lie of the ground on the Langemark side of the road. There are open views out to the left to Langemark church.

Go to the Guynemer memorial roundabout, go right round it and head back to Vancouver Corner and turn left, this time heading towards Dochy Farm CWGC. At Winnipeg crossroads **(6)**, about a kilometre from

Taken from the same area, showing New Houses, the battalion headquarters of 2/Ox & Bucks.

Vancouver Corner, turn left up onto the 's-Graventafel Ridge along St Juliaanstraat. There are extensive views to left and right all along this road.

At the **(7)** T junction (which marked the right boundary of the Worcesters on the 21st); [***switch to the second map for this tour***] turn right, with good views towards Poelkapelle on the left (even the tower of the church at Westrozebeke is visible) and Zonnebeke on the right. It is worth pausing at the high point of the ridge by the recently erected memorial, on your left, to the 15th Battalion (48th Highlanders of Canada) CEF, to profit from these views; but the road is narrow and the traffic can be fast moving, so try and ensure that you get your car off the road sufficient to allow the passage of other vehicles. At the New Zealand memorial, pause. Elements of 3/Coldstream managed to get on to the ridge on 21 October but were forced to pull back as 7th Division, on the left, came under very heavy pressure.

Turn right and head down to Kansas Cross, signposted Sint Jan and Ieper. After the Hanebeek is crossed there is a confusing sign 'Langemark', though that is well to the northwest from this point. At Kansas Cross (sparing a thought for Ma Jeffreys trying to persuade the French general and his staff officers to take shelter in the roadside ditch) turn left, signposted 'Museum Passchendaele 1917'. Stop at Dochy Farm CWGC **(8)** and look at the views up towards Tyne Cot and to the left of Zonnebeke. The ground is still quite close to the north and east, but it was much more so in October 1914, when there were confusing night time patrol actions during the period covered by this book. Over to the east the outskirts of Zonnebeke can be seen – the town has expanded significantly from its 1914 boundaries; 2/Queen's held a refused flank here on the night of the 21st.

Shortly after the cemetery there is a sign 'Zonnebeke'. Continue towards the site of Zonnebeke Station **(9)** on the left – currently there is parking before it (though building work was in progress in late 2013); the name of the station remains on the building. There are views right across to Polygon Wood from here. Immediately behind the parking area is a road running to the north east, Albertstraat, fifty metres before the station and next to a business selling tiles; walk beyond this for a hundred metres on to the top of the rising ground – the windmill **(10)**

The road in to Zonnebeke from the station; compare this to the pre-war photograph of the same road on p. 36.

187

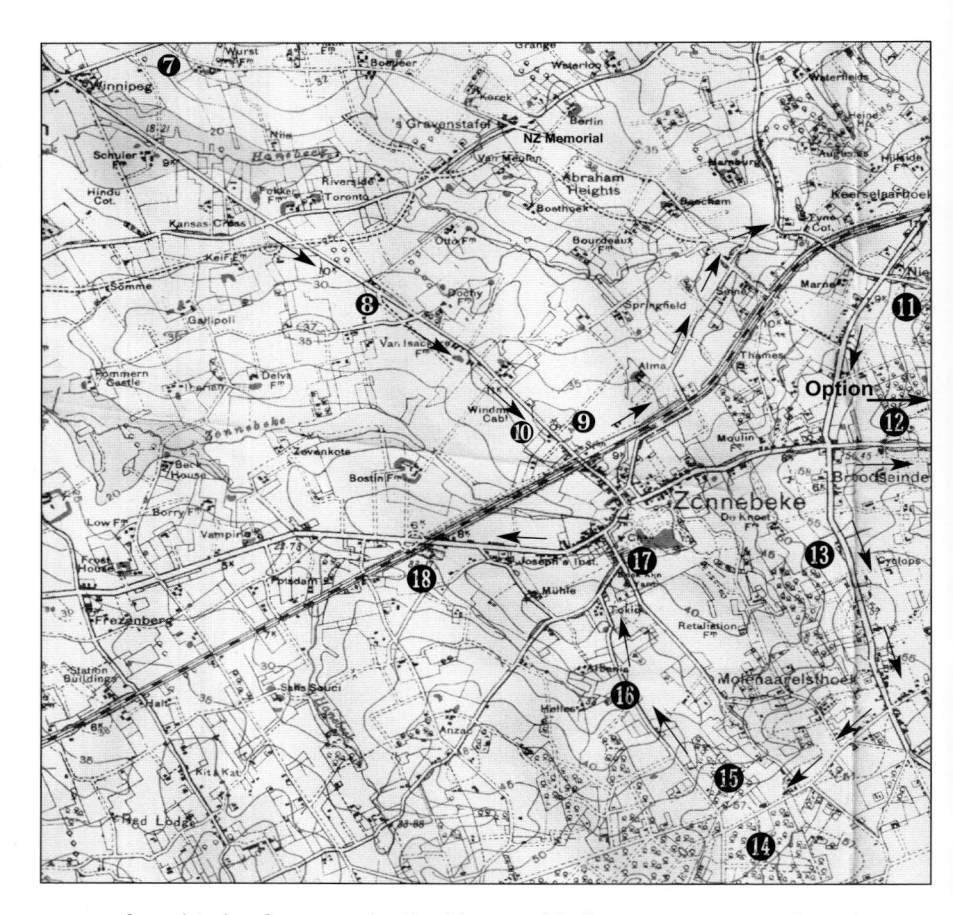

referred to by, for example, the Master of Belhaven, was approximately here, on the east side of the road. Return to your car and take Albertstraat; continue to a junction and turn left onto Schipstraat and then immediately right onto Vijfwegstraat and head towards Tyne Cot. At a junction, the cemetery is to your left front; turn right onto Tyne Cot Straat, keeping right, crossing the old Roulers railway line and arrive at the Passendale - Broodseinde road. The area of this busy intersection **(11)** was marked as Nieuwemoelen (sic); today it is a little further to the east. Elements of 6 (Cavalry) Brigade and of the 7th Division held positions around here on 19 and 20 October. Turn right onto Passendalestraat signposted 'Museum Passchendaele 1917'. Continue to the roundabout at Broodseinde crossroads and go straight on, signposted Beselare.

Optional Diversion: Take the left (eastern) exit at the roundabout (Moorslede) and proceed some three kilometres on to the high ground; take the second turning on the left **(12)**, a minor road, signposted to Passendale. Proceed a couple of hundred yards and find a safe space to stop (it is a rather narrow road and quite well used). From here there is an excellent view from the German perspective of the British 7th Division defenders on 20 October (see maps on pages 23, 27 and 41) and the line defended by, eg the Warwicks, the RWF and the South Staffs. The view extends from Passendale to the north to Beselare to the south. A number of the positions were forward of Broodseinde Ridge. It will be recalled that communications were poor amongst the defenders because of the length of line that had to be held and the weight of German fire.

Continuation of Tour:
After about five hundred yards the 7th Division memorial is on the right, with space to get off the road **(13)**. (The 1:25000 Belgian IGN map describes this as an Australian memorial...) The Division also has a similar memorial in Italy. This is an appropriate spot for the Division's memorial in France; just consider for a moment that its line ran, at one stage, from a kilometre or so north of here to Zandvoorde, eight kilometres and more as the crow flies. Its casualties, by the time it was withdrawn from the battle, were ferociously high. There are good views down into Zonnebeke itself and across to Polygon Wood; and over to the east as well.

The 7th Division's memorial on the Western Front. The distinctive tower of Zonnebeke Church is off the photograph to the left.

From the memorial continue south towards Noordeindhoek; after just under a kilometre turn right on to Spilstraat, just before a sign 'Beselare', signposted De Akkerwinde. Exit the built up area and the views towards Polygon Wood open up. Signs to Den Doel (ie Polygon Wood) and then the road swings sharply right as you come close to Polygon Wood. It is worth stopping **(14)** just before the swing to the right and walking up the field track on the left from where there are good views of Reutelbos. Polygon Wood was rather more extensive in 1914. These views will prepare you for the next volume in the series, where Polygon Wood and Reutel have prominent places. At the tip of Polygon Wood follow the road north west (ie away from the wood and the two CWGC cemeteries), along Citernestraat. If you can safely stop near this junction **(15)** there are views to Langemark church and also the ground immediately south of Zonnebeke and Polygon Wood, where 22 Brigade withdrew on the night of 20 October. There is also a network of small fields here, reminiscent of the situation in 1914 when Reserve Infantry Regiments 238 and 240, together with Reserve Jäger Battalion 23 of 52nd Reserve Division attempted to advance either side of Broodseinde and to the south of Zonnebeke on 21 October. On the left, on the way to Zonnebeke, you pass the site of Helles Farm **(16)**, which was behind the current farm building. 22 Brigade was deployed more or less along this road, extending back to the west. Helles was on the boundary between the Queen's and South Staffs.

At the first road junction in Zonnebeke, a right turn leads to the museum **(17)**, which makes use of the rebuilt Zonnebeke Chateau. It is a pleasant spot and might prove useful as a lunch stop as well as giving the opportunity to visit this excellent museum, recently extended. The museum concentrates on Passchendaele 1917, but still has interesting exhibits and information relating to this early period of the war. The car parking is not extensive, but there is usually space on the streets in the town if it is full and there is an alternative entrance from the Ypres road.

For the tour, go straight ahead (this is a post Great War road) and then turn left on the main road, Ieperstraat. The tour ends at the roundabout where the old Ieper - Roeselare railway crossed the road **(18)**, a fall back position for the British on 21 and 22 October; from here you can easily proceed to Ypres or to your next destination.

Cemeteries

A most important development in recent years in locating burials and commemorations from Britain, the Dominions and the Empire has been the much improved website and casualty database of the Commonwealth War Graves Commission (cwgc.org). It is now possible to search it, for example, to find members from a regiment killed on a particular date or between dates; or to locate all those from a regiment in a chosen cemetery or on a memorial; and so it goes on. It has limitations – thus a man's battalion was often not on the original record from which the Commission was then working, so you would not get a full return by looking up, for example, 1/Coldstream Guards between 20 and 24 October 1914. Granted this, the new tool, readily available to visitors, means that there is less need to provide a full cemetery section as was the case in the earlier Battleground Europe books.

For this book we have selected several CWGC cemeteries in the area (with one exception) where there is at least one fatality from the fighting in the 20 – 24 October period; very few are actually where they were originally buried as most have been concentrated from isolated graves or small burial plots; or have been transferred from German cemeteries.

It is an unfortunate fact that so many of those killed in the BEF during First Ypres have no known grave. Taking the official dates for the battle, 19 October to 22 November 1914 and applying these to the Menin Gate memorial, the result is 7,014 names. If you do the same search, but using the dates and the country where the commemoration is located (ie Belgium), the total comes to 10,229, which gives you approximately 70% with no known grave. This total includes those commemorated on the Ploegsteert Memorial, for example, which is beyond the area of First Ypres if the boundary is taken to be the Douve River and which gives a total of 1,587 for the same dates. Why a man is located on a particular memorial is not an exact science and it is not uncommon to find someone killed outside the 'catchment' area of a memorial to be found on it. But, always allowing for this fact, the figures would suggest that about 8,700 were killed in the Salient and of these some 80% have no known grave. There are also, of course, cemeteries in Belgium south of the 1st Ypres battlefield as well, though the number of casualties that fall within the date parameters are relatively few. One final observation: a number were evacuated to hospitals on the coast, the UK or in France and died there, and so these figures should only be regarded as an indicator. The Official History figures for the battle do not exist for First Ypres alone, as the calculation includes the whole of BEF from 14 October – 30 November and includes a very substantial number of missing.

St Julien Dressing Station
This cemetery, situated at the south east end of St Juliaan, a short distance off the Ypres road, was started during Third Ypres, in September 1917, and now has 420 burials, of which 180 are identified. St Juliaan is of interest in this book because it was a support line centre for the initial assault on 21 October by I Corps and also had at least one dressing station at the time – the Ox & Bucks, for example, refer to evacuating their wounded there. There are good views to the north east from the cemetery, which underwent extensive maintenance work for a couple of years prior to 2014. Besides a complete horticultural renovation, much of the boundary wall was demolished and then completely rebuilt from the foundations up, with new drainage installed.

Those brought here after the war from scattered and isolated burial sites are to be found in Plots II and IV. The only one who fits our

Structural renovation at St Julien Dressing Station; this involved a complete rebuild of the perimeter walls with deeper foundations and improved drainage.

category is Lieutenant Frederick **Pollock**, 1/Coldstream, who died on 22 October 1914 (II F 13), two days shy of his 29th birthday. Joining the army in 1904 and promoted to lieutenant in 1907, he spent a number of years (between 1909 and February 1914) seconded to the West African Frontier Force. There are four other identified casualties of First Ypres buried here.

Cement House Cemetery

The cemetery is to be found a short distance to the west of Langemark, on the road to Boezinge; the pill box, after which it is named, is a large, ivy enshrouded, structure well inside the yard of the neighbouring farm on the east side of the cemetery. The original burials (starting at the end of August 1917, during Third Ypres) can be easily identified by the irregular layout in Plot I. Post war the cemetery was identified as suitable as a concentration cemetery for the isolated graves to be found in such profusion in the areas of Langemark, east of Pilkem and Poelkapelle; and these are to be found in Plots II to XV.

Plots XVI - XVIII originally contained about 500 French graves, presumably for the most part, if not entirely, casualties of the French efforts made on the left of Gough's Fifth Army, an all but ignored part of Third Ypres. Of course it is also possible that there might well have been French casualties from First Ypres through to Second Ypres, when the French army held the line in the area. These graves were removed in 1922, we assume to St Charles de Potyze French Military Cemetery, a couple of kilometres east of Ypres. This area has been filled over the years by further concentrations. There are now 3,592 men buried or commemorated in the cemetery, of whom 2,425 are unidentified. In addition there are twenty two men from the Second World War who have found their final resting place here, of whom five are unidentified.

All but one of the fifteen identified First Ypres casualties buried in this cemetery were killed in our time frame; the exception is Captain **Mervyn Crawshay** of 5/DG (VIIA F6), killed (or died) on 31 October, when his regiment was engaged in the defence of Messines. There are numerous possible explanations as to why he should have ended up in this cemetery: since his burial place is so far from the action of his regiment on this (and indeed preceding) days, that he died of wounds in the

German rear areas and was buried by them with his body moved here in the post war concentrations; or that he was attached to a different unit/formation, away from his regiment; or fortune dictated where his isolated grave should be concentrated, especially if his body was found in the later post war years, when Cement House was one of the major cemeteries open for such discoveries (another, for example, was Bedford House). This latter hypothesis seems the most likely, especially as he is buried in Plot VIIA, an extension of Plot VII, which came into use when Plots XVI – XVIII had been filled. He was 33 when he was killed and was one of the army's outstanding horsemen.

Another burial that took our interest was that of Sir Robin **Duff**, 2nd Life Guards, killed on 16 October 1914. He has an unusual epitaph, taken from Milton's *Samson Agonistes* and with the whole quote below:

> *Nothing is here for tears, nothing to wail*
> *Or knock the breast, no weakness, no contempt,*
> *Dispraise, or blame; nothing but well and fair,*
> *And what may quiet us in a death so noble.*

A large number of this group (nine men) were concentrated from Elverdinghe Churchyard, almost certainly nine of the ten burials in VIIA E1 – E10, which number includes Lieutenant **George Chisnall**, the Camerons' medical officer (E 10). He was 28 when he died of his wounds, hit when tending 'a wounded man in the open'. When we visited the headstone was being replaced; unfortunate but a good indicator of the continuing work of maintenance undertaken by the Commission. The solitary British officer killed in October 1914 and moved here from Oostnieuwerke Churchyard, where he was originally buried by the Germans, a couple of kilometres east of Westrozebeke, is likely to be Second Lieutenant Maurice Williams, 1/Queen's (XIX A 6), who died between 22 and 24 October.

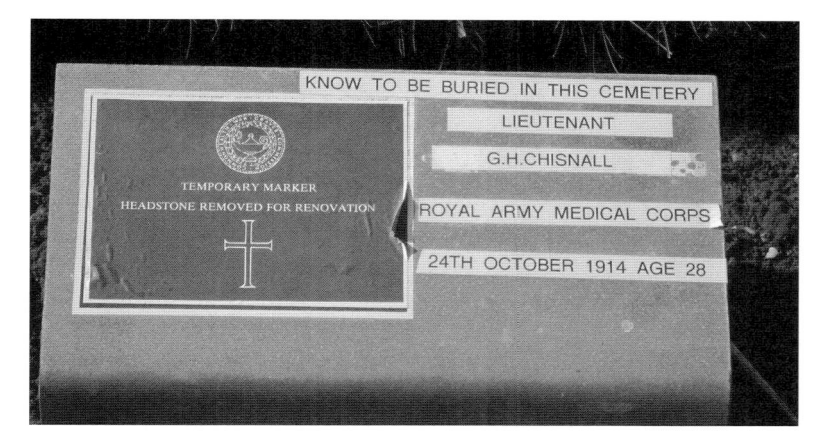

Plot VIIA is to be found on the east side of the Great Cross, right up by the boundary wall.

Poelcapelle British Cemetery

Parking is not easy here; we recommend, approaching from Poelkapelle, that you do not use the formal entrance, which is at the eastern end of the cemetery, but use the one at the western end, where you will first come across the cemetery's boundary wall. At the beginning of the fighting that October, hordes of German troops would have been seen moving along this road from Westrozebeke.

This cemetery, with thirty two identified First Ypres casualties, was created after the war as a place to concentrate isolated graves or those brought in from small cemeteries. One major exception to 'small' was the German Poelcapelle No 2 Cemetery, which was about a mile south east of the village; ninety six BEF casualties of 1914 and 1915 were brought in from it. Amongst them were four Ox & Bucks casualties, row XLV B, all killed on 21 October; Lieutenant **Turbutt** (see

A plinth indicating German cemeteries where men were known to have been buried but whose remains could not be identified when BEF casualties were relocated here.

p. 103), Special Memorial 1, is one who was known to be buried there but whose body could not be identified. Commemorated nearby, Special Memorial 3, is an officer, Hugh **Langton**, killed during Third Ypres, who has what the CWGC believes is a unique epitaph; a bar of music. It is thought that this is taken from an American song, *After the Ball is Over*. He was a well-trained violinist, having studied under some of the great names in Europe. His father died very shortly after the war, so it was probably his wife who chose the epitaph.

The two 1st (Royal) Dragoons, LIV A 18 and 19, were in 6 (Cavalry) Brigade, part of Rawlinson's IV Corps. The two 3/Coldstream, IA (close to our recommended point of entrance) C 4 and 7, killed on 21 October, were likely brought into the cemetery some years after the war ended, as their plot is an obvious addition to the original design.

The two officers from the Loyals, Second Lieutenant **Kingsley** (XLV E 19) and Captain **Miller** (XLV F 8), were killed on 23 October in the action at Kortekeer Cabaret. Kingsley had been commissioned in June 1914. 'He had acted in a most gallant manner when we had captured the German trenches. He was getting his platoon together for a further advance and was shot, death being instantaneous'. For more details on the Loyals' action, see pages 110-119.

Although there are few identified 1914 casualties in this vast cemetery, with 7,429 BEF casualties, of whom 6,230 are unidentified, ie getting on for 85%, it is likely that there are a significant number of unidentified casualties here from the fighting around Langemark in October 1914. Of all these unknown, only eight are known to be buried here (hence the Special Memorials) but whose bodies could not be identified.

Tyne Cot Cemetery

In this vast cemetery there are seventy five identified casualties of First Ypres, nearly all from 7th Division's 21 and 22 Brigades: thus there are three RWF in XIX E 13-15 (20 October); there are quite a few in row LXI K and LV H. Interestingly enough, there are no officers.

Perth (China Wall) Cemetery

Although this cemetery, situated on the road between Zillebeke and the Menin Road, is well outside the geographical boundaries of this book, there are a large number of First Ypres casualties buried here (166), of whom ninety three were killed between 21 and 24 October, including a substantial number as a result of the fighting covered in this book. The reason why so many have found their way to this cemetery is because of the concentrations into what had been a small (130 casualties) cemetery at the end of the war to the 2,791 casualties that are now buried here, approximately half of whom are unidentified.

Amongst the German cemeteries which contained British casualties who were relocated here are Keerselare West German Cemetery, Weidendrift German Cemetery (situated in the farm of that name), Broodseinde German cemetery, St Julien East German Cemetery, Schreiboom German Cemetery – all places which saw the BEF in action during the period covered by this book - and the unusually named Hans

Kirchner German Cemetery, situated about a mile south east of Poelkapelle. At first we considered that it was named after Hans Kirchner, a *kriegsfreiwilliger* (volunteer) who was killed on 22 October and is now buried in Menen German Cemetery, Block H Grave 158. We could not recall seeing a German cemetery named after an individual before. Whilst checking this with Aurel Sercu in Belgium, a keen Great War historian, he pointed out that this name was due to an error in paperwork at the time the introduction to the cemetery was written; for it should not be 'Hans' but 'Haus'. This is a lesson that one should check all the available evidence – a shame, really, as other pieces of the story fitted nicely with the original idea.

In this cemetery there are seventeen Camerons, seven Northamptons, twelve Royal Scots Fusiliers, eight South Wales Borderers and nine Worcesters, along with men from other relevant battalions, identified and buried here or else commemorated on memorials (all the relevant ones of these latter are to the immediate right as you enter the cemetery). The First Ypres' casualties tend to be concentrated in the area on the left of the cemetery, in what seem to be later burials, in Plots X and XII (Rows A, B and C), Plots XIV (B and C) and XV (A and B).

There are four officers buried here within our time frame:

Captain William **Curgenven**, 1/SWB, killed 21 October, XV B 2, commanded No 4 Company. He was first wounded in the arm and almost immediately afterwards shot in the head. Just short of his thirty eighth birthday when he was killed, he entered the regiment from the militia in 1897, saw service in the South African War and spent several years, from 1909 – 1913, as an instructor at Sandhurst (in topography).

Lieutenant Ivan **Sprot** Camerons, XII B 6, was killed in the fighting around Kortekeer Cabaret; aged 25, his last words before he was shot in the temple by a sniper were reputed to be: 'Come on boys, come on! Let's at them!' His older brother was killed on 11 November, serving with 1/Black Watch, but was only reported at the time as missing and it was many months before his death could be confirmed. His body was never recovered and so he is commemorated on the Menin Gate. Yet another brother, in the Gordon Highlanders, was badly wounded.

Captain the Hon. Charles **Monck**, 3/Coldstream, St Julien East German Cemetery Memorial, was also thirty seven when he was killed, shot through the heart, 'at St Julien' on 21 October; at the time of his death he was the senior captain in the Battalion. He, too, entered his regiment through the militia, in 1897; and also served in the South African War.

Finally, there is another RAMC fatality: Captain Rupert **Nolan** was thirty two when he died. He was serving as the medical officer of 2/Worcesters and originally buried at Keerselaere West German Cemetery (which was west of the Zonnebeke – Langemark road) but whose body could not be identified and he is therefore commemorated by the appropriate memorial headstone. He was commissioned into the RAMC in January 1909.

* * * *

The tours section in this book takes the visitor to the relatively rarely visited **Vladslo German Cemetery**, which is described there; Langemark and Menen German cemeteries will be covered in *The Menin Road* in this trilogy. The explanatory note below will appear in each of the books.

The Care of German Casualties
The *Volksbund Deutsche Kriegsgräberfürsorge e.V.*, usually abbreviated to *Volksbund*, is the body charged with the care of German war graves in countries outside the Federal Republic of German. It is a charity and depends almost entirely on donations from individuals and organisations for its funding, though it receives occasional grants to cover the cost of particular projects. In other words, it is not financed like the Commonwealth War Graves Commission and, as a result, there are limits to its ability to fulfil both its primary duties and also act as a clearing house for information concerning the German fallen. Nevertheless, it is possible to consult its data base on line. If a casualty has a known grave, it will be listed by cemetery, block and grave number and it will be possible to locate it. Unfortunately a great many casualties have no known grave, there are no memorials to the missing and the *Volksbund* does not list them systematically either. In addition, large numbers of bodies were repatriated to Germany after the war at the expense of relatives and, unless they were reburied in places such as the *Waldfriedhof* in Stuttgart which voluntarily supplies the *Volkbund* with information, there will be no easily accessible record of such burials.

That said, it is possible to search online for one of the 4.6 million German burials which are listed. Do an internet search for *Volksbund*, then look in the top right hand corner of the home page for *Gräbersuche Online*. Click on this and you will be taken to a page with several questions. The fields ask for *Nachname* = surname, *Vorname* = given name, *Geburtsdatum* = date of birth, *Todes/Vermisstendatum* = date of death or date went missing and *Geburtsort* = place of birth. It is not necessary to know all this information, but the surname is an absolute minimum and, for a common name, such as Müller, the more accurate the date the man died the better. You then press the button *Suche beginnen* and, if you are fortunate, you will be shown one or more possibilities. N.B. This response may be preceded by a page asking for your personal details. This is not sinister, but simply a way for the *Volksbund* to target its requests for support. It is also possible to search for all the casualties from a town or village, but this is of little use for First World War casualties; relatively few have their place of birth listed.

More often than not, you will see a page stating in a green panel *Die Recherche war leider erfolglos* [Unfortunately the search was unsuccessful]. There can be all sorts of reasons for this, ranging from inaccurate record keeping to simple lack of information as outlined above. On the other hand, sometimes a simple search can be very revealing. As an experiment try typing *Nachname* Zech and *Todes/Vermisstendatum* 1914 and every relevant detail of Graf [Count] Julius von Zech auf Neuhofen, who is buried at Menen will appear - except, frustratingly, his regiment. This is a weakness of both the data base and cemetery registers and makes researching casualties a time-consuming and difficult-to-impossible matter. Sometimes a search involving a common name will produce so many hits of men of the same rank that it is not possible to distinguish between them at all.

The *Volksbund* carries out its onerous task diligently to the best of its ability and according to its resources. If you care about the preservation of such sites, never pass a *Volksbund* collection box without donating. Only with such support can the work be carried on.

Langemarck: German Skeleton Order of Battle

All formations were under the overall command of the German Fourth Army, commanded by Duke Albrecht of Württemberg.

What is evident here is that the Germans had to throw together disparate formations and units to put into the attack, rather as the French and particularly the British were forced to 'putty up' in the defence of their line.

Initial Attacks:
XXVI Reserve Corps
51st Reserve Division
101 Reserve Infantry Brigade (Reserve Infantry Regiments 233 & 234)
102 Reserve Infantry Brigade (Reserve Infantry Regiments 235 & 236)

52nd Reserve Division
103 Reserve Infantry Brigade (Reserve Infantry Regiments 237 & 238)
104 Reserve Infantry Brigade (Reserve Infantry Regiments 239 & 240)
Reserve Jäger Battalion 23

From 22 October:
Elements of XXIII Reserve Corps in reinforcing role.
46th Reserve Division
91 Reserve Infantry Brigade (Reserve Infantry Regiments 213 & 215)
92 Reserve Infantry Brigade (Reserve Infantry Regiments 214 & 216)
Reserve Jäger Battalion 18

From 23 October:
45th Reserve Division
89 Reserve Infantry Brigade (Reserve Infantry Regiments 211 & 212)
90 Reserve Infantry Brigade (Reserve Infantry Regiments 209 & 210)

From 2 November:
Elements of III Reserve Corps, withdrawn from west of the Yser in relieving/reinforcing role
5th Reserve Division
9 Reserve Infantry Brigade (Reserve Infantry Regiments 8 & 48)
10 Reserve Infantry Brigade (Reserve Infantry Regiments 12 & 52)
Reserve Jäger Battalion 3

6th Reserve Division
11 Reserve Infantry Brigade (Reserve Infantry Regiments 20 & 24)
12 Reserve Infantry Brigade (Reserve Infantry Regiments 26 & 35)

From 3 November
Elements of XXII Reserve Corps, withdrawn from west of the Yser in relieving/reinforcement role.
44th Reserve Division
87 Reserve Infantry Brigade (Reserve Infantry Regiments 205 & 206)
88 Reserve Infantry Brigade (Reserve Infantry Regiments 207 & 208)

From 8 November
Elements of V Reserve Corps, withdrawn from Verdun to renew the attack from the east under command of III Reserve Corps.
9th Reserve Division
17 Reserve Infantry Brigade (Reserve Infantry Regiments 6 & 7 (- two battalions))
19 Reserve Infantry Brigade (Reserve Infantry Regiments 19 + one battalion Reserve Infantry Regiment 7)

Bibliography

Anglesey, The Marquess of, *A History of the British Cavalry 1816 – 1919:* Vol 7, *The Curragh Incident and the Western Front, 1914*, 1996

Anon ('By a Regimental Committee'), *Historical Records of the Queen's Own Cameron Highlanders*, Vol 3, 1931

Anon: *Ypres 1914*, Battery Press, n.d.

Atkinson, CH, *The Seventh Division 1914 – 1918*, 1927

Atkinson, CH, *The History of the South Wales Borderers 1914 – 1918*, 1931

Bickersteth, JB, *History of the Sixth Cavalry Brigade 1914 – 1918*, 1920

Craster, JM (ed), *Fifteen Rounds a Minute*, 1976

Edmonds, JE: *Military Operations France and Belgium Vols 1 and 2*. Macmillan and Co., 1922 and 1929

Ewart, W (et al), *The Scots Guards in the Great War 1914 -1918*, 1925

Hamilton, Lord E, *The First Seven Divisions*, 1916

Hare, S, *The Annals of the King's Royal Rifle Corps*, Vol V: *The Great War*, 1932

Hyndson, Captain JGW, *From Mons to the First Battle of Ypres*, 1932

Jourdain, HFN and Fraser, E: *The Connaught Rangers Volume I*. Naval & Military Press, n.d.

Kipling, R, *The Irish Guards in the Great War* Vols I and II, 1923

Master of Belhaven (Ralph Hamilton), *The War Diary of the Master of Belhaven 1914 - 1918*, 1924

Mockler-Ferryman, AF (comp and ed), The Oxfordshire and Buckinghamshire Light Infantry Chronicle 1914 – 1915, n.d.

Murland, J, *Aristocrats go to war: uncovering the Zillebeke Churchyard cemetery*, 2010

Ponsonby, Sir F, *The Grenadier Guards in the Great War of 1914 – 1918*, Vol I, 1920

Ross-of-Bladensburg, Sir J, *The Coldstream Guards 1914 – 1918*, 1928

Sheffield, G and Bourne, J (eds), *Douglas Haig: War Diaries and Letters 1914 – 1918*, 2005

Sheldon, J: *The German Army at Ypres, 1914*. Pen and Sword, 2010

Stacke, H Fitz M, *The Worcestershire Regiment in the Great War*, 1928

Ward, CH Dudley, *Regimental Records of the Royal Welch Fusiliers*, Vol III, 1928

Wauchope, AG, *A History of the Black Watch (Royal Highlanders) in the Great War, 1914 – 1918*, Vol One, 1925

Wylly, HC, *History of the Queen's Royal (West Surrey) Regiment in the Great War*

Wylly, HC, *The Loyal North Lancashire Regiment*, Vol II 1914 – 1919, 1933

Wyrall, E, *The History of the Second Division*, N&M reprint, n.d.

Acknowledgements

We should like to acknowledge the assistance of these Belgian experts in the writing of this book:

Aurel Sercu for information concerning the German Haus Kirchner cemetery.

Eddy Lambrecht for advice and providing personal information concerning Luitenant Victor Callemeyn of the Belgian 10th Infantry Regiment.

Particular thanks are due to Sabine Declercq-Couvet who was most helpful as regards photographs; and to the Memorial Museum Passchendaele 1917. We strongly recommend a visit to this museum, which also has 1914 interest.

* * *

Dedication

To the members – and particularly the Administrators – of the internet Great War Forum. This is an excellent and helpful resource for all with an interest in the Great War.

Index

Ackand-Allen Lt 39
Aisne 10-11, 13-14, 98
Albrecht Generaloberst Duke 9, 135
Allenby Lieutenant General 11, 45
Antwerp 6, 8, 10-11
Army Group Fabeck 123
Arras 8
Ashoop 80
Aubers Ridge 14
Basdow Oberst v. 132
Beaulieu-Marconnay Oberst Freiherr v 26
Becelaere/Beselare 17, 21, 31, 42, 73, 155
Beerst 20, 160, 165
Beeuswaert Mill 171
Bellewaarde Farm 109
Beselar General v. 145
Béthune 11
Bidon General 70
Birkenstock Major 127
Bixschoote/Bikschote 21, 43, 60-2, 73-4, 79-83, 85, 88, 90, 95-6, 118, 124-30, 134, 136, 144, 146, 149, 159, 169, 171-4, 177, 179
Black Watch Corner 155
Blücher Major v. 34
Boeschepe 27
Boesinge/Boezinge 20, 28, 44, 55-6, 78-9, 95, 109, 117, 193
Bowes-Lyon Lt 117
Bredt Major 92

British Army
Corps
I 6, 13-15, 20, 26, 39, 45, 60-2, 70, 79, 83, 109, 118-19, 192; **II** 11; **III** 11; **IV** 13-16, 22, 29, 60, 73-4, 197; **Cavalry** 11, 14; **Indian** 11

Divisions
1st 13-14, 26-7, 29, 45, 49, 51, 54-7, 61-2, 73-4, 77, 79, 90, 105, 107, 109, 119-20, 179, 181-2, 184; **2nd** 20, 26-7, 29, 40, 45, 49, 54, 56, 73-4, 77, 90, 96, 120, 143, 184; **3rd (Cavalry)** 13-17, 20, 23, 29, 45; **7th** 10, 13-17, 20, 22-3, 27, 30, 35, 40-2, 45, 55, 61, 74, 120, 187, 189, 197; **8th** 11

Brigades
1 (Guards) 55, 57, 61, 80, 117, 119; **2** 55, 58, 90, 109, 117; **3** 13-14, 49, 53, 55, 58-9, 79-80, 109, 119; **4 (Guards)** 20, 27, 40-1; **5** 28, 40, 49, 74-5, 77, 100-101, 106, 184, 186; **6** 40, 54, 74, 99, 110; **6 (Cavalry)** 16, 24, 197; **7 (Cavalry)** 16; **19** 15; **21** 16, 22, 73-4, 197; **22** 15-17, 22, 24, 30, 40, 42, 73-4, 190, 197

Regiments
1/Black Watch 60, 80, 86-7, 89, 109, 116, 176-7
1/Cameron Highlanders 60-2, 83-4, 86, 90, 107, 109-10, 112-13, 115-19, 174, 177
1/Coldstream Guards 59, 61, 79, 86-7, 89-90, 107-109, 178

2/Coldstream Guards 27, 40-2, 74, 96
3/Coldstream Guards 27, 41, 75, 99, 118, 187
2/Connaught Rangers 49-50, 75, 99, 184-5
1/Glosters 56-7, 59-60, 107-109, 178-80
2/Grenadier Guards 41-2, 75, 97-100
2/Highland Light Infantry 49, 52, 54, 104, 106, 184
1/Irish Guards 39, 41-2, 74, 96
2/KRRC 90, 109-10, 113, 115
1/Loyal N Lancs 55, 90, 109-11, 113, 115
1/Northampton 89-90, 109-10, 115, 118
2/Ox & Bucks Light Infantry 49, 51, 53-4, 56, 58, 76, 101, 103, 105, 185-6, 192
1/Queen's 56-7, 59, 109-10, 113, 115, 117, 180-1, 190, 195
2/Queen's 17, 24, 31, 37, 39
1/Royal Berkshire 54
2/Royal Scots Fusiliers 22
1/Royal Welch Fusiliers 17, 25, 31, 35, 40, 189
1 Scots Guards 59-61, 90, 118
1/South Staffs 24-5, 31, 35, 39-40, 189-90
2/South Staffs 90, 109-10
1/South Wales Borderers 13-14, 49, 51, 56-9, 79, 107, 181-2, 184
2/Warwicks 17, 35, 39, 189
1/Welch 107
2/Welch 58-9, 107-108, 180
2/Wiltshires 23
1/Worcesters 118
2/Worcesters 28, 49-50, 52, 75, 99-101, 184-5
15/Hussars 41
26 Battery RGA 110
26 Field Company RE 80, 107, 180

Brielen 71
Broenbeek see Kortebeek
Bronisch Oberstleutnant 33
Broodseinde 17, 24-6, 30-1, 34-5, 39, 43, 71, 73, 80, 93, 106, 190
Bruges 13, 20
Bulfin Brigadier General 90, 109, 115, 119
Busse Oberstleutnant v. 122, 141-3
Byng Major-General 14, 23, 45
Callemeyn Luitenant 159
Capper Major-General 14, 45
Carter Major 111
Cassel 14

Cemeteries
British
Cement House 114, 193-4
Dochy Farm New British 184, 186-7
New Irish Farm 117
Perth (China Wall) 197
Poelcapelle British 112-13, 195-6
St Julien Dressing Station 192
Tyne Cot 24, 187, 197-9

German
Vladslo 161

206

Comines Canal 70, 73
Courtrai 20
Dancox Frederick VC 180
Davies Lt Col 51, 53, 76, 101, 185
Dieringshofen Generalleutnant v. 147
Dillon Capt 52, 102-106, 185
Dixmude/Diksmuide 20, 74, 79, 119, 132, 136, 157, 160, 165, 168
Dochy Farm 42
Dorrer Generalleutnant v. 130
Doullens 14
Draaibank 82, 128-9, 168-9, 174-5
Eden Major 54
Elverdinghe 27, 29, 55-6
Esen 160, 163
Etaples 14
Falkenhayn 8-9, 134
Feilding Lt Col 41
Fère en Tardenois 14
FitzClarence Brigadier General 60
Foch General 14

French Army
Groupe des Armées du Nord 14
Détachment d'Armée de Belgique 29
II (Cavalry) Corps 20, 60
IX Corps 70
7th (Cavalry) Division 59, 61
17th Division 96
42nd Division 29
87th Division 20, 70, 73, 79
33 Brigade 98
41e Infantry Regiment 22
96e Infantry Regiment 128

French FM Sir John 10-11, 70
Frezenberg 54
Fromelles 14-15

German Army
Armies
Fourth 9, 21, 30, 42, 73, 77, 94, 124, 130, 135; **Sixth** 8, 135

Corps
III Reserve 6, 8, 10, 130, 134, 144-5, 149, 152; **V Reserve** 134; **VIII** 152; **XXIII Reserve** 21-2, 42, 73, 95, 119, 132, 172; **XXVI Reserve** 10, 21, 26, 29, 66, 71, 73, 77, 95, 133, 135; **XXVII Reserve** 21, 29, 31, 73, 133
Higher Cavalry Commanders 1,2 & 4 8

Divisions
5th Reserve 130-3, 145, 149; **6th Reserve** 130-2, 137, 144; **9th Reserve** 6, 10, 134-5, 137-9, 144, 182; **44th Reserve** 130, 132-3, 146-7, 149; **45th Reserve** 88, 95, 124, 127, 132; **46th Reserve** 42, 57, 73, 77-8, 80-1, 95, 106, 122-5, 127, 132-3, 172; **51st Reserve** 21-2, 30-1, 42-4, 46, 62, 65-6, 71, 73, 75, 78, 80, 94, 106, 123-4, 127, 131, 137, 141, 158, 181; **52nd Reserve** 21, 26, 30, 43, 71, 73, 78, 80, 91, 190

Reserve Infantry Brigades
9 131, 145; **10** 131; **12** 131; **89** 126; **90** 126; **91** 128; **92** 127; **101** 141-2

Reserve Infantry Regiments
6 137, 140, 144; 7 140; **12** 144; **19** 134, 137, 139-40, 142-3; **24** 144, 146; **26** 131, 134, 144; **35** 131-2, 141, 144; **48** 131, 134, 145-6; **52** 131, 133; **201** 160; **205** 147-9; **206** 147, 149; **207** 163; **208** 149; **209** 95, 126-7, 129 ; **210** 126; **211** 88, 95, 126-7, 174; **212** 126, 132; **213** 80-2, 95-6, 127-9, 169, 173, 172; **214** 80, 95, 127; **215** 80-2, 87, 95, 127-8, 172; **216** 80, 95, 127-8; **233** 47, 64, 68, 121-2; **234** 43, 4, 12, 87, 121-2, 124, 141, 143; **235** 22, 33, 44, 46, 62, 65-6, 68, 91, 121-2, 124, 141-2; **236** 43-4, 47, 65-6, 68, 121-2, 124, 181; **237** 26, 30-1, 33, 93; **238** 26, 31, 33, 150, 40, 93, 190; **239** 26, 30, 32-3, 93-4, 121-2; **240** 26, 31, 33-4, 40, 93, 190

Reserve Jäger Battalions
3 145-6; **15** 160; **16** 147, 149; **18** 81-2, 88, 95-6, 127-8, 172; **23** 22, 43, 94, 141-2, 190; **24** 31, 43, 93

Reserve Field Artillery Regiments
44 134; **51** 43-4, 47; **52** 94
Bavarian Foot Artillery Battalion 2 146
Reserve Pioneer Company 51 143

Gheluvelt/Geluveld 130, 155
Ghent 9, 13-14
Gilsa Oberst v. 91-2, 121
Grimm Major 121
Grossetti General 29
Group Poelcapelle 123-4
Grutesaele Farm 60
Haanixbeek 76, 131, 184
Haig Lieutenant General Sir Douglas 13, 20, 26-7, 45, 70, 74
Halte 100-101
Hamilton Major 24, 31
Handzame Canal 160
Hanebeek 41, 51, 54, 83, 87, 187
Harden Capt 53
Hazebrouck 11, 13, 15, 27
Helles Farm 39, 190
Hell-Fire Corner 101
Hely d'Oissel General 61, 182
Het Sas 43-4, 110, 134, 147
Hoge Roker 180-2
Hollebeke 74, 130
Hooge 109
Hoskyns Lt 39
Houthulst Wood 21-3, 42-3, 57, 60-1, 79-81, 151, 158, 169
Hügel Gen der Inf Freiherr v. 21, 135
Iron Cross 60
Jeffreys Major 42, 98-9, 187
Joffre General 11, 20, 70, 120
Kansas Cross 40, 99, 187
Keiberg 26, 34, 80
Kerselaar 71, 137
Klein Zillebeke 74
Kleist Oberst v. 145

207

Klerken 160
Koblenz 22
Koekuit 43, 57, 59-62, 107, 158, 170, 180
Kollwitz Käthe 163
Kollwitz Peter 163
Kortebeek/Broenbeek 6, 59-60, 73, 79-82, 95-6, 106-107, 128, 131, 133, 179-80
Kortekeer Cabaret 43, 60-2, 79, 81, 83-4, 107, 109, 117-19, 124, 133-4, 146, 149, 169, 171-2, 177
Krumbiegel-Möllmann Major 142
Landon Brigadier General 55
Langemarck/Langemark *passim*
Lawford Brigadier General 25, 39
Le Havre 13
Lekkerboterbeek 139, 185-6
Lennox Major The Lord 98
Lille 8, 11, 14
Limé 14
Loesen Major v. 95, 129
Lomax Major-General 55, 60
Lombartzyde 20
Lorraine 8
Luzerne 78
MacEwen Lt Col 62, 119
Madonna 158-9, 170
Mangelaere/Mangelare 22, 59-60, 78, 81, 106, 121, 169, 175, 180
Markham Major 96
Marseilles 11
Menin 15-16, 20, 132
Menin Road 10, 120, 155
Markejevaert 126
Miller Capt 112-13
Minoterie 165
Mitry General de 20, 23, 70
Monro Major-General 77
Mons 13, 110
Moorslede 16-17, 21, 26, 35, 40, 71
Mosselmarkt 71
Moussy General 98
Nachtegaal 80-1
Namur Crossing 180-1
New Houses 76, 186
Nieuport 8, 17, 29, 119
Nieuwemolen 23
Nonne Bosschen 31, 40
Oertzen Oberst v. 82, 87
Oostnieuwkerke 21-2
Orr Capt 85
Ostend 9
Ottmer Oberst 129
Paris 10
Passchendaele 24-6, 30, 45, 51, 70, 93, 98-9
Pilckem (Ridge) 28, 43-4, 49, 90-1, 109-10, 114
Ploegsteert 8
Poelcappelle/Poelkapelle 16, 22, 24, 33, 43-6, 53-4, 56, 58-60, 64-6, 68-70, 73, 76, 78, 80, 92-3, 104, 106, 121-2, 131, 137, 140, 157, 178-80, 182, 186-7
Polygon Wood 31, 42, 74, 120, 155, 183, 187, 189-90
Poperinghe 20, 27-9, 55, 118
Pritchard Major 107

Pulteney Major-General 11
Rawlinson Lieutenant General 13-14, 39, 70, 197
Remy Farm 117
Reutel 31, 73-4, 190
Rising Capt 107
Rohden Generalmajor Herhudt v. 88
Ronarc'h Admiral 166
Roulers 16, 30
Rupprecht Generaloberst Crown Prince 8-9
Schleinitz Oberst Freiherr v. 147
Schoepflin Generalleutnant 88
Schreiber Lt Col 107
's-Gravenstafel Ridge 33, 41, 75, 187
Smalian Oberst 137
Smith-Dorrien General 11
Sorel-Cameron Major 89
St Eloi 136
St Jansbeek 60, 83, 85-6, 88, 96, 133, 175-6
St Jean 27, 74, 91, 101, 109
St Julien 27, 33, 41, 49-50, 54-5, 73, 76, 80, 101
St Omer 8, 11
Staden 21, 59, 131
Steenbeek 6
Steenstraat 28-9, 43, 61-2, 78-9, 118, 134, 147-9
Steenevoorde 55
Stroombeek 78
Terhand 16, 23
't Goed ter Veste Farm 43, 181
Thourout 20
Trench of Death 167
Urbal General d' 29
Urquhart 117
Vancouver Corner 40, 49, 184, 186-7
Varna Farm 60, 107, 180
Veldhoek 133
Verdun 6, 10, 130, 134
Vladslo 160-1
Vlamertinghe 15
Vyvyan Capt 39
Wartenberg Oberstv. 33
Wasielewski Generalleutnant 126
Wechmar General v. 94-5, 106
Wedel Oberst v. 95
Weidendrift 124, 128-9, 145, 170, 176-8
Weidenrest 43
Westmacott Lt Col 77
Westroosebeke 22-4, 43, 45-6, 57, 66-7, 71, 135, 187, 195
Wieltje 29, 40, 54, 99, 101
Wilhelmi Oberst 65-6, 121
Winnipeg Crossroads 186
Woumen 160
Wunsch Oberst 122
Y Farm 89
Ypres 6-8, 10, 13-15, 20, 24, 26, 30, 42, 55, 70, 100-101, 105-106, 120, 123, 132, 136-7, 152, 190
Yser 6, 8, 10, 12, 14, 17, 30, 42-3, 56, 61, 70, 78, 119, 133, 136-7, 145-6
Zandvoorde 20, 189
Zeebrugge 10
Zillebeke 97-9, 120
Zonnebeke 16, 20-1, 25-7, 31-2, 34, 36-42, 54, 62, 70, 74, 96-7, 99, 155, 183, 187, 189-90